THE GROLIER LIBRARY
OF
SCIENCE BIOGRAPHIES

VOLUME 5

Haüy–Klitzing

Grolier Educational
Sherman Turnpike, Danbury, Connecticut 06816

Published 1997 by
Grolier Educational
Danbury Connecticut 06816

Copyright © 1996 by Market House Books Ltd.
Published for the School and Library market exclusively
by Grolier Educational, 1997

Compiled and Typeset by Market House Books Ltd, Aylesbury, UK.

General Editors
    John Daintith BSc, PhD
    Derek Gjertsen BA

Market House Editors
    Elizabeth Martin MA
    Anne Stibbs BA
    Fran Alexander BA
    Jonathan Law BA
    Peter Lewis BA, DPhil
    Mark Salad

Picture Research
    Linda Wells

Contributors
    Eve Daintith BSc
    Rosalind Dunning BA
    Garry Hammond BSc
    Robert Hine BSc, MSc
    Valerie Illingworth BSc, MPhil
    Sarah Mitchell BA
    Susan O'Neill BSc
    W. J. Palmer MSc
    Roger F. Picken BSc, PhD
    Carol Russell BSc
    W. J. Sherratt BSc, MSc, PhD
    Jackie Smith BA
    B. D. Sorsby BSc, PhD
    Elizabeth Tootill BSc, MSc
    P. Welch DPhil
    Anthony Wootton

Published by arrangement with
The Institute of Physics Publishing
Bristol BS1 6NX
UK

ISBN   Volume 5   0-7172-7631-7
        Ten-Volume Set 0-7172-7626-0
Library of Congress Catalog Number: 96-31474
Cataloging Information to be obtained directly from Grolier Educational.
First Edition
Printed in the United States of America

CONTENTS

PREFACE

ABOUT THE GROLIER LIBRARY OF SCIENCE BIOGRAPHIES

The 19th-century poet and essayist Oliver Wendell Holmes wrote:

> Science is a first-rate piece of furniture for a man's upper chamber, if he has common sense on the ground floor.
>
> *The Poet at the Breakfast-Table* (1872)

While it has been fashionable in this century to assume that science is capable of solving all human problems, we should, perhaps, pause to reflect on Holmes's comment. Scientific knowledge can only be of value to the human race if it is made use of wisely by the men and women who have control of our lives.

If this is true, all thinking people need a solid piece of scientific furniture in their upper chambers. For this reason the editors and publishers of this series of books have set out to say as much about science itself as about the scientists who have created it.

All the entries contain basic biographical data – place and date of birth, posts held, etc. – but do not give exhaustive personal details about the subject's family, prizes, honorary degrees, etc. Most of the space has been devoted to their main scientific achievements and the nature and importance of these achievements. This has not always been easy; in particular, it has not always been possible to explain in relatively simple terms work in the higher reaches of abstract mathematics or modern theoretical physics.

Perhaps the most difficult problem was compiling the entry list. We have attempted to include people who have produced major advances in theory or have made influential or well-known discoveries. A particular difficulty has been the selection of contemporary scientists, in view of the fact that of all scientists who have ever lived, the vast majority are still alive. In this we have been guided by lists of prizes and awards made by scientific societies. We realize that there are dangers in this – the method would not, for instance, catch an unknown physicist working out a revolutionary new system of mechanics in the seclusion of the Bern patent office. It does, however, have the advantage that it is based on the judgments of other scientists. We have to a great extent concentrated on what might be called the "traditional" pure sciences – physics, chemistry, biology, astronomy, and the earth sciences. We also give a more limited coverage of medicine and mathematics and have included a selection of people who have made important contributions to engineering and technology. A few of the entries cover workers in such fields as anthropology and psychology, and a small number of philosophers are represented.

A version of this book was published in 1993 by the Institute of Physics, to whom we are grateful for permission to reuse the material in this set. Apart from adding a number of new biographies to the Institute of Physics text, we have enhanced the work with some 1,500 photographs and a large number of quotations by or about the scientists themselves. We have also added a simple pronunciation guide (the key to which will be found on the back of this page) to provide readers with a way of knowing how to pronounce the more difficult and unfamiliar names.

Each volume in this set has a large biographical section. The scientists are arranged in strict alphabetical order according to surname. The entry for a scientist is given under the name by which he or she is most commonly known. Thus the American astrophysicist James Van Allen is generally known as Van Allen (not Allen) and is entered under V. The German chemist Justus von Liebig is commonly referred to as Liebig and is entered under L. In addition, each volume contains a section on "Sources and Further Reading" for important entries, a glossary of useful definitions of technical words, and an index of the whole set. The index lists all the scientists who have entries, indicating the volume number and the page on which the entry will be found. In addition scientists are grouped together in the index by country (naturalized nationality if it is not their country of origin) and by scientific discipline. Volume 10 contains a chronological list of scientific discoveries and publications arranged under year and subject. It is intended to be used for tracing the development of a subject or for relating advances in one branch of science to those in another branch. Additional information can be obtained by referring to the biographical section of the book.

JD
DG 1996

PRONUNCIATION GUIDE

A guide to pronunciation is given for foreign names and names of foreign origin; it appears in brackets after the first mention of the name in the main text of the article. Names of two or more syllables are broken up into small units, each of one syllable, separated by hyphens. The stressed syllable in a word of two or more syllables is shown in **bold** type.

We have used a simple pronunciation system based on the phonetic respelling of names, which avoids the use of unfamiliar symbols. The sounds represented are as follows (the phonetic respelling is given in brackets after the example word, if this is not pronounced as it is spelled):

a *as in* bat
ah *as in* palm (pahm)
air *as in* dare (dair), pear (pair)
ar *as in* tar
aw *as in* jaw, ball (bawl)
ay *as in* gray, ale (ayl)
ch *as in* chin
e *as in* red
ee *as in* see, me (mee)
eer *as in* ear (eer)
er *as in* fern, layer
f *as in* fat, phase (fayz)
g *as in* gag
i *as in* pit
I *as in* mile (mIl), by (bI)
j *as in* jaw, age (ayj), gem (jem)
k *as in* keep, cactus (**kak**-tus), quite (kwIt)
ks *as in* ox (oks)
ng *as in* hang, rank (rangk)
o *as in* pot

oh *as in* home (hohm), post (pohst)
oi *as in* boil, toy (toi)
oo *as in* food, fluke (flook)
or *as in* organ, quarter (**kwor**-ter)
ow *as in* powder, loud (lowd)
s *as in* skin, cell (sel)
sh *as in* shall
th *as in* bath
th as in feather (**fe*th***-er)
ts *as in* quartz (kworts)
u *as in* buck (buk), blood (blud), one (wun)
u(r) *as in* urn (but without sounding the "r")
uu *as in* book (buuk)
v *as in* van, of (ov)
y *as in* yet, menu (**men**-yoo), onion (**un**-yon)
z *as in* zoo, lose (looz)
zh *as in* treasure (**tre**-zher)

The consonants b, d, h, l, m, n, p, r, t, and w have their normal sounds and are not listed in the table.

In our pronunciation guide a consonant is occasionally doubled to avoid confusing the syllable with a familiar word, for example, -iss rather than -is (which is normally pronounced -iz); -off rather than -of (which is normally pronounced -ov).

Ha

Haüy, René Just

(1743–1822)

FRENCH MINERALOGIST

Haüy (a-oo-**ee**), whose father was a poor clothworker, was born in St. Just in France. His interest in church music attracted the attention of the prior of the abbey, who soon recognized Haüy's intelligence and arranged for him to receive a sound education. While in Paris, his interest in mineralogy was awakened by the lectures of Louis Daubenton. He became professor of mineralogy at the Natural History Museum in Paris in 1802. His *Traité de mineralogie* (Treatise on Mineralogy) was published in five volumes in 1801 and *Traité de cristallographie* (Treatise on Crystallography) in three volumes in 1822.

Haüy is regarded as the founder of the science of crystallography through his discovery of the geometrical law of crystallization. In 1781 he accidentally dropped some calcite crystals onto the floor, one of which broke, and found, to his surprise, that the broken pieces were rhombohedral in form. Deliberately breaking other and diverse forms of calcite, he found that it always revealed the same form whatever its source. He concluded that all the molecules of calcite have the same form and it is only how they are joined together that produces different gross structures. Following on from this he suggested that other minerals should show different basic forms. He thought that there were, in fact, six different primitive forms from which all crystals could be derived by being linked in different ways. Using his theory he was able to predict in many cases the correct angles of the crystal face. The work aroused much controversy and was attacked by Eilhard Mitscherlich in 1819 when he discovered isomorphism in which two substances of different composition can have the same crystalline form. Haüy rejected Mitscherlich's arguments.

Haüy also conducted work in pyroelectricity. The mineral *haüyne* was named for him.

Hawking, Stephen William

(1942–   )

BRITISH THEORETICAL PHYSICIST AND COSMOLOGIST

Even as he [Hawking] sits helpless in his wheelchair, his mind seems to soar even more brilliantly across the vastness of space and time to unlock the secrets of the universe.

—Time (1988)

I was again fortunate in that I chose theoretical physics, because that is all in the mind. So my disability has not been a serious handicap.

—A Brief History of Time (1988)

Why does the universe go to all the bother of existing? Is the unified theory so compelling that it brings about it's own existence? Or does it need a creator, and, if so, does he have any other effect on the universe? And who created him?

—As above

Hawking, who was born in Oxford, England, graduated from the university there and obtained his PhD from Cambridge University. After holding various Cambridge posts, he became professor of gravitational physics in 1977 and, in 1979, was appointed Lucasian Professor of Mathematics.

Hawking has worked mainly in the field of cosmology, in particular the theory of black holes. In 1965 Roger Penrose had shown that a star collapsing to form a black hole would ultimately form a singularity – a point at which the density of matter is infinite and at which there is an infinite curvature of space–time. Hawking realized that by reversing the time in Penrose's theory he could show that the big bang originating the Universe must also have come from a singularity. Similarly, if the Universe were to stop expanding and start contracting it would eventually end at a singularity – the so-called "big-crunch." Penrose and Hawking published these results in 1970. The results of Hawking's work using general relativity were summarized in a book with George Ellis, *The Large Scale Structure of Spacetime* (1973).

In fact, at a singularity, with infinite curvature of space–time, the general theory of relativity breaks down and consequently it cannot be applied to the origin of the Universe. This led Hawking to the application of quantum theory to the gravitational interaction. Of the four fundamental interactions, the strong, weak, electromagnetic, and gravitational interactions, the gravitational interaction is the only one not described by quantum theory. The others occur at distances comparable to the sizes of atomic particles and quantum effects are important. Gravitational interactions between masses over long distances are important in cosmology and can be described by the nonquantum theory of relativity. However, at the vanishingly small distances necessarily occurring just after the big bang (or just before a total collapse), quantum effects would be important. Hawking and others turned their attention to "quantum gravity."

So far, the general application of quantum mechanics to gravitational interactions has had limited success. One notable discovery has been Hawking's theory showing that black holes are not in fact "black" – they effectively emit energy as if they were a hot body.

The basis of the mechanism behind "hot" black holes is the Heisenberg uncertainty principle. According to this, free space cannot be empty because a point in space would then have zero energy at a fixed time and this would contradict the principle. In space, pairs of virtual particles and antiparticles are constantly forming and annihilating. One member of the pair has a positive energy and the other has a negative energy. Under normal conditions a virtual particle does not exist in isolation and is not detected. However, Hawking has shown that in the vicinity of a black hole it is possible for the particles to separate. The negative-energy particle can fall into a black hole and its partner may escape to infinity, appearing as emitted energy.

The theory resolves a problem concerning the thermodynamics of black holes. If matter of high entropy falls into a black hole then there has been a net entropy loss unless the black hole itself gains entropy. One interpretation of the entropy of a black hole is its area, which increases whenever matter falls into the hole. However, if a black hole has an entropy it must also have a temperature. Hawking showed that the emission of energy from a black hole was distributed as if it were radiated from a black body at the appropriate temperature.

A black hole produced by a collapsing star would have a temperature within a few millionths of a degree above absolute zero. Hawking has speculated on the existence of "mini black holes" weighing a billion tons but having a size no bigger than a proton (about 10^{-15} meter). These could be produced during the early stages of the big bang and are consequently known as "primordial black holes." Because of their small size they would radiate gigawatts of energy in the X-ray and gamma-ray regions of the electromagnetic spectrum. So far there is no experimental evidence for their existence.

Hawking has innovatively applied quantum gravity to the question of the origin of the Universe, making various modifications to the inflationary theory first proposed by Alan Guth. He has also put forward an original proposal for the origin and evolution of the Universe applying the "sum over histories" formalism of quantum mechanics of Richard Feynmann. Hawking's model of the Universe is conceptually difficult. It involves a Euclidean space–time in which time is an imaginary quantity (in the mathematical sense). There are no singularities at which the laws of physics break down; space–time is finite but closed, having no boundaries and no beginning or end.

Hawking is generally regarded as one of the foremost theoretical physicists of this century despite a severe physical handicap. In the early 1960s he developed motor neuron disease and for the past twenty years he has been confined to a wheelchair. Most of his communication is through a computer speech synthesizer. Of this, Hawking has said that he "was fortunate in that I chose theoretical physics, because that is all in the mind." In 1988 Hawking published a popular account of cosmology, *A Brief History of Time*. The book and its author captured the public imagination and made Hawking an international celebrity, even to noncosmologists. In it he looks forward to a time when a complete theory could be found understandable to everyone. "If we find the answer to that, it would be the ultimate triumph of human reason – for then we would know the mind of God."

Haworth, Sir (Walter) Norman

(1883–1950)

BRITISH CHEMIST

Haworth, who was born in Chorley, in northwest England, began work in a linoleum factory managed by his father. This required some knowledge of dyes, which led Haworth to chemistry. Despite his family's objections he persisted in private study until he was sufficiently qualified to gain admission to Manchester University in 1903, where he studied under and later worked with William Perkin, Jr. on terpenes. Haworth did his postgraduate studies at Göttingen where, in 1910, he gained his PhD. In 1912 he joined the staff of St. Andrews University and worked with Thomas Purdie and James Irvine on carbohydrates. He remained there until 1920 when, after five years at the University of Durham, he was appointed Mason Professor of Chemistry at Birmingham, where he remained until his retirement in 1948.

Emil Fischer had dominated late 19th-century organic chemistry and, beginning in 1887, had synthesized a number of sugars, taking them to be open-chain structures, most of which were built on a framework of six carbon atoms. Haworth however succeeded in showing that the carbon atoms in sugars are linked by oxygen into rings: either there are five carbon atoms and one oxygen atom, giving a pyranose ring, or there are four carbon atoms and one oxygen atom, giving a furannose ring. When the appropriate oxygen and hydrogen atoms are added to these rings the result is a sugar. He went on to represent the carbohydrate ring by what he called a "perspective formula," today known as a *Haworth formula*.

With Edmund Hirst he went on to establish the point of closure of the ring using the technique of Irvine and Purdie of converting the sugar into its methyl ester. He later investigated the chain structure of various polysaccharides. In 1929 he published his views in *The Constitution of the Sugars*.

In 1933 Haworth and his colleagues achieved a further triumph. Albert Szent-Györgyi had earlier isolated a substance from the adrenal cortex and from orange juice which he named hexuranic acid. It was in fact vitamin C and Haworth, again in collaboration with Hirst, succeeded in synthesizing it. He called it ascorbic acid.

For this work, the first synthesis of a vitamin, Haworth shared the 1937 Nobel Prize for chemistry with Paul Karrer.

Hays, James Douglas

(1933–   )

AMERICAN GEOLOGIST

Hays was born in Johnstown, New York, and educated at Harvard, Ohio State, and Columbia universities, obtaining his PhD from the last in 1964. He joined Columbia's Lamont–Doherty Geological Observatory, New York, in 1967 as director of the deep-sea sediments core laboratory and in 1975 was appointed professor of geology.

In 1971 Hays reported that from his study of 28 deep-sea piston cores from high and low latitudes it was shown that during the last 2.5 million years eight species of radiolaria had become extinct. Prior to extinction these species were widely distributed and their sudden extinction, in six out of eight cases, was in close proximity to a magnetic reversal, a change in the Earth's magnetic polarity. Hays concluded that the magnetic reversals influenced the radiolarians' extinction.

Heaviside, Oliver

(1850–1925)

BRITISH ELECTRONIC ENGINEER AND PHYSICIST

> Should I refuse a good dinner simply because
> I do not understand the process of digestion?
> —On being criticized for using formal
> mathematical manipulations, without
> understanding how they worked

Heaviside, a Londoner, was a nephew of Charles Wheatstone. Being very deaf, he was hampered in school, and was largely self-taught. He was interested in the transmission of electrical signals and used Maxwell's equations to develop a practical theory of cable telegraphy, introducing the concepts of self-inductance, impedance, and conductance. However, his early results were not recognized, possibly because the papers were written using his own notation.

After radio waves had been transmitted across the Atlantic in 1901, he suggested (1902) the existence of a charged atmospheric layer that reflected the waves. The same year Arthur Kennelly independently suggested the same explanation. The *Heaviside layer* (sometimes called the Kennelly–Heaviside layer) was detected experimentally in 1924 by Edward Appleton.

Later in life his fame grew and he was awarded an honorary doctorate at Göttingen and was elected a fellow of the Royal Society in 1891.

Hecataeus of Miletus

(*c.* 550 BC–*c.* 476 BC)

GREEK GEOGRAPHER

Hecataeus (hek-a-**tee**-us), who was born in Miletus (now in Turkey), flourished during the time of the Persian invasion of Ionia, and was one of the ambassadors sent to Persia. One of the earliest geographical works, the *Periegesis* (Tour Round the World), is attributed to him but only fragments of this now exist. It reportedly contained a map showing the world as Hecataeus believed it to be – a flat disk surrounded by ocean. The work was used by the ancients, notably by the Greek historian Herodotus (who also ridiculed it). Even fewer fragments remain of Hecataeus's other surviving work, *Historiai* (Histories), which gave an account of the traditions and mythology of the Greeks.

Hecht, Selig

(1892–1947)

AMERICAN PHYSIOLOGIST

Hecht (hekt) was born in the Austrian town of Glogow and brought to America in 1898. He was educated at the City College, New York, and at Harvard where he obtained his PhD in 1917. After several junior posts and a prolonged traveling fellowship, Hecht was appointed professor of biophysics at Columbia in 1926, a post he retained until his death.

Hecht is best remembered for his photochemical theory of visual adaptation formulated in the mid-1920s. That the eye can readily adapt to changes in brightness is a familiar experience but the exact mechanism behind this response is far from clear. Hecht proposed that in bright light the visual pigment rhodopsin is somewhat bleached while regeneration takes place in the dark. Under steady illumination the amount of rhodopsin bleached would be balanced by that regenerated. Adaptation is thus simply equated with the amount of rhodopsin in the retinal rods.

Heezen, Bruce Charles

(1924–1977)

AMERICAN OCEANOGRAPHER

Born in Vinton, Iowa, Heezen was educated at Iowa State University, graduating in 1948, and at Columbia, New York, where he received his PhD in 1957. He worked at the Lamont Geological Observatory at Columbia from 1948.

Heezen's work has contributed significantly to knowledge of the ocean floor and the processes that operate within the oceans. In 1952 he produced convincing evidence for the existence of turbidity currents, i.e., currents caused by a mass of water full of suspended sediment. Their existence had been suggested by Reginald Daly in 1936 and proposed as the cause of submarine canyons. Heezen used precise records available from the 1929 Grand Bank earthquake to study these currents. As the area off the Grand Bank was rich with communication cables, exact records of the disturbance caused by the earthquake had been obtained. He was able to reconstruct the movement down the bank of about 25 cubic miles (100 cubic km) of sediment moving with speeds approaching 50 miles per hour (85 km per hour).

In 1957, in collaboration with William Ewing and Marie Tharp, the existence of the worldwide ocean rift was demonstrated and its connection with seismic activity postulated. In 1960 Heezen argued for an expanding Earth in which new material is emerging from the rift, increasing the oceans' width and pushing the continents further apart. Such a view, based on the grounds that the gravitational constant decreases slowly with time, had been suggested earlier by Paul Dirac, but received little support in the early 1960s, particularly when a more plausible mechanism was suggested by Harry H. Hess in 1962.

Heidelberger, Michael

(1888–1991)

AMERICAN IMMUNOLOGIST

Heidelberger (**hI**-del-ber-ger) was born in New York City and educated at Columbia where he obtained his PhD in 1911. He first worked at the Rockefeller Institute from 1912 until 1927 when he moved to Columbia, where he served as professor of immunochemistry from 1948 until his retirement in 1956. He then took up the position of adjunct professor of pathology at the New York University Medical School, where he continued to work in his lab when over 100.

Heidelberger in his long career worked on many immunological problems. Between 1928 and 1950 he did much to reveal the chemical structure of antibody and complement, two of the key parts of the immune system.

He also collaborated with a colleague at Rockefeller, Oswald Avery, and in a famous experiment (1923) demonstrated that the specific antigenic properties of pneumococci are due to certain polysaccharides in their capsules.

Heisenberg, Werner Karl

(1901–1976)

GERMAN PHYSICIST

Heisenberg (**hI**-zen-berg), whose father was a professor of Greek at the University of Munich, was born in Würzburg, Germany. He was educated at the universities of Munich and Göttingen, where in 1923 he obtained his doctorate. After spending the period 1924–26 in Copenhagen working with Niels Bohr, he returned to Germany to take up the professorship of theoretical physics at the University of Leipzig. After the war, Heisenberg returned to Göttingen, where he reestablished the Kaiser Wilhelm Institute for Physics. This was renamed the Max Planck Institute and in 1958 it moved to Munich with Heisenberg as its director, a post he occupied until 1970 when he resigned on the grounds of ill health.

In 1925 Heisenberg formulated a version of quantum theory that became known as matrix mechanics. It was for this work, which was later shown to be formally equivalent to the wave mechanics of Erwin Schrödinger, that Heisenberg was awarded the 1932 Nobel Prize for physics. Heisenberg began in a very radical way, much influenced by Ernst Mach. Considering the various bizarre results emerging in quantum theory, such as the apparent wave–particle duality of the electron, his first answer was that it is simply a mistake to think of the atom in visual terms at all. What we really know of the atom is what we can observe of it, namely, the light it emits, its frequency, and its intensity. The need therefore was to be able to write a set of equations that would permit the correct prediction of such atomic phenomena. Heisenberg succeeded in establishing a mathematical formalism that permitted accurate predictions to be made. The method was also developed by Max Born and Pascual Jordan. As they used the then relatively unfamiliar matrix mathematics to develop this system, it is not surprising that physicists preferred the more usual language of wave equations used in the equivalent system of Schrödinger.

In 1927 Heisenberg went on to explore a deeper level of physical understanding when he formulated his fundamental "uncertainty principle": that it is impossible to determine exactly both the position and momentum of such particles as the electron. He demonstrated this by simple "thought experiments" of the following type: if we try to locate the exact position of an electron we must use rays with very short wavelengths such as gamma rays. But by so illuminating it the electron's momentum will be changed by its interaction with the energetic gamma rays. Alternatively a lower-energy wave can be used that will not disturb the momentum of the electron so much but, as lower energy implies longer wavelength, such radiation will lack the precision to provide the exact location of the electron. There seems to be no way out of such an impasse and Heisenberg went on to express the limits of the uncertainty mathematically:

$$\Delta x . \Delta p \geq h/4\pi$$

where Δx is the uncertainty in ascertaining the position in a given direction, Δp is the uncertainty in ascertaining the momentum in that direction, and h is the Planck constant. What the equation tells us is that the product of the uncertainties must always be about as great as the Planck constant and can never disappear completely. Further, any attempt made to reduce one element of uncertainty to the minimum can only be done at the expense of increasing the other. The consequence of this failure to know the *exact* position and momentum is an inability to predict accurately the future position of an electron. Thus, like Max Born, Heisenberg had found it necessary to introduce a basic indeterminacy into physics.

After his great achievements in quantum theory in the 1920s Heisenberg later turned his attention to the theory of elementary particles. Thus in 1932, shortly after the discovery of the neutron by James Chadwick, Heisenberg proposed that the nucleus consists of both neutrons and protons. He went further, arguing that they were in fact two states of the same basic entity – the "nucleon." As the strong nuclear force does not distinguish between them he proposed that they were "isotopes" with nearly the same mass, distinguished instead by a property he called "isotopic spin." He later attempted the ambitious task of constructing a unified field theory of elementary particles. Although he published a monograph on the topic in 1966 it generated little support.

Unlike many other German scientists Heisenberg remained in Germany throughout the war and the whole Nazi era. He was certainly no Nazi himself but he thought it essential to remain in Germany to preserve traditional scientific values for the next generation. At one time he came under attack from the Nazis for his refusal to compromise his support for the physics of Einstein in any way. Thus when, in 1935, he wished to move to the University of Munich to succeed Arnold Sommerfeld he was violently attacked by the party press and, eventually, the post went to the little-known W. Müller.

With the outbreak of war in 1939 Heisenberg was soon called upon to come to Berlin to direct the program to construct an atom bomb. His exact role in the program has become a matter of controversy. He has claimed that he never had any real intention of making such a bomb, let alone giving it to Hitler. As long as he played a key role he was, he later claimed, in a position to sabotage the program if it ever looked like being a success. He even went so far as to convey such thoughts to Niels Bohr in 1941 when he met him in Copenhagen, hinting that the Allies' physicists should pursue a similar policy. Bohr later reported that if such comments had been made to him they were done so too cryptically for him to grasp; he was rather under the impression that Heisenberg was trying to find out the progress made by the Allies.

New information on the role of Heisenberg and other senior German scientists was released in 1992. The Allies had gathered the scientists in a bugged house, Farm Hall, near Cambridge and recorded their conversation for six months. When the possibility of microphones was put to Heisenberg, he casually dismissed the suggestion: "Microphones installed? (Laughing) Oh no, they're not as cute as all that...they're a bit old fashioned in that respect."

Heisenberg learned of the Hiroshima bomb on 6 August 1945. His first reaction was of disbelief. He insisted that the announcement could refer only to high explosives. During further discussion he declared: "I never thought we would make a bomb." He felt that as a bomb could not have been completed before the war's end, he lacked the urgency to argue the case strongly enough before the military and politicians. He was also arrogant enough to believe that the Allies would do no better. The question of having to make a moral choice, of deliberately sabotaging a German nuclear program simply never arose.

Helmholtz, Hermann Ludwig von

(1821–1894)

GERMAN PHYSIOLOGIST AND
PHYSICIST

> Whoever, in the pursuit of science, seeks after immediate practical utility may rest assured that he seeks in vain.
>
> —*Academic Discourses* (1862)

> The first discovery of a new law...is of the same quality as the highest performances of artistic perception in the discovery of new types of expression.
> —"On Thought in Medicine" in *Popular Lectures on Scientific Subjects* (1884)

Born in Potsdam, Germany, Helmholtz (**helm**-holts) studied medicine at the Friedrich Wilhelm Institute in Berlin and obtained his MD in 1842. He returned to Potsdam to become an army surgeon, but returned to civilian life in 1848 and was appointed assistant at the Anatomical Museum in Berlin. He then held a succession of chairs at Königsberg (1849–55), Bonn (1855–58), Heidelberg (1858–71), and Berlin (1871–77) and later became director of the Physico-Technical Institute at Berlin Charlottenburg.

Helmholtz made major contributions to two areas of science: physiology and physics. In physiology he invented (1851) the ophthalmoscope for inspecting the interior of the eye and the ophthalmometer for measuring the eye's curvature. He investigated accommodation, color vision, and color blindness. His book *Handbuch der physiologische Optik* (Handbook of Physiological Optics) was published in 1867. Helmholtz also worked on hearing, showing how the cochlea in the inner ear resonates for different frequencies and analyzes complex sounds into harmonic components. In 1863 he published *Die Lehre von den Tönemfindungen als physiologische Grundlage für die Theorie der Musik* (The Sensation of Tone as a Physiological Basis for the Theory of Music). Another achievement was his measurement of the speed of nerve impulses (1850).

One of Helmholtz's interests had been muscle action and animal heat and this, inspired by his distaste for vitalism, led him to his best-known discovery – the law of conservation of energy. This was developed independently of the work of James Joule and Julius von Mayer and published as *Über die Erhaltung der Kraft* (1847; On the Conservation of Force). He showed that the total energy of a collection of interacting particles is constant, and later applied this idea to other systems.

Helmholtz also worked in thermodynamics, where he introduced the concept of free energy (energy available to perform work). In electrodynamics he attempted to produce a general unified theory. Heinrich Hertz, who discovered radio waves in 1888, was Helmholtz's pupil.

Helmont, Jan Baptista van

(1579–1644)

FLEMISH CHEMIST AND PHYSICIAN

A citizen being by a Peer openly disgraced and injured; unto whom he might not answer a word without fear of his utmost ruine; in silence dissembles and bears the reproach: but straightway after, an Asthma arises.
—*Ortus medicinae* (1648; Origin of Medicine)

Van Helmont (**hel**-mont), who came from a noble Brussels family, was educated at the Catholic University of Louvain in medicine, mysticism, and chemistry, but declined a degree from them. Rejecting all offers of employment, he devoted himself to private research at his home. In 1621 he was involved in a controversy with the Church over the belief that it was possible to heal a wound caused by a weapon by treating the weapon rather than the wound. Van Helmont did not reject this common belief but insisted that it was a natural phenomenon containing no supernatural elements. He was arrested, eventually allowed to remain under house arrest, and forbidden to publish without the prior consent of the Church. He wrote extensively and after his death his collected papers were published by his son as the *Ortus medicinae* (1648; Origin of Medicine).

Van Helmont rejected the works of the ancients, although he did believe in the philosopher's stone. He carried out careful observations and measurements, which led him to discover the elementary nature of water. He regarded water as the chief constituent of matter. He pointed out that fish were nourished by water and that substantial bodies could be reduced to water by dissolving them in acid. To demonstrate his theory he performed a famous experiment in which he grew a willow tree over a period of five years in a measured quantity of earth. The tree increased its weight by 164 pounds despite the fact that only water was added to it. The soil had decreased by only a few ounces.

Van Helmont also introduced the term "gas" into the language, deriving it from the Greek for chaos. When a substance is burned it is reduced to its formative agent and its gas and van Helmont believed that when 62 pounds of wood is burned to an ash weighing 1 pound, 61 pounds have escaped as water or gas. Different substances give off different gases when consumed and van Helmont identified four gases, which he named gas carbonum, two kinds of gas sylvester, and gas pingue. These we would now call carbon dioxide, carbon monoxide, nitrous oxide, and methane.

Hempel, Carl Gustav

(1905–　)

AMERICAN PHILOSOPHER OF SCIENCE

Hempel was born in Oranienburg, Germany, and educated at Göttingen, Heidelberg, Vienna, and Berlin, where he completed his doctorate in 1934. Alarmed by political conditions in Germany, he moved to Holland and finally emigrated to America in 1938. He became a naturalized citizen in 1944. Hempel then taught in Chicago, New York, and Yale before finally settling at Princeton as professor of philosophy, a position he held until his retirement in 1973.

Hempel established his reputation with a paper, *Studies in the Logic of Confirmation* (1945), which challenged the foundations of inductive logic. He pointed out that if we accept the equivalence condition, namely, that whatever confirms either of two equivalent propositions confirms the other, and the rule that positive instances confirm, then a simple paradox follows. For example, the generalization:

(1) All ravens are black

is confirmed by

(2) Anything that is a raven and black.

But (1) is equivalent to:

(3) All nonblack things are nonravens.

By the equivalence principle whatever confirms (3) must also confirm (1). But a green pencil, as something that is a nonblack nonraven, confirms (3) and therefore it must also confirm (1). Thus at least according to the rules of inductive logic, it seems that the fact that a pencil is green has confirmed the generalization that all ravens are black. The point can be pushed further to the absurd conclusion that whatever is neither black nor a raven, such as red flags and blue skies, confirms the proposition that all ravens are black.

Hempel went on, in a paper written in collaboration with Paul Oppenheim, *Studies in the Logic of Explanation* (1948), to propose a model of scientific explanation, the Hypothetico-Deductive method (HD), which dominated discussion for a generation. Scientific explanations are seen as deductive consequences from a set of laws and initial conditions. For example, from the initial conditions describing the positions of the Sun, Moon, and Earth together with Newton's laws of motion, the date of a future eclipse can be deduced. The laws and the initial conditions constitute an explanation of the eclipse.

For the reasoning to be valid, Hempel stressed, four conditions must be satisfied, namely, the conclusion must follow logically from the hypotheses, the hypotheses must contain a statement of a law of nature, they must have empirical content, and they must be true. Yet, later critics have argued, even if all conditions are satisfied, the HD method can still lead to error. Further, many explanations in science lie outside the HD framework. Finally, Hempel seems to ignore the crucial question of how the hypotheses are established in the first place. His work is more an account of how scientific discoveries are reported or rationalized; not of how they are arrived at or justified.

Hench, Philip Showalter

(1896–1965)

AMERICAN BIOCHEMIST

Born in Pittsburgh, Pennsylvania, Hench was educated at Lafayette College and the University of Pittsburgh, where he obtained his MD in 1920. He spent most of his career working at the Mayo Clinic, becoming head of the section for rheumatic diseases in 1926. Hench was also connected with the Mayo Foundation and the University of Minnesota, where he became professor of medicine in 1947.

For many years Hench had been seeking a method of treating the crippling and painful complaint of rheumatoid arthritis. He suspected that it was not a conventional microbial infection since, among other features, it was relieved by pregnancy and jaundice. Hench therefore felt it was more likely to result from a biochemical disturbance that is transiently corrected by some incidental biological change. The search, he argued, must concentrate on something patients with jaundice had in common with pregnant women. At length he was led to suppose that the antirheumatic substance might be an adrenal hormone, since temporary remissions are often induced by procedures that stimulate the adrenal cortex. Thus in 1948 he was ready to try the newly prepared "compound E," later known as cortisone, of Edward Kendall on 14 patients. All showed remarkable improvement, which was reversed on withdrawing the drug.

For this development of the first steroid drug Hench shared the 1950 Nobel Prize for physiology or medicine with Kendall and Tadeus Reichstein.

Henderson, Thomas

(1798–1844)

BRITISH ASTRONOMER

Born in Dundee, Scotland, Henderson started as an attorney's clerk who made a reputation as an amateur astronomer. In 1831 he accepted an appointment as director of a new observatory at the Cape of Good Hope in South Africa. While observing Alpha Centauri he found that it had a considerable proper motion. He realized that this probably meant that the star was comparatively close and a good candidate for the measurement of parallax – the apparent change in position of a (celestial) body when viewed from spatially separate points, or from one point on a moving Earth. All major observational astronomers had tried to detect this small angular measurement and failed. Henderson at last succeeded in 1832 and found that Alpha Centauri had a parallax of just less than one second of arc. The crucial importance of this was that once parallax was known, the distance of the stars could be measured successfully for the first time. Alpha Centauri turned out to be over four light years away. Unfortunately (for Henderson), he delayed publication of his result until it had been thoroughly checked and rechecked. By this time Friedrich Bessel had already observed and published, in 1839, the parallax of 61 Cygni.

In 1834 Henderson became the first Astronomer Royal of Scotland.

Henle, Friedrich Gustav Jacob

(1809–1885)

GERMAN PHYSICIAN, ANATOMIST, AND PATHOLOGIST

> A rational system of histology must employ the transformations of the cells as a principle of classification, so that groups of tissue can be formed according to whether, for example, the cells remain discrete or join lengthwise in rows, or expand into star shapes, or split into fibers, and so forth.
> —*Allgemeine Anatomie* (1841; General Anatomy)

Henle (**hen**-lee), a merchant's son from Fürth, in Germany, was educated at the universities of Heidelberg and Bonn where he obtained his MD in 1832. He began his career as assistant to Johannes Müller in Berlin and, despite various political troubles (he was tried for treason in Berlin), served as professor of anatomy and physiology at the universities of Zurich (1840–44) and Heidelberg (1844–52) before moving to a similar post at Göttingen where he remained until his death.

By the beginning of the 19th century the humoral theory of disease had been finally expelled from orthodox medicine. It was far from clear, however, what to put in its place. A cogent and comprehensive theory, as developed by Louis Pasteur and Henle's own pupil, Robert Koch, would not be available for a further 40 years. Henle however took some preliminary steps, notably his declaration that contagious substances are not only organic but indeed are living organisms. He distinguished between miasmas, which arise from the environment, and contagions, which spread from person to person. Such theorizing had little immediate impact on medicine, largely because of the difficulty in providing experimental support. His work consequently was largely ignored as speculative.

Henle also produced two standard and highly influential textbooks: *Allgemeine Anatomie* (1841; General Anatomy) and *Handbuch der rationelle Pathologie* (2 vols., 1846–53; Handbook of Rational Pathology). In them he first described and emphasized the microscopic structure of the epithelium, the cells that cover the internal and external surface of the human body. He has thus frequently been referred to as the founder of modern histology.

As an anatomist Henle's name has been preserved in the *loop of Henle*, a part of the nephron, or urine-secreting tubules, in the kidney.

Henry, Joseph

(1797–1878)

AMERICAN PHYSICIST

One great object of science is to ameliorate our present condition, by adding to those advantages we naturally possess...by a combination of theoretical knowledge with practical skill, machines have been constructed no less useful in their productions than astonishing in their operations.
—*Albany Argus and City Gazette* (1826)

One of the first great American scientists, Henry came from a poor background in Albany, New York, and had to work his way through college. He was educated at the Albany Academy, New York, where he first studied medicine, changing to engineering in 1825. A year later he was appointed a professor of mathematics and physics at Albany. In 1832 he became professor of natural philosophy at Princeton (then the College of New Jersey) where he taught physics, chemistry, mathematics, and geological sciences, and later astronomy and architecture.

Henry is noted for his work on electricity. In 1829 he developed a greatly improved form of the electromagnet by insulating the wire that was to be wrapped around the iron core, thus allowing many more coils, closer together, and greatly increasing the magnet's power. Through this work he discovered, in 1830, the principle of electromagnetic induction. Soon after, and quite independently, Michael Faraday made the same observation and published first. Faraday is thus credited with the discovery but Henry has the unit of inductance (the *henry*) named for him. However, Henry did publish in 1832 – prior to Faraday and Heinrich Lenz – his discovery of self-induction (in which the magnetic field from a changing electric current induces an electromotive force opposing the current). Earlier (in 1829) he had invented and constructed the first practical electric motor. In 1835 he developed the electric relay in order to overcome the problem of resistance that built up in long wires. This device had an immediate social impact for it was the key step in the invention of the long-distance telegraph, which played a large part in the opening up of the North American continent. In 1846 he became the first secretary of the Smithsonian Institution, which he formed into an extremely efficient body for liaison between scientists and government support of their research. He also did work on solar radiation and on sunspots.

Henry, William

(1774–1836)

BRITISH PHYSICIAN AND CHEMIST

Henry's father, Thomas Henry, was a manufacturing chemist in Manchester, England, and an analytical chemist of some repute. Initially qualifying as a physician from Edinburgh University, Henry practiced for five years in the Manchester Infirmary. Later he took over the running of the chemical works established by his father.

In 1801 he formulated the law now known as *Henry's law*, which states that the solubility of a gas in water at a given temperature is proportional to its pressure. His close friend John Dalton was encouraged by this finding, seeing it as a confirmation of his own theory of mixed gases, and the two men discussed the methods of experimentation in detail.

Henry also researched into the hydrocarbon gases, following Dalton in clearly distinguishing methane from ethylene (ethene). He determined the molecular formula of ammonia by exploding it with oxygen. He also described the preparation, purification, and analysis of coal gas, and developed a method of analyzing gas mixtures by fractional combustion. His textbook, *Elements of Experimental Chemistry* (1799), went through 11 editions in 30 years.

Hensen, Viktor

(1835–1924)

GERMAN PHYSIOLOGIST AND
OCEANOGRAPHER

Hensen (**hen**-zen) was born in Schleswig, Germany, and studied science and medicine at the universities of Würzburg, Berlin, and Kiel, graduating from the latter in 1858. He remained at Kiel to work in the physiology department and later served as professor of physiology (1871–1911).

Hensen worked on comparative studies of vision and hearing but also discovered, independently of Claude Bernard, the compound glycogen. He is better remembered however for his work on plankton. He introduced the term plankton in 1887 to describe the minute drifting animals and plants in the oceans. Moreover he advanced beyond the descriptive stage and introduced numerical methods into marine biology, notably in constructing the *Hensen net*, a simple loop net designed to filter a square meter of water. This enabled the number of plankton in a known area of water to be counted. Hensen tested his equipment in the North Sea and the Baltic in 1885.

Satisfied with his techniques, he made a more ambitious trip in 1889 covering more than 15,000 miles of the Atlantic. One of his more surprising results was the greater concentration of plankton in temperate than in tropical waters.

Heracleides of Pontus

(*c.* 390 BC–*c.* 322 BC)

GREEK ASTRONOMER

Heracleides of Pontus, when he drew the circle of Venus, and also of the Sun, and assigned a single center to both circles, showed that Venus is sometimes above, sometimes below the Sun.

—Calcidius (5th century AD)

Heracleides (her-a-**kII**-deez), who was born in Heraclea, now in Turkey, was an associate and possibly a pupil of Plato. Although none of his writings have survived, two views that were unusual for the time have been attributed to him. The philosopher Simplicius of Cilicia, a usually reliable source, reports that "Heracleides supposed that the Earth is in the center and rotates while the heaven is at rest." If this is accurate he must have been the first to state that the Earth rotates, a view that found as little support in antiquity as it did in the medieval period. The second doctrine attributed to him is that Mercury and Venus move around the Sun, which moves around the Earth – a view adopted later by Tycho Brahe in the 16th century.

Heraclitus of Ephesus

(about 500 BC)

GREEK NATURAL PHILOSOPHER

If you do not expect the unexpected, you will not find it; for it is hard to be sought out, and difficult.

—Quoted in C. H. Khan, *The Art and Thought of Heraclitus* (1979)

Virtually nothing is known of the life of Heraclitus (her-a-**kII**-tus), and of his book *On Nature* only a few rather obscure fragments survive. His doctrines contrast with those of his near contemporary Parmenides for whom, on purely logical grounds, change of any kind was totally impossible. For Heraclitus, everything is continually in a state of change, hence his characteristic aphorism: "We cannot step twice into the same river," and his selection of fire as the fundamental form of matter. The mechanism behind such unremitting change was the constant tension or "strife" between contraries or opposites.

Hermite, Charles

(1822–1901)

FRENCH MATHEMATICIAN

Hermite (air-**meet**) was born in Dieuze, France. His mathematical career was almost thwarted in his student days, since he was incapable of passing exams. Fortunately his talent had already been recognized and his examiners eventually let him scrape through. Hermite obtained a post at the Sorbonne where he was an influential teacher.

Hermite began his mathematical career with pioneering work on the theory of Abelian and transcendental functions, and he later used the theory of elliptic functions to give a solution of the general equations of the fifth degree – the quintic. One long-standing problem solved was proving that the number "e" is transcendental (i.e., not a solution of a polynomial equation). He also introduced the techniques of analysis into number theory. His most famous work is in algebra, in the theory of *Hermite polynomials*. Although Hermite himself had little interest in applied mathematics this work turned out to be of great use in quantum mechanics.

Hero of Alexandria

(about 62 AD)

GREEK MATHEMATICIAN AND INVENTOR

> Hero is no scientist, but a practical technician and surveyor.
> —J. L. Heiberg, *History of Mathematics and Science in Classical Antiquity* (1925)

Hero (**heer**-oh) produced several written works on geometry, giving formulas for the areas and volumes of polygons and conics. His formula for the area of a triangle was contained in *Metrica* (Measurement), a work that was lost until 1896. This book also describes a method for finding the square root of a number, a method now used in computers, but known to the Babylonians in 2000 BC. In another of Hero's books, *Pneumatica* (Pneumatics), he wrote on siphons, a coin-operated machine, and the aeolipile – a prototype steam-powered engine that he had built. The engine consisted of a globe with two nozzles positioned so that steam jets from the inside made it turn on its axis. Hero also wrote on land-surveying and he designed war engines based on the ideas of Ctesibius. Yet another of his works, *Mechanica* (Mechanics), was quoted by Pappus of Alexandria.

Herophilus of Chalcedon

(about 300 BC)

GREEK ANATOMIST AND PHYSICIAN

Herophilus (her-**off**-i-lus), a pupil of Praxagoras of Cos, was one of the founders of the Alexandrian medical school set up at the end of the 4th century BC under the patronage of Ptolemy I Soter. Although none of his works have survived, Galen lists some eight titles of which the *Anatomica* (Anatomy) was probably the most significant.

Herophilus is widely, even notoriously, remembered as the result of a famous passage in Celsus reporting that, with Erasistratus, he practiced vivisection on criminals. The passage has been regarded as suspect by many scholars on the grounds that no such reference occurs in any extant, earlier Greek text. It is however certain that from the results attributed to him he must have undertaken both human and animal dissection. For example, he described a passage from the stomach to the intestines as being "12 finger widths" (*dodekadaktylon*) or in its Latin form, the duodenum; he also named the retina and the prostate and did much work on the brain.

It has been claimed that Herophilus was the first to distinguish between sensory and motor nerves. Nerves, or neura, for Herophilus were simply channels that carried the pneuma or vital air to different parts of the body. Thus while he probably identified sensory nerves it is unlikely that he was able to distinguish between motor nerves and tendons.

Herophilus was reported to have advanced Praxagoras's work on the pulse by counting its frequency against a water clock. Also, according to Galen, he made the important observation that the arteries carried blood as well as pneuma.

Héroult, Paul Louis Toussaint

(1863–1914)

FRENCH CHEMIST

Héroult (ay-**roo**), who was born at Thury-Harcourt in France, was a student at the St. Barge Institute in Paris and later worked at the Paris School of Mines. In 1886 he discovered a process for extracting aluminum by electrolysis of molten aluminum oxide, with cryolite (sodium aluminum fluoride) added to lower the melting point. Charles Hall developed a similar process independently in America at about the same time.

Herring, William Conyers

(1914–)

AMERICAN PHYSICIST

Herring was born in Scotia, New York, and educated at the University of Kansas where he obtained a BA in astronomy in 1933. He did research in mathematical physics at Princeton and obtained his PhD at Princeton in 1937. During World War II he worked on underwater warfare and then joined the Bell Telephone Laboratories in 1946. Herring remained with Bell as a research physicist until 1978 when he was appointed professor of applied physics at Stanford, California, a post he held until his retirement in 1981.

Herring has worked on a wide range of theoretical problems in solid-state physics, including electrical conduction, surface tension of solids, anisotropic effects in superconducting materials, and the magnetic properties of solids.

Herschbach, Dudley Robert

(1932–   )

AMERICAN CHEMIST

Herschbach (**hersh**-bahk), who was born in San José, California, was educated at the University of Stanford and at Harvard University, where he gained his PhD in 1958. After teaching at the University of California, Berkeley for four years, he returned to Harvard in 1963 as professor of chemistry.

Herschbach has worked on the details of chemical reactions; for example, a simple reaction in which potassium atoms and iodomethane molecules form potassium iodide and methyl radicals as products, that is:

$$K + CH_3I \rightarrow KI + CH_3\cdot$$

He decided to use molecular beams to examine the nature of the reaction. The reagent molecules were formed into two collimated beams at a sufficiently low pressure to make collisions within the beams a negligible event. The beams were allowed to collide and the direction and velocity of the product molecules measured.

Herschbach was able to draw some conclusions about the reaction. He demonstrated, for example, that the reagents would only react if the incoming potassium atoms struck the iodomethane molecules at the iodide end. As techniques were refined and extended Herschbach demonstrated that the study of molecular beams could throw considerable light on reaction dynamics. For his work in this field he shared the 1986 Nobel Prize for chemistry with Yuan Lee and John Polanyi.

Herschel, Caroline Lucretia

(1750–1848)

GERMAN–BRITISH ASTRONOMER

Caroline Herschel (**her**-shel), who was born in Hannover, Germany, was the sister and colleague of William Herschel. Having joined her brother as his housekeeper in Bath in 1772, she rapidly graduated to being his assistant and then to original astronomical research of her own. In 1786 she observed her first comet and before 1797 had detected seven more. She also discovered many new nebulae. Her devotion to her brother and his work must have been completely unconditional judging by the many hundreds of nights spent observing. There is a story that she once slipped and fell on a hook attached to the telescope but made no cry lest she disturb her brother's observations. After his death in 1822 she returned to Hannover where she prepared a catalog of about 2,500 nebulae and star clusters. Although it was never published she received the Gold Medal of the Royal Astronomical Society in 1828 for it.

Herschel, Sir (Frederick) William

(1738–1822)

GERMAN–BRITISH ASTRONOMER

> I saw, with the greatest pleasure, that most of the nebulae...yielded to the force of my light and power, and were resolved into stars.
> —On the great light-gathering power of his large telescopes

Herschel, who was born in Hannover, Germany, started life in the same occupation as his father – an oboist with the band of the Hannoverian footguards. He moved permanently to England in 1757, where he worked as a freelance itinerant musician until in 1767 he was appointed as organist of a church in Bath. His sister Caroline Herschel joined him in Bath in 1772. He was led by his interest in musical theory to a study of mathematics and ultimately astronomy. Herschel made his own telescopes and his early observations were significant enough to be drawn to the attention of George III in 1782. The king, who had a passionate interest in astronomy and clockwork, was sufficiently impressed with Herschel to employ him as his private astronomer at an initial salary of £200 a year and to finance the construction of very large telescopes. At first Herschel settled at Datchet, near Windsor, but in 1786 he moved to Slough where he remained for the rest of his life.

Herschel's contributions to astronomy were enormous. He was fortunate to live at a time when prolonged viewing with a large reflector could not but be fruitful and he took full advantage of his fortune. He made his early reputation by his discovery in 1781 of the first new planet since ancient times. He wished to name it after his patron as "Georgium Sidus" (George's Star) but Johann Bode's suggestion of "Uranus" was adopted. Herschel's work is notable for the unbelievable comprehensiveness with which he extended the observations of others. Thus he extended Charles Messier's catalog of just over 100 nebulae by a series of publications listing over 2,000 nebulae. He not only began the study of double stars but cataloged 800 of them. He also discovered two satellites of Uranus – Titania and Oberon (1787) – and two of Saturn; Mimas and Enceladus (1789–90). He built a large number of telescopes of various sizes, culminating in his enormous 40-foot (12-m) reflector. This cost George III £4,000 plus £200 a year for its upkeep. The eyepiece was attached to the open end, thus eliminating the loss of light caused by the secondary mirror used in the Newtonian and Gregorian reflectors. The disadvantage was the danger of climbing up to the open end of the 40-foot instrument in the dark. One eminent astronomer, Giuseppe Piazzi, failing to master this skill, fell and broke his arm. It was finally dismantled in 1839 while William's son John conducted his family in a special requiem he had composed for the occasion.

Herschel produced not only observational work but theoretical contributions on the structure of the universe. He established the motion of the Sun in the direction of Hercules and tried to calculate its speed (1806). But, above all, he was the first to begin to see the structure of our Galaxy. Conducting a large number of star counts, he established that stars are much more numerous in the Milky Way and the plane of the celestial equator, becoming progressively fewer toward the celestial poles. He explained this by supposing that the Galaxy is shaped like a grindstone. If we look through its short axis we see few stars and much dark space; through its long axis we see a stellar multitude. Herschel was supported in his astronomical life by his sister Caroline. His son John also became an astronomer of note.

Herschel, Sir John Frederick William

(1792–1871)

BRITISH ASTRONOMER

John Herschel, who was born at Slough in the southeast of England, read mathematics at Cambridge University and then began to study law. Although he was the son of the astronomer William Herschel he did not take up astronomy seriously until 1816 when he began, somewhat reluctantly, to assist his father with his observations.

John Herschel went to South Africa in 1834 to make a comprehensive survey of the skies of the southern hemisphere, and succeeded Thomas Henderson as director of the Cape of Good Hope Observatory, doing for the southern skies what his father had done for the northern. He discovered and described some 2,000 nebulae and some 2,000 double stars, publishing the results of his surveys in 1847. He seems to have given up astronomical observation on his return from South Africa in 1838, instead becoming interested in photography (introducing the terms "positive" and "negative") and pioneering the use of photographic techniques in astronomy. He also experimented on the spectral lines discovered by Joseph von Fraunhofer because he began to see a connection between the absorption and emission lines. He was also a major figure in the regeneration and reorganization of British science in the first half of the 19th century. He was one of the founder members of the Royal Astronomical Society in 1830, and took on many public duties, becoming, like Newton, master of the mint from 1850 to 1855. This, however, proved too taxing for him and he suffered a nervous breakdown, which led to his retirement from public life. His study of scientific method *Discourse on the Study of Natural Philosophy* (1830) influenced the philosopher John Stuart Mill and Charles Darwin.

Hershey, Alfred Day

(1908–   )

AMERICAN BIOLOGIST

Hershey was born in Owosso, Michigan, and graduated from Michigan State College in 1930, remaining there to do his PhD thesis on the chemistry of *Brucella* bacteria. Having received his doctorate in 1934, he taught at Washington University, St. Louis, until 1950, when he moved to the Genetics Research Unit of the Carnegie Institute, Washington. In 1962 he became director of the unit, a position he retained until his retirement in 1974.

Hershey, along with Salvador Luria and Max Delbrück, was one of the founders in the early 1940s of the so-called "phage group." In 1945, independently of Luria, he demonstrated that spontaneous mutations must occur in bacterial viruses (phage). In the following year he established, at the same time as Delbrück, that genetic recombination takes place between phages present in the same cell.

Hershey is best known, however, for the experiment conducted with Martha Chase and reported in their 1952 paper, *Independent Functions of Viral Proteins and Nucleic Acid in Growth of Bacteriophage*. At the time it was still uncertain whether genes were composed of protein, nucleic acid, or some complex mixture of the two. They utilized the fact that DNA contains phosphorus but no sulfur, while phage protein has some sulfur in its structure but no phosphorus. Phage with a protein coat labeled with radioactive sulfur and DNA with radioactive phosphorus was allowed to infect bacteria. After infection the bacteria were spun in a blender. The labeled protein was stripped off the bacteria while the radioactive DNA remained inside the bacterial cell. When allowed to incubate, the bacteria proved capable of producing a new phage crop. The experiment would seem to show that DNA was more involved than protein in the process of replication.

For his fundamental contributions to molecular biology, Hershey received the 1958 Albert Lasker Award and the 1965 Kimber Genetics Award. However, it was not until 1969 that Hershey, together with Delbrück and Luria, was awarded the Nobel Prize for physiology or medicine.

Hertz, Gustav

(1887–1975)

GERMAN PHYSICIST

A nephew of the distinguished physicist Heinrich Hertz (herts), Gustav Hertz was born in Hamburg, Germany, and educated at the universities of Munich and Berlin. He taught in Berlin and Halle before his appointment in 1928 to the professorship of experimental physics at the Technical University, Berlin. Hertz, as a Jew, was dismissed from his post in 1935. He worked for the Siemens company from 1935 until 1945, somehow managing to survive the war, when he was captured by the Russians. He reemerged in 1955 to become director of the Physics Institute in Leipzig, then in East Germany.

In 1925 Hertz was awarded the Nobel Prize for physics for his work with James Franck on the quantized nature of energy transfer.

Hertz, Heinrich Rudolf

(1857–1894)

GERMAN PHYSICIST

One cannot escape the feeling that these mathematical formulae have an independent existence and an intelligence of their own, that they are wiser than we are, wiser even than their discoverers, that we get more out of them than was originally put into them.

—Quoted by E. T. Bell in *Men of Mathematics*

Hertz came from a prosperous and cultured Hamburg family. In 1875 he went to Frankfurt to gain practical experience in engineering and after a year of military service (1876–77) spent a year at the University of Munich. He had decided on an academic and scientific career rather than one in engineering, and in 1878 chose to continue his studies at the University of Berlin under Hermann von Helmholtz. Hertz obtained his PhD in 1880 and continued as Helmholtz's assistant for a further three years. He then went to work at the University of Kiel. In 1885 he was appointed professor of physics at Karlsruhe Technical College and in 1889 became professor of physics at the University of Bonn. His tragic early death from blood poisoning occurred after several years of poor health and cut short a brilliant career.

Hertz's early work at Berlin was diverse but included several pieces of research into electrical phenomena and equipment. With no laboratory facilities at Kiel he had considered more theoretical aspects of physics and had become more interested in the recent work of James Clerk Maxwell on electromagnetic theory. Helmholtz had suggested an experimental investigation of the theory to Hertz in 1879 but it was not until 1885 in Karlsruhe that Hertz found the equipment needed for what became his most famous experiments. In 1888 he succeeded in producing electromagnetic waves using an electric circuit; the circuit contained a metal rod that had a small gap at its midpoint, and when sparks crossed this gap violent oscillations of high frequency were set up in the rod. Hertz proved that these waves were transmitted through air by detecting them with another similar circuit some distance away. He also showed that like light waves they were reflected and refracted and, most important, that they traveled at the same speed as light but had a much longer wavelength. These waves, originally called *Hertzian waves* but now known as radio waves, conclusively confirmed Maxwell's prediction on the existence of electromagnetic waves, both in the form of light and radio waves.

Once at Bonn Hertz continued his analysis of Maxwell's theory, publishing two papers in 1890. His experimental and theoretical work put the field of electrodynamics on a much firmer footing. It should also be noted that in 1887 he inadvertently discovered the photoelectric effect whereby ultraviolet radiation releases electrons from the surface of a metal. Although realizing its significance, he left others to investigate it.

Hertz's results produced enormous activity among scientists but he died before seeing Guglielmo Marconi make his discovery of radio waves a practical means of communication. In his honor the unit of frequency is now called the hertz.

Hertzsprung, Ejnar

(1873–1967)

DANISH ASTRONOMER

Hertzsprung (**hairt**-spruung) was born in Frederiksberg, Denmark, the son of a senior civil servant who had a deep interest in mathematics and astronomy but who was anxious to see that his son received a more practical education. Consequently Hertzsprung was trained as a chemical engineer at the Copenhagen Polytechnic, graduating in 1898. He worked as a chemist in St. Petersburg and then studied photochemistry under Wilhelm Ostwald in Leipzig before returning to Denmark in 1902. His first professional appointment as an astronomer was in 1909 at the Potsdam Observatory. The bulk of his career, from 1919 to 1944, was spent at the University of Leiden where from 1935 he served as director of the observatory. After his retirement in 1944 he returned to Denmark where he continued his studies for a further 20 years.

Hertzsprung's name is linked with that of Henry Russell as independent innovators of the Hertzsprung–Russell (H–R) diagram. In the late 19th and early 20th centuries, techniques used in photographic spectroscopy were being greatly improved. With his background in photochemistry, Hertzsprung was able to devise methods by which he could determine the intrinsic brightness, i.e., luminosity, of stars. He showed that the luminosity of most of the stars he studied decreased as their color changed from white through yellow to red, i.e., as their temperature decreased. He also found that a few stars were very much brighter than those of the same color. Hertzsprung thus discovered the two main groupings of stars: the highly luminous giant and supergiant stars and the more numerous but fainter dwarf or main-sequence stars. Hertzsprung published his results, although not in diagrammatic form, in 1905 and 1907 in an obscure photographic journal. His work therefore did not become generally known and credit initially went to Russell who published the eponymous diagram in 1913. It would be difficult to exaggerate the importance or usefulness of the H–R diagram, which has been the starting point for discussions of stellar evolution ever since.

Much of Hertzsprung's work concerned open clusters of stars. In 1911 he published the first color-magnitude diagrams of the Pleiades and Hyades clusters, showing how the color of member stars varied with observed brightness. He also measured the proper motions of stars, i.e., their angular motions in a direction perpendicular to the observer's line of sight, and used the results to establish membership of clusters.

One other major achievement of Hertzsprung was the development of a method for the determination of stellar and galactic distances. In the 19th century Friedrich Bessel and Friedrich Georg Struve had been the first to use measurements of annual parallax to calculate stellar distances but this was only accurate up to distances of about a hundred light-years. In 1913, when Hertzsprung announced his results, astronomers had made little progress in measuring distances. The work of Henrietta Leavitt in 1912 had shown that the period of light variation of a group of stars known as Cepheid variables was related to their observed mean brightness. These Cepheids lay in the Magellanic Clouds. Hertzsprung assumed that at the great distance of the Clouds all member stars could be considered to have approximately the same distance. Since observed and intrinsic brightness of a star are directly linked by its distance, the periods of light variation of Cepheids in the Clouds were thus also related to their intrinsic brightness. By extrapolation, Cepheids could thus be an invaluable means of measuring the distance of any group of stars containing a Cepheid by observing the period and apparent brightness of the Cepheid.

The work of establishing the period-luminosity relation on a numerical basis was begun by Hertzsprung and continued by Harlow Shapley. Hertzsprung determined the distances of several nearby Cepheids from

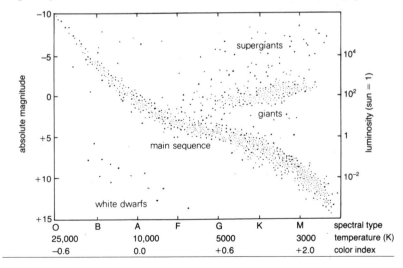

HERTZSPRUNG–RUSSELL DIAGRAM *An example of an H–R diagram for bright stars.*

measurements of their proper motions. Using his results and Leavitt's values for the periods and apparent brightness of Cepheids in the Small Magellanic Cloud (SMC) he was then able to calculate the distance to the SMC. Although somewhat smaller than today's value, this was the first measurement of an extragalactic distance.

Herzberg, Gerhard

(1904–   )

CANADIAN SPECTROSCOPIST

Born in Hamburg, Germany, Herzberg (**herts**-berg) was educated at the universities of Göttingen and Berlin. He taught at the Darmstadt Institute of Technology from 1930 until 1935 when, with the rise to power of the Nazis, he emigrated to Canada where he was research professor of physics at the University of Saskatchewan from 1935 until 1945. He returned to Canada in 1948 after spending three years as professor of spectroscopy at the Yerkes Observatory, Wisconsin. From 1949 until his retirement in 1969 he was director of the division of pure physics for the National Research Council in Ottawa.

Herzberg is noted for his extensive work on the technique and interpretation of the spectra of molecules. He has elucidated the properties of many molecules, ions, and radicals and also contributed to the use of spectroscopy in astronomy (e.g., in detecting hydrogen in space). His work includes the first measurements of the Lamb shifts (important in quantum electrodynamics) in deuterium, helium, and the positive lithium ion.

Herzberg has written a number of books, notably the two classic surveys *Atomic Spectra and Atomic Structure* (1937) and *Molecular Spectra and Molecular Structure* (4 vols. 1939–79). He received the Nobel Prize for chemistry in 1971 for his "contributions to the knowledge of electronic structure and geometry of molecules, particularly free radicals."

Hess, Germain Henri

(1802–1850)

SWISS–RUSSIAN CHEMIST

Hess, who was born at Geneva in Switzerland, was taken to Russia as a child by his parents. He studied medicine at the University of Dorpat (1822–25) and started his career by practicing medicine in Irkutsk. In 1830 he moved to St. Petersburg, becoming professor of chemistry at the Technological Institute of the university. While there he wrote a chemistry textbook in Russian, which became a standard work.

Hess worked on minerals and on sugars, but his main work was on the theory of heat. By carefully measuring the heat given off in various chemical changes, he was able to conclude in 1840 that in any chemical reaction, regardless of how many stages there are, the amount of heat developed in the overall reaction is constant. *Hess's law*, also called the law of constant heat summation, is in fact a special case of the law of conservation of energy.

Hess, Harry Hammond

(1906–1969)

AMERICAN GEOLOGIST

Hess was born in New York City and educated at Yale, graduating in 1927, and Princeton where he gained his PhD in 1932. He worked first as a field geologist in Northern Rhodesia (now Zambia) in the period 1928–29. After a year at Rutgers in 1932 he moved to Princeton in 1934, becoming professor of geology in 1948.

Hess was a key figure in the postwar revolution in the Earth sciences. He was the first to draw up theories using the considerable discoveries on the nature of the ocean floor that were made in the postwar period. Hess himself discovered about 160 flat-topped summits on the ocean bed, which he named guyots for an earlier Princeton geologist, Arnold Guyot. As they failed to produce atolls he dated them to the Precambrian, 600 million years ago, before the appearance of corals. But in 1956 Cretaceous fossils, from only 100 million years ago, were found in Pacific guyots. The whole of the ocean floor was discovered to be surpris-

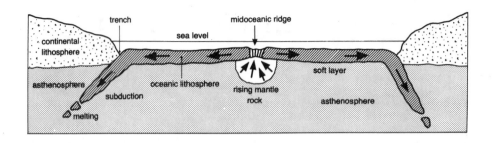

SEA-FLOOR SPREADING *Magma rises from the Earth's mantle to the surface along the midoceanic ridge and cools to form the new oceanic crust. H. H. Hess estimated the oceanic crust to be spreading apart along the midoceanic ridge at the rate of about 1 to 2 inches (2.5–5 cm) a year.*

ingly young, dating only as far back as the Mesozoic, while the continental rocks were much older.

In 1962 Hess published his important paper, *History of Ocean Basins*. The ocean floors were young, he argued, as they were constantly being renewed by magma flowing from the mantle up through the oceanic rifts, discovered by William Morris Ewing, and spreading out laterally. This became known as the sea-floor spreading hypothesis and was a development of the convection-currents theory proposed by Arthur Holmes in 1929. The hypothesis has been modified since its proposal, notably through the work of Drummond Hoyle Matthews and Frederick Vine on magnetic anomalies, but remains largely accepted.

Hess, Victor Francis

(1883–1964)

AUSTRIAN–AMERICAN PHYSICIST

Hess, the son of a forester, was born at Waldstein in Austria and educated at the University of Graz where he obtained his doctorate in 1906. He worked at the Institute for Radium Research, Vienna, from 1910 to 1920 and then took up an appointment at the University of Graz where he became professor in 1925. In 1931 he set up a cosmic-ray observatory near Innsbruck but in 1938 he was dismissed from all his official positions as he was a Roman Catholic. Leaving Nazi Austria, he emigrated to America where he served as professor of physics at Fordham University, New York, from 1938 to 1956.

In 1911–12 Hess made the fundamental discovery of cosmic rays, as they were later called by Robert Millikan in 1925. For this work he shared the Nobel Prize for physics with Carl Andersen in 1936. The work stemmed from an attempt to explain why gases are always slightly ionized; thus a gold-leaf electroscope, however well insulated it might be, will discharge itself over a period of time. Radiation was clearly coming from somewhere and the most likely source was the Earth itself. To test this, attempts were made to see if the rate of discharge decreased with altitude. But both T. Wulf, who took an electroscope to the top of the Eiffel Tower in 1910, and A. Gockel, who took one up in a balloon in 1912, failed to obtain any clear results.

However when Hess ascended in a balloon to a height of 16,000 feet (4,880 m) he found that although the electroscope's rate of discharge decreased initially up to about 2,000 feet (610 m), thereafter it increased considerably, being four times faster at 16,000 feet than at sea level. He concluded that his results were best explained by the assumption that a radiation of very great penetrating power enters our atmosphere from above.

He was able to eliminate the Sun as the sole cause for he found that the effect was produced both by day and at night. Further, in 1912, he made a balloon ascent during a total eclipse of the Sun and found that during the period when the Sun was completely obscured there was no significant effect on the rate of discharge. Hess however failed to convince everyone that cosmic rays came from outside the Earth's atmosphere as it could still be argued that the source of the radiation was such atmospheric disturbances as thunderstorms. It was left to Millikan in 1925 finally to refute this objection.

Hess, Walter Rudolf

(1881–1973)

SWISS NEUROPHYSIOLOGIST

The son of a physics teacher from Frauenfel in Switzerland, Hess was educated at the universities of Lausanne, Bern, Berlin, Kiel, and Zurich where he obtained his MD in 1906. Although he actually began as an ophthalmologist, building up a prosperous practice, he decided in 1912 to abandon it for a career in physiology. After junior posts in Zurich and Bonn he was appointed in 1917 to the directorship of the physiology department at the University of Zurich, where he remained until his retirement in 1951.

In the early 1920s Hess began an important investigation of the interbrain and hypothalamus. To do this he inserted fine electrodes into the brains of cats, and used these to stimulate specific groups of cells. His most startling discovery was that when electrodes in the posterior interbrain were switched on this would instantaneously turn a friendly cat into an aggressive spitting creature – a transformation instantly reversed by a further press of the switch. Other areas found by Hess would induce flight, sleep, or defecation.

Less dramatic perhaps but no less significant were the two main areas identified by Hess in the hypothalamus. Stimulation of the posterior region prepared the animal for action but stimulation of the anterior region tended to cause relaxation. Hess had discovered the control center for the sympathetic and parasympathetic systems.

Hess's work was enormously influential and led to a detailed mapping of the interbrain and hypothalamus by many different workers in various centers over a number of years. For his discovery of "the functional organization of the interbrain" Hess was awarded the 1949 Nobel Prize for physiology or medicine, sharing it with Antonio Egas Moniz.

Hevelius, Johannes

(1611–1687)

GERMAN ASTRONOMER

I prefer the unaided eye.

Hevelius (hay-**vay**-lee-uus) was the son of a prosperous brewer from Danzig (now Gdańsk in Poland). He followed his father in the family business as well as devoting himself to civic duties. After studying in Leiden, he established his own observatory on the rooftops of several houses overlooking the Vistula, an observatory which soon gained him an international reputation.

He published several major works of observational astronomy. Four years' telescopic study of the Moon, using telescopes of long focal power, led to his *Selenographia* (1647; Pictures of the Moon). Making his own engravings of the Moon's surface he assigned names to the lunar mountains, craters, and plains taken from the Earth, placing, with what the writer Sir Thomas Browne called "witty congruity," "...the Mediterranean Sea, Mauritania, Sicily, and Asia Minor in the Moon." This system of naming, apart from the Alps, did not survive long, Giovanni Riccioli's alternative system of scientific eponomy being preferred. His star catalog *Prodromus astronomiae* (Guide to Astronomy) was published posthumously in 1690.

Hevelius is today best remembered for his "aerial" telescopes of enormous focal length and his rejection of telescopic sights for stellar observation and positional measurement. He was widely criticized for the latter eccentricity and in 1679 was paid a famous visit by Edmond Halley who had been instructed by Robert Hooke and John Flamsteed to persuade him of the advantages of the new telescopic sights. Hevelius claimed he could do as well with his quadrant and alidade. Halley tested him thoroughly, finding to his surprise that Hevelius could measure both consistently and accurately. He is therefore the last astronomer to do major observational work without a telescope.

Hevesy, George Charles von

(1885–1966)

HUNGARIAN–SWEDISH CHEMIST

Hevesy (**he**-ve-shee) came from a family of wealthy industrialists in Budapest, the Hungarian capital. He was educated in Budapest and at the University of Freiburg where he obtained his doctorate in 1908. He then worked in Zurich, Karlsruhe, Manchester, and Copenhagen, before his appointment to the chair of physical chemistry in 1926 at Freiburg. In 1935 he left Germany for Denmark, fleeing from the Nazis who caught up with him once more in 1942, when he sought refuge in Sweden at the University of Stockholm.

In 1923 Hevesy discovered the new element hafnium in collaboration with Dirk Coster. His most important work, however, began in 1911 in the Manchester laboratory of Ernest Rutherford, where he worked on the separation of "radium D" from a sample of lead. In fact radium D was a radioactive isotope of lead (lead–210) and could not be separated by chemical means. Hevesy was quick to see the significance of this and began exploring the use of radioactive isotopes as tracers. In 1913, with Friedrich Adolph Paneth, he used radioactive salts of lead and bismuth to determine their solubilities. In 1923 Hevesy made the first application of a radioactive tracer – Pb–212 – to a biological system. The Pb–212 was used to label a lead salt that plants took up in solution. At various time intervals plants were burned and the amount of lead taken up could be determined by simple measurements of the amount of radioactivity present. The drawback of this technique was the high toxicity of lead to most biological systems and it was only with the discovery of artificial radioactivity by Irène and Frédéric Joliot-Curie in 1934 that Hevesy's radioactive tracers developed into one of the most widely used and powerful techniques for the investigation of living and of complex systems. For his work in the development of radioactive tracers Hevesy was awarded the 1943 Nobel Prize for chemistry.

Hewish, Antony

(1924–)

BRITISH RADIO ASTRONOMER

Hewish was born at Fowey in Cornwall, England, and studied at Cambridge University. He obtained his BA in 1948 and his PhD in 1952 after wartime work with the Royal Aircraft Establishment, Farnborough. He lectured in physics at Cambridge until in 1969 he was made reader and in 1971 professor of radio astronomy, becoming professor emeritus in 1989. In 1974 he was awarded the Nobel Prize for physics jointly with Martin Ryle.

One of Hewish's research projects was the study of radio scintillation using the 4.5-acre telescope, which consisted of a regular array of 2,048 dipoles operating at a wavelength of 3.7 meters. Radio scintillation is a phenomenon, similar to the twinkling of visible stars, arising from random deflections of radio waves by ionized gas. The three types of scintillation are caused by ionized gas in the interstellar medium, in the interplanetary medium, and in the Earth's atmosphere. All three types were discovered at Cambridge and Hewish was involved in their investigation. In 1967 a research student, Jocelyn Bell, noticed a rapidly fluctuating but unusually regular radio signal that turned out to have a periodicity of 1.33730113 seconds. She had discovered the first pulsar.

To determine the nature of the signal, Hewish's first job was to eliminate such man-made sources as satellites, radar echoes, and the like. Measurements indicated that it must be well beyond the solar system. It seemed possible that it had been transmitted by an alien intelligence and the LGM (Little Green Men) hypothesis, as it became known, was seriously considered at Cambridge, but with the rapid discovery of three more pulsars it was soon dropped.

Hewish did however manage to establish some of the main properties of the pulsar from a careful analysis of its radio signal. Apart from its striking regularity (it was later shown to be slowing down very slightly) it was extremely small, no more than a few thousand kilometers, and was situated in our Galaxy.

By the end of February 1968 Hewish was ready to publish. His account received wide publicity in the popular press and stimulated much thought among astronomers as to the possible mechanism. The proposal made by Thomas Gold and others that pulsars were rapidly rotating neutron stars has since won acceptance.

Heymans, Corneille Jean François

(1892–1968)

BELGIAN PHYSIOLOGIST AND PHARMACOLOGIST

Heymans (**hI**-mahns) was educated at the university in his native city of Ghent, where his father was professor of pharmacology, obtaining his MD in 1920. He began as a pharmacology lecturer there in 1923 and in 1930 succeeded his father, holding the chair until his retirement in 1963.

In 1924 Heymans began a series of important cross-circulation experiments. The relationship between respiration and blood pressure had been known for some time – high arterial pressure (hypertension) inhibited respiration while low pressure (hypotension) stimulated it – but the mechanism of such a response was far from clear. Heymans's basic experiment consisted of separating the head of a dog from its body in such a way that its only remaining contact with the body was the nervous supply to the heart. The body of the dog could be made to respire artificially while its head could be linked up to the blood supply of a second dog. Even in such circumstances, hypotension produced an increase in the rate of respiration while hypertension inhibited it. This suggested to Heymans that the process was due not to direct action of the blood pressure on the respiratory center but to nervous control.

Heymans went on to show the important role played in the regulation of heart rate and blood pressure by the carotid sinus, an enlargement of the carotid artery in the neck. By severing the sinus from its own blood supply while maintaining its nervous connection and linking it up to the blood supply of another animal he was able to show that changes of pressure initiated nervous reflexes that automatically reversed the process. The sinus was in fact a sensitive pressure receptor. He also demonstrated that a nearby glandlike structure, the glomus caroticum, was a chemoreceptor, responding to changes in the oxygen/carbon dioxide ratio in the blood.

For his work on the regulation of respiration Heymans was awarded the 1938 Nobel Prize for physiology or medicine.

Heyrovský, Jaroslav

(1890–1967)

CZECH PHYSICAL CHEMIST

The reason why I keep some 38 years to... the dropping mercury electrode is its exquisite property as electrode material.
—Nobel Prize address, 1959

Heyrovský (**hay**-rawf-skee), the son of an academic lawyer, was educated at Charles University in his native Prague and at University College, London. He joined the staff of Charles University in 1919 where he served as professor of physics from 1919 until 1954. From 1950 he was also head of the Central Polarographic Institute, which, since 1964, has borne his name.

Heyrovský is best known for his discovery and development of polarography, which he described in 1922. This is one of the most versatile of all analytical techniques. It depends on the fact that in electrolysis the ions are discharged at an electrode and, if the electrode is small, the current may be limited by the rate of movement of ions to the electrode surface. In polarography the cathode is a small drop of mercury (constantly forming and dropping to keep the surface clean). The voltage is increased slowly and the current plotted against voltage. The current increases in steps, each corresponding to a particular type of positive ion in the solution. The height of the steps indicates the concentration of the ion. For his work, Heyrovský was awarded the Nobel Prize for chemistry in 1959.

Higgins, William

(1763–1825)

IRISH CHEMIST

Born at Colooney in Ireland, Higgins worked in London as a young man with his uncle, Bryan Higgins, the chemist. He studied at Oxford University from 1786 and on his return to Ireland became, in 1791, chemist to the Apothecaries Company of Ireland. He moved to Dublin in 1795 to become chemist and librarian to the Royal Dublin Society, this post being made into a professorship in 1800. From 1795 to 1822 he was chemist to the Irish Linen Board.

Higgins is remembered for his contributions to the new atomic theory and for his claim to have anticipated John Dalton. His claim is based on his work *A Comparative View of the Phlogistic and Antiphlogistic Theories with Inductions* (1789), which was written as a reply to Richard Kirwan's work.

He introduced a clearer symbolism system than that of Dalton but did not follow up his work on atomism until he published a strong attack on Dalton's work in his eight-volume work *Experiments and Observations on the Atomic Theory and Electrical Phenomena* (1814).

Higgins spent the intervening years between these publications trying to introduce new chemical technology into Ireland. In 1799 he published an *Essay on the Theory and Practice of Bleaching*, a work written specifically for the bleachers themselves.

Higgs, Peter Ware

(1929–   )

BRITISH THEORETICAL PHYSICIST

Higgs was born at Bristol in the west of England and educated at Kings College, London, where he completed his PhD in 1955. He worked initially at the University of London but moved to Edinburgh University in 1960 and was elected professor of theoretical physics there in 1980.

Along with many other physicists in the 1960s, Higgs worked on proposals to unify the weak and the electromagnetic forces into a single electroweak theory. At very high temperatures the two forces and their carriers, photons for the electromagnetic force and the W and Z bosons for the weak force, would be indistinguishable. But, at lower temperatures, the symmetry breaks down and massless photons are obviously distinct from the massive W and Z bosons. In 1964 Higgs worked out a mechanism for the breakdown in symmetry, since known as the *Higgs field*, which would endow the bosons with mass. At the same time, he noted, the mechanism would also produce another massive particle, the *Higgs boson*.

The existence of this particle, it has been claimed, will be the ultimate test of the correctness of the electroweak theory, and of the standard model of particle physics itself. Yet no sign of the particle has so far been detected. The failure is normally explained away by pointing out that the Higgs boson probably has a mass in excess of 1 TeV (10^9 electron volts), well beyond the capacity of any current accelerator. It will therefore be the first task of the Superconducting Proton Synchotron, with an expected capacity of 20 TeV, if ever completed, to search for the Higgs boson.

Hilbert, David

(1862–1943)

GERMAN MATHEMATICIAN

Physics is much too hard for physicists.
—Quoted by Constance Reid in *Hilbert* (1970)

One hears a good deal nowadays of the hostility between science and technology. I don't think that is true, gentlemen. I am quite sure that it isn't true, gentlemen. It almost certainly isn't true. It really can't be true. *Sie haben ja gar nichts einander zu tun* [They have nothing whatever to do with one another].
—Quoted by J. R. Oppenheimer in *Physics in the Contemporary World*

Hilbert (**hil**-bairt) studied at the university in his native city of Königsberg (now Kaliningrad in Russia) and at Heidelberg; he also spent brief periods in Paris and Leipzig. He took his PhD in 1885, the next year became *Privatdozent* at Königsberg, and by 1892 had become professor there. In 1895 he moved to Göttingen to take up the chair that he occupied until his official retirement in 1930.

Hilbert's mathematical work was very wide ranging and during his long life there were few fields to which he did not make some contribution and many he completely transformed. His attention was first turned to the newly created theory of invariants and in the period 1885–88 he virtually completed the subject by solving all the central problems. However, his work on invariants was very fruitful as he created entirely new methods for tackling problems in the context of a much wider general theory. The fruit of this work consisted of many new and fundamental theorems in algebra and in particular in the theory of polynomial rings. Much of his work on invariants turned out later to have important application in the new subject of homological algebra.

Hilbert now turned to algebraic number theory where he did what is probably his finest research. Hilbert and Minkowski had been asked to prepare a report surveying the current state of number theory but Minkowski soon dropped out, leaving Hilbert to produce not only a masterly account but also a substantial body of original and fundamental new discoveries. The work was presented in the *Zahlbericht* (1897; Report on Numbers) with an elegance and lucidity of exposition that has rarely been equaled.

Hilbert then moved to another area of mathematics and wrote the *Grundlagen der Geometrie* (1899; Foundations of Geometry), giving an account of geometry as it had developed through the 19th century. Here his interest lay chiefly in expounding and illuminating the work of others in a systematic way rather than in making new developments of the subject. He devised an abstract axiomatic system that could admit many different geometries – Euclidean and non-Euclidean – as models and by this means go much further than had previously been done in obtaining consistency and independence proofs for various sets of geometrical axioms. Apart from its importance for pure geometry his work led to the development of a number of new algebraic concepts and was particularly important to Hilbert himself because his experience with the axiomatic method and his interest in consistency proofs shaped his approach to mathematical logic and the foundations of mathematics.

In mathematical logic and the philosophy of mathematics Hilbert is a key figure, being one of the major proponents of the formalist view, which he expounded with much greater precision than had his 19th-century precursors. This philosophical view of mathematics had a formative impact on the development of mathematical logic because of the central role it gave to the formalization of mathematics into axiomatic systems and the study of their properties by metamathematical means.

Hilbert aimed at formalizing as much of mathematics as possible and finding consistency proofs for the resulting formal systems. It was soon shown by Kurt Gödel that *Hilbert's program*, as this proposal is called, could not be carried out, at least in its original form, but it is nonetheless true that Gödel's own revolutionary metamathematical work would have been inconceivable without Hilbert. Hilbert's contribution to mathematical logic was important, especially to the development of proof theory, as further developed by such mathematicians as Gerhard Gentzen.

Hilbert also made notable contributions to analysis, to the calculus of variations, and to mathematical physics. His work on operators and on *Hilbert space* (a type of infinite-dimensional space) was of crucial importance to quantum mechanics. His considerable influence on mathematical physics was also exerted through his colleagues at Göttingen who included Minkowski, Hermann Weyl, Erwin Schrödinger, and Werner Heisenberg.

In 1900 Hilbert presented a list of 23 outstanding unsolved mathematical problems to the International Congress of Mathematicians in Paris. A number of these problems still remain unsolved and the mathematics that has been created in solving the others has fully vindicated his deep insight into his subject. Hilbert was an excellent teacher and during his time at Göttingen continued the tradition begun in the 19th century and built the university into an outstanding center of mathematical research, which it remained until the dispersal of the intellectual community by the Nazis in 1933. Hilbert is generally considered one of the greatest mathematicians of the 20th century and indeed of all time.

Hildebrand, Joel Henry

(1881–1983)

AMERICAN CHEMIST

> A child of the new generation
> Refused to learn multiplication.
> He said, "Don't conclude
> That I'm stupid or rude;
> I am simply without motivation."
> —*Perspectives in Biology and Medicine* (1970)

Hildebrand was born in Camden, New Jersey, and educated at the University of Pennsylvania and at the University of Berlin, where he obtained his PhD in 1906. He returned to Pennsylvania in 1907, but moved to the University of California, Berkeley, in 1913 and served there as professor of chemistry from 1918 until his retirement in 1952.

Hildebrand, the author with R. Powell of a widely read textbook, *Principles of Chemistry* (1964; 7th edition), was engaged in chemical research for virtually the whole of the century. He worked on fluorine chemistry, intermolecular forces, and, above all, on the theory of solubility. Even in his nineties Hildebrand continued with his researches, producing in 1976 a substantial monograph on the subject of viscosity and diffusion.

Hilditch, Thomas Percy

(1886–1965)

BRITISH CHEMIST

A Londoner, Hilditch was educated at the University of London, where he was awarded a DSc in 1911. After further studies in Jena and Geneva he joined the research laboratories of Joseph Crosfield and Sons Ltd., a soap and chemical manufacturer (1911–25). There he began his studies of fat chemistry for which he is best known. He published over 300 papers in this field and produced two standard works, *The Chemical Constitution of Natural Fats* (1940) and *Industrial Chemistry of Fats and Waxes* (1927).

In 1926 Hilditch became the first John Campbell Brown Professor of Industrial Chemistry at Liverpool University, where he remained until his retirement in 1951. He established a large research school of fat chemistry at Liverpool, where with his coworkers he established the fatty acid and glyceride composition of a large number of fats and oils – over 1,450 such substances were dealt with in the fourth edition of his 1940 work published in 1964.

Hill, Archibald Vivian

(1886–1977)

BRITISH PHYSIOLOGIST AND
BIOCHEMIST

Born at Bristol in the west of England, Hill was professor of physiology at Manchester University (1920–23) and then Jodrell Professor at University College, London, from 1923 to 1925 (and honorary professor from 1926 to 1951). He was Foulerton Research Professor of the Royal Society (1926–51), of which he was also for some years both secretary and foreign secretary. From 1940 until 1946 he was the Independent Conservative member of Parliament for Cambridge University and a member of the War Cabinet Scientific Advisory Committee.

Hill's major research was directed toward accurately recording the minute quantities of heat produced during muscle action. For this he used thermocouples, which recorded the smallest variations in heat generated after the muscle had completed its movement. He was able to show that oxygen was only consumed *after* muscular contraction, and not during it, indicating that molecular oxygen is required only for muscle recovery. In 1922 he shared the Nobel Prize for physiology or medicine (with Otto Meyerhof) for this work on the physiology of muscular contraction.

Hill, James Peter

(1873–1954)

BRITISH EMBRYOLOGIST

Hill, the son of a farmer from Kennoway in Scotland, was educated at the University of Edinburgh and the Royal College of Science, London. He taught in Australia at the University of Sydney from 1892 until 1906 when he returned to England as Jodrell Professor of Zoology at University College, London. In 1921 he became professor of embryology and histology, a post he retained until his retirement in 1938.

Beginning during his time in Australia, Hill spent most of his life working on monotreme and marsupial embryology, a virtually unexplored area. Hill totally dominated the field and in his numerous monographs on the subject revealed the evolutionary relationships between the primitive mammals.

Hillier, James

(1915–)

CANADIAN–AMERICAN PHYSICIST

Born in Brantford, Ontario, Hillier was educated at the University of Toronto, where he gained successively his BA (1937), MA (1938), and PhD in physics (1941). He went to live and work in America in 1940 and became a naturalized citizen in 1945. From 1940 to 1953 he worked for the Radio Corporation of America (RCA) Laboratories as a research physicist, primarily on the development of the electron microscope.

Many efforts were being made around the world to develop a commercial electron microscope that could offer higher resolution than optical microscopes. It had been known since the 1920s that a shaped magnetic field could act as a "lens" for electrons, and in the 1930s the first electron micrographs had been taken. Hillier and his colleagues at RCA designed and built the first successful high-resolution electron microscope in America in 1940; they had in fact been anticipated by Ernst Ruska and Max Knoll who had produced a similar machine for the Siemens and Halske Company in Germany in 1938. The outbreak of war prevented commercial development and exploitation of the German machine.

Hillier made many instrumental advances to the electron microscope. By 1946 he had achieved resolutions (magnifications) approaching close to the theoretical limits. He also involved himself in the development of techniques for the preparation of viral and bacteriological samples for examination.

Hillier's career at RCA continued with only a short break to his present position of executive vice-president for research engineering. He is now principally concerned with research management, and has served on various American governmental, research, and engineering committees.

Hinshelwood, Sir Cyril Norman

(1897–1967)

BRITISH CHEMIST

Hinshelwood, a Londoner, was educated at Oxford University, where he was elected to a fellowship in 1920 and obtained his doctorate in 1924. In 1937 he became Dr. Lee's Professor of Chemistry at Oxford. He retired in 1964 when he moved to Imperial College, London, as a senior research fellow.

Hinshelwood worked mainly in the field of chemical reaction kinetics. He produced a major text on the subject, *The Kinetics of Chemical Change in Gaseous Systems* (1926) and, in 1956, shared the Nobel Prize for chemistry with Nicolay Semenov for his work. He later applied his work to a relatively new field in his book, *The Chemical Kinetics of the Bacterial Cell* (1954).

In some papers published earlier, in 1950, Hinshelwood came very close to the true meaning of DNA, established by Jim Watson and Francis Crick three years later. He declared that in the synthesis of protein the nucleic acid guides the order in which the various amino acids are laid down. Little attention was paid to Hinshelwood's proposal at the time although Crick later declared it to be the first serious suggestion of how DNA might work.

Hinshelwood was a linguist and classical scholar as well as a scientist; he had the unique distinction of serving as president of both the Royal Society (1955–60) and the Classical Association. He was knighted in 1948.

Hipparchus

(*c.* 170 BC–*c.* 120 BC)

GREEK ASTRONOMER AND GEOGRAPHER

Born at Nicaea, which is now in Turkey, Hipparchus (hi-**par**-kus) worked in Rhodes, where he built an observatory, and in Alexandria. None of his works have survived but many of them were recorded by Ptolemy. In 134 BC he observed a new star in the constellation of Scorpio. This led him to construct a catalog of about 850 stars. By comparing the position of the stars of his day with those given 150 years earlier he found that Spica, which was then 6° from the autumn equinox, had previously been 8°. He used this observation to deduce not the movement of Spica but the east to west precession (motion) of the equinoctial point. He calculated the rate of the precession as about 45 seconds of arc a year – a value close to the 50.27 seconds now accepted. He also introduced the practice of dividing the stars into different classes of magnitude based on their apparent brightness. The brightest stars he classed as first magnitude and those just visible to the naked eye he classed as sixth magnitude.

As a theorist Hipparchus worked on the orbits of the Sun and Moon. He established more accurate lengths of both the year and the month and was able to produce more accurate eclipse predictions. One of his lasting achievements was the construction of a table of chords, which virtually began the discipline of trigonometry. The concept of a sine had not yet been developed. Instead, Hipparchus calculated the ratio of the chord to the diameter of its own circle, which was divided into 120 parts. Thus if a chord produced by an angle of 60° is half the length of the radius, it would have, for Hipparchus, 60 parts. He much improved the geography of Eratosthenes, fixing the parallels astronomically.

Hipparchus of Cos

(*c.* 460 BC–*c.* 370 BC)

GREEK PHYSICIAN

We must turn to nature itself, to the observations of the body in health and disease to learn the truth.
—*Aphorisms*

Science is the father of knowledge, but opinion breeds ignorance.
—*The Canon Law*

Very little is known of the life of Hippocrates (hi-**pok**-ra-teez) except that he was born on the Greek island of Cos. The main source, Soranus, dates from the second century AD and was clearly telling a traditional tale rather than writing a biography. Hippocrates is reported to have studied under his father Heraclides, also a physician, and with the atomist Democritus and the sophist Gorgias. He then seems to have spent most of his life traveling around the Greek world curing the great of obscure diseases and ridding grateful cities of plagues and pestilence.

After the fantasy of his life there is the reality of the *Corpus Hippocraticum* (The Hippocratic Collection). This consists of some 70 works though whether any were actually written by Hippocrates himself will probably always remain a matter of speculation. What is clear, on stylistic and paleographic grounds, is that the corpus was produced by many hands in the second half of the fifth century and the first part of the fourth. Nor do the works represent a single "Hippocratic" point of view but, it has been suggested, probably formed the library of a physician and acquired the name of its first owner or collector.

Of more importance is the character of these remarkable works. They are surprisingly free of any attempt to explain disease in theological, astrological, diabolic, or any other spiritual terms. Diseases in the *Corpus* are natural events, which arise in a normal manner from the food one has eaten or some such factor as the weather. The cause of the disease is for the Hippocratic basically a malfunction of the veins leading to the brain which, though no doubt false, is the same kind of rational, material, and verifiable claim that could be found in any late 20th-century neurological textbook.

Such rationality was not to rule for many years for in the fourth century BC new cults entered Greece and with them the dream, the charm, and other such superstitions entered medicine. More successful in the length of its survival was the actual theory of disease contained in the *Corpus*. This was the view, first formulated by Alcmaeon in the fifth century BC, that health consists of an *isonomia* or equal rule of the bodily elements rather than a *monarchia* or domination by a single element. By the time of Hippocrates it was accepted that there were just four elements, earth, air, fire, and water with their corresponding qualities, coldness, dryness, heat, and wetness. If present in the human body in the right amounts in the right places health resulted, but if equilibrium was destroyed then so too was health.

A new terminology developed to describe such pathological conditions, a terminology still apparent in most western languages. Thus an excess of earth, the cold/dry element, produced an excess of black bile, or in Greek melancholic, in the body; too much water, the cold/moist element, made one phlegmatic.

One striking contrast between Hippocratic and later medicine is the curious yet impressive reluctance of the former to attempt cures for various disorders: the emphasis is rather on prognosis. For example, the *Epidemics* describes the course, but not treatment, of various complaints. At least knowing the expected course and outcome of an illness helped the practitioner to inform his patient what to expect, information that could be useful and reassuring. Further, if it is known which conditions lead to a disease such conditions could sometimes be avoided.

The works *Regimen in Acute Diseases* and *Regimen in Health*, which deal specifically with therapy, tend to restrict themselves to diet, exercise, bathing, and emetics. Thus the Hippocratic doctor may not have cured many of his patients but he was certainly less likely than his 18th-century counterpart to actually kill them.

Hirsch, Sir Peter Bernhard

(1925–)

BRITISH METALLURGIST

Hirsch, who was born in Berlin, Germany, gained his doctorate from Cambridge University in 1951. Continuing at Cambridge he lectured in physics from 1959 and took a readership in 1964. In 1966 he moved to the University of Oxford where he was Isaac Wolfson Professor of Metallurgy from 1966 to 1992. His research interests include the development of the Oxford field-emission scanning transmission electron microscope, the weak-beam technique of electron microscopy, and electron microscopy of the chemical behavior of metal oxides. Hirsch is known principally for his pioneering work in applying the electron microscope to the study of imperfections in the crystalline structure of metals, and in relating these defects to mechanical properties. He showed, for instance, that dislocations (faults) play an important part in theories of work-hardening.

Hirst, Sir Edmund Langley

(1898–1975)

BRITISH CHEMIST

Hirst, the son of a baptist minister from Preston in the north of England, was educated at St. Andrews University, where he worked with Norman Haworth and obtained his PhD in 1921. He continued working with Haworth at the universities of Durham and Birmingham, where

Hirst served as reader in natural products from 1934 until 1936 when he was appointed professor of organic chemistry at Bristol University. He moved to Manchester in 1944 but held the chair of organic chemistry there only until 1947 when he accepted a similar post at the University of Edinburgh. Here he remained until his retirement in 1968.

Hirst worked mainly in the field of carbohydrate chemistry, collaborating with Haworth over a long period in working out the structure and synthesis of various sugars. He succeeded in showing that the ring structure of stable methyl glycosides, for example of xylose, rhamnose, arabinose, and glucose, are actually six-membered and not, as previously assumed, five-membered. That is, they have the pyranose rather than the furanose ring structure.

Hirst is also known for determining the structure of vitamin C and, in collaboration with Haworth, managing to synthesize this compound – the first chemical synthesis of a vitamin.

His, Wilhelm

(1831–1904)

SWISS ANATOMIST AND
PHYSIOLOGIST

His (hiss), a merchant's son from Basel in Switzerland, studied at a number of German and Swiss universities before graduating from the university in his native city in 1854. He served on the staff there as professor of anatomy and physiology from 1857 until 1872 when he moved to a comparable post at the University of Leipzig, which he retained until his death.

His did much to redirect embryological research onto a more fruitful track by arguing powerfully against the so-called biogenetic law as formulated by Ernst Haeckel. His detailed how, starting from the assumption that the embryonic layers are basically elastic sheets, the principal organs could be constructed by such straightforward processes as cutting, bending, pinching, and folding. He was the first to describe accurately the development of the human embryo. His also worked on the development of the nervous system and was able to show that nerve fibers grow from specialized kinds of cell he termed "neuroblasts."

He had earlier, in 1866, introduced into science that invaluable instrument the microtome. This permitted the cutting of extremely thin slices, a few microns thick, for staining and microscopic examination.

One discovery frequently attributed to His, namely the *bundles of His* – a specialized bundle of fibers connecting the cardiac auricles and ventricles – have nothing to do with him. They were in fact first described by his son, also named Wilhelm, professor of medicine at the University of Berlin.

Hisinger, Wilhelm

(1766–1852)

SWEDISH MINERALOGIST

Hisinger (**hee**-sing-er) was the son of a wealthy iron foundry owner from Skinnatersberg in Sweden. Following his father's death he ran the family business and also devoted himself to private geological research.

One of his iron mines at Bastnäs produced a mineral with an unexpectedly high density and Hisinger studied this mineral over the years, sending samples to some of the most expert analysts of Europe. Martin Klaproth who examined it in 1803 became convinced that it contained a new element. Shortly afterwards both Jöns Berzelius and Hisinger isolated a new element from it, which they called cerium, after the new minor planet Ceres, discovered by Giussepe Piazzi in 1801.

Hisinger also made major contributions to the growth of geological knowledge, publishing a geological map of southern and central Sweden (1832) and an account of the fossils of Sweden (1837–41).

Hitchings, George Herbert

(1905–   )

AMERICAN PHARMACOLOGIST

Hitchings, the son of a naval architect, was born in Hoquiam, Washington, and educated at the University of Washington and at Harvard where he obtained his PhD in 1933 and where he taught until 1939. He then moved briefly to Western Reserve University until in 1942 he joined the Wellcome Research Laboratories where he spent the rest of his career, serving as vice president in charge of research from 1966 until his retirement in 1975.

Hitchings has been one of the most productive of modern chemical pharmacologists. He began in 1942 with the study of purines and pyrimidines on the grounds that, as important ingredients in cell metabolism, their manipulation could lead to the control of important diseases at the cellular level. This insight led to the synthesis in 1951 of the purine analog, 6-mercaptopurine (6MP), which, as it inhibited DNA synthesis and thus cellular proliferation, proved valuable in the treatment of cancer, particularly leukemia.

In 1959 6MP was found to inhibit the ability of rabbits to produce antibodies against foreign proteins. A less toxic form, azathioprine or Imuran, was quickly developed by Hitchings and used in 1960 by the surgeon Roy Calne to control rejection of transplanted kidneys.

One further drug was developed from work on 6MP when it was realized that it was broken down in the body by the enzyme xanthine oxydase, the same enzyme that converts purines into uric acid. As gout is caused by an excess of uric acid Hitchings developed allopurinol, which blocks uric acid production by competing for xanthine oxydase.

Other drugs developed by Hitchings include the malarial prophylactic pyrimethamine, or Daraprim, and the antibacterial, trimethoprim.

Hittorf, Johann Wilhelm

(1824–1914)

GERMAN CHEMIST AND PHYSICIST

Born at Bonn in Germany, Hittorf (**hit**-orf) became professor of chemistry and physics at the University of Münster in 1852 and later became director of laboratories there (1879–89).

He carried out fundamental work on electrolytes, publishing, in 1853, his paper *The Migration of Ions during Electrolysis*. Hittorf showed that changes in concentration around electrodes during electrolysis could be understood if it was assumed that not all ions move with the same speed. He showed how the relative speeds of ions could be calculated from changes in concentration. He also introduced the ideas of complex ions and transport numbers (sometimes called the Hittorf numbers). The transport number of a given ion in an electrolyte is the fraction of total current carried by that ion.

Hittorf was also one of the first to experiment on cathode rays, noting as early as 1868 that obstacles put in their way would cast shadows.

Hitzig, Eduard

(1838–1907)

GERMAN PSYCHIATRIST

I believe that intelligence, or more accurately, the storage of ideas, is to be looked for in all portions of the cerebral cortex, or rather in all parts of the brain.
—*Über die Funktionen der Grosshirnrinde* (1874;
On the Function of the Cerebral Cortex)

Incorrigible conceit and vanity complicated by Prussianism.
—Anon. on Hitzig

Hitzig (**hit**-sik), the son of a Berlin architect, was educated at the university there and obtained his MD in 1862. He was later appointed, in 1875, director of the Berghölzi asylum and professor of psychiatry at the University of Zurich. In 1885 Hitzig moved to similar posts at the University of Halle, posts he retained until his retirement in 1903.

In 1870, in collaboration with Gustav Fritsch, Hitzig published a fundamental paper, *On the Excitability of the Cerebrum*, which provided the first experimental evidence for cerebral localization. Following the important work of Pierre Flourens in 1824 it was widely accepted that, despite the discoveries of Paul Broca and John Neethlings Jackson, the cerebral hemispheres constituted a unity, the seat of intelligence, sensation, and volition and not the source of movement.

This was shown to be false when Hitzig and Fritsch electrically stimulated the cerebral cortex of a dog and elicited distinct muscular contractions. They identified five localized centers, which produced various movements on the side of the dog opposite to the side of the brain stimulated. Their work was soon confirmed by David Ferrier and opened up a vast research program, still, a century later, unfinished.

Hitzig himself continued with this work and in 1874 tried to define what soon became known as the motor area of the dog and the monkey. He also tried to identify, though less successfully, the site of intelligence, in the sense of abstract ideas, in the frontal lobes.

Hjelm, Peter Jacob

(1746–1813)

SWEDISH CHEMIST AND METALLURGIST

Hjelm (yelm), who was born at Sunnerbo, Sweden, studied at the University of Uppsala and became assay master of the Royal Mint in Stockholm in 1782. In the same year he discovered the element molybdenum. At the time, the term "molybdaena" (a Latin form of a Greek word for "lead") was used for a number of substances, including the substances now known as graphite and molybdenite. Carl Scheele showed that the mineral molybdenite with nitric acid produced sulfuric acid and an insoluble residue, which he suspected contained a new element. Lacking the appropriate equipment to reduce this, he called on the assistance of Hjelm, who obtained the metallic element molybdenum. This was later obtained in pure form by Jöns Berzelius in 1817.

Hoagland, Mahlon Bush

(1921–   )

AMERICAN BIOCHEMIST

Hoagland was born in Boston, Massachusetts, the son of Hudson Hoagland, a distinguished neurophysiologist. Having obtained his MD from Harvard in 1948, he joined the Huntington Laboratories of the Massachusetts General Hospital. He then served in the Harvard Medical School from 1960 until 1967 when he became professor of biochemistry at Dartmouth. From 1970 to 1985 he was scientific director of the Worcester Institute for Experimental Biology, founded by his father and Gregory Pincus in 1944.

In early 1955 Francis Crick published his "adaptor" hypothesis to explain protein synthesis by the cell. Unaware of this work, Hoagland, in collaboration with Paul Zamecnik and Mary Stephenson, provided the experimental confirmation in 1956. It had earlier been shown by George Palade that protein synthesis occurred outside the nucleus in the ribosomes. Hoagland and Zamecnik discovered that before the amino acids reach the ribosomes to be synthesized into protein, they are first activated by forming a bond with the energy-rich adenosine triphosphate (ATP).

What happened in the ribosome was unveiled by forming a cell-free mixture of ATP, the radioactively labeled amino acid leucine, enzymes, and some of the small soluble RNA molecules found in the cytoplasm. At this point they discovered the crucial step, predicted by Crick, in between the activation of the amino acid and its appearance in the protein; the amino acid became tightly bound to the soluble RNA. Shortly afterward the labeled leucine was no longer bound to the RNA but present in the protein. The discovery of transfer RNA (or tRNA as it soon became known) was also made independently by Paul Berg and Robert Holley.

In his autobiography *Toward the Habit of Truth* (1990), Hoagland described his work as a molecular biologist and sketched the history of the Worcester Institute.

Hodge, Sir William Vallance Douglas

(1903–1975)

BRITISH MATHEMATICIAN

Hodge studied at the university in his native city of Edinburgh and then at Cambridge. He later taught at Bristol University (from 1926) and in America at Princeton (1931–32). Most of his career was spent in Cambridge, England, where in 1936 he took up the Lowndean Chair in Mathematics.

Hodge's mathematical work belongs almost entirely to algebraic geometry and although no expert on analysis or physics his work had immense impact in both these fields. Hodge's principal contribution was to the theory of harmonic forms. One of his central results was a uniqueness theorem showing that there is a unique harmonic form with prescribed periods. In general Hodge helped to initiate the shift of focus in mathematics from a search for purely local results to the more ambitious global approach now so influential.

Hodgkin, Sir Alan Lloyd

(1914–)

BRITISH PHYSIOLOGIST

Born at Banbury in England, Hodgkin graduated from Cambridge University and became a fellow in 1936. He spent World War II working on radar for the Air Ministry. He then worked at the physiological laboratory at Cambridge, where he served as Foulerton Research Professor from 1952 to 1969 and as professor of biophysics from 1970 until 1981. He also served from 1978 to 1984 as master of Trinity College, Cambridge; he was knighted in 1972.

In 1951, with Andrew Huxley and Bernard Katz, he worked out the sodium theory to explain the difference in action and resting potentials in nerve fibers. Using the single nerve fiber (giant axon) of a squid, they were able to demonstrate that there is an exchange of sodium and potassium ions between the cell and its surroundings during a nervous impulse, which enables the nerve fiber to carry a further impulse. Hodgkin also showed that the nerve fiber's potential for electrical conduction was greater during the actual passage of an impulse than when the fiber is resting. For their work on the "sodium pump" mechanism and the chemical basis of nerve transmission Hodgkin, Huxley, and John Eccles shared the Nobel Prize for physiology or medicine in 1963. He is the author of *Conduction of the Nervous Impulse* (1964). In 1992 he published his autobiography *Chance and Design: Reminiscences of Science in Peace and War*.

Hodgkin, Dorothy Crowfoot

(1910–1994)

BRITISH CHEMIST

> I'm really an experimentalist. I used to say "I think with my hands." I just like manipulation.
> —Quoted by L. Wolpert and A. Richards in *A Passion for Science* (1988)

Born Dorothy Crowfoot in Cairo, Egypt, she was educated at Somerville College, Oxford. After a brief period as a postgraduate student at Cambridge University, she returned to Oxford in 1934 and spent her entire academic career there. She served as Wolfson Research Professor of the Royal Society from 1960 until 1977.

Hodgkin had the good fortune to fall under the influence of the inspiring and scientifically imaginative physicist J. D. Bernal at Cambridge. Bernal was eager to use the technique of x-ray diffraction analysis, introduced by Max von Laue in 1912, to investigate important complex organic molecules. He gathered around him a group of enthusiastic scientists to work out the appropriate techniques. Of the Bernal group, Hodgkin was probably the most talented; she also possessed a greater single-mindedness than Bernal himself and, despite the demands of three young children and a busy political life, it was her persistence and talent that produced some of the first great successes of x-ray analysis.

Her first major result came in 1949 when, with Charles Bunn, she published the three-dimensional structure of penicillin. This was followed by the structure of vitamin B_{12} (by 1956) and, in 1969, that of insulin. For her work on vitamin B_{12} she was awarded the Nobel Prize for chemistry in 1964.

Hodgkin, Thomas

(1798–1866)

BRITISH PATHOLOGIST

Hodgkin, the son of the grammarian John Hodgkin, was born in London and graduated in medicine from Edinburgh in 1823. After further study abroad and practice in London he was appointed in 1825 as pathologist at Guy's Hospital. He resigned in 1837 to devote himself to his practice and, increasingly, to the affairs of the Aborigines' Protection Society, which he helped to found in 1838.

Hodgkin is widely known for his description of lymphadenoma, first described in his paper *On Some Morbid Appearances of the Absorbent Glands and the Spleen* (1832), and named Hodgkin's disease by Samuel Wilks in 1865. Hodgkin reported six cases, in all of whom he found enlargement of the glands in the neck, armpit, and groin together with, in five of the cases, a diseased spleen. However, later studies by Wilks employing the microscope, which Hodgkin did not use, revealed that some of Hodgkin's cases were actually different conditions.

Hoff, Marcian Edward

(1937–   )

AMERICAN COMPUTER ENGINEER

> It's like a light bulb. When it's broken, unplug it, throw it away and plug in another.
>
> —When asked how he would repair a chip

Hoff gained his doctorate in 1962 at Stanford, where he worked for a further six years as a research associate. In 1968 he was invited by Robert Noyce to join his newly formed semiconductor firm, Intel.

Noyce had earlier shown how to assemble a large number of transistors into an integrated circuit (IC). Shortly after joining Intel, Hoff was asked to help some Japanese engineers design a number of IC chips to be used in desktop calculators.

Hoff proposed a calculator that could perform simple hardware instructions but could store complex sequences of these instructions in read-only memory (ROM) on a chip. The result of his idea was the first microprocessor – the Intel 4004 – released in 1971. Despite initial debate about its use and marketability, it became the forerunner of a whole range of advanced microprocessors, leading to a new generation of computers.

Hoff left Intel in 1982 to move to the computer company Atari to investigate new products. When Atari was sold in 1984 Hoff set up as an independent consultant.

Hoffmann, Friedrich

(1660–1742)

GERMAN PHYSICIAN

The son of a physician, Hoffman (**hof**-mahn) was born in Halle, Germany, and studied medicine at the University of Jena where he qualified in 1681. After a period of travel and further study in Holland and England, Hoffmann returned to Germany where he practiced medicine in Minden and Halberstadt. In 1693 Hoffmann was appointed professor of medicine at the University of Halle where he remained for the rest of his life apart from two periods, 1709–12 and 1734, when he served as physician at the Brandenburg court.

Hoffmann belonged to the period of medical history that had come to reject the humoral theory of disease, being one of the new generation of theorists who tried to reconstruct some alternative scheme out of the mechanical philosophy of René Descartes. He declared that medicine can only be a science insofar as it uses the four mechanical principles of physics – size, shape, motion, and rest. All natural phenomena and effects may be explained by resort to these principles. However, after this radical start he slipped back, believing the body consisted of an indeterminate number of elements. Various mixtures of these explained temperament, and imbalance accounted for disease.

It is clear that Hoffmann had simply translated ancient medicine into a modern terminology – there had in fact been no radical break with the past.

Hoffmann, Roald

(1937–   )

POLISH–AMERICAN CHEMIST

Born in Zloczow, Poland (now Zolochez in Ukraine), Hoffmann was moved at the age of four with his family to a labor camp. His father was executed for trying to escape, but Hoffmann and his mother were smuggled out in 1943 and spent the rest of the war hiding in the attic of a schoolhouse. Hoffmann has noted that only 80 of the 12,000 Jews of Zloczow survived the war. Following the liberation in mid-1944, Hoffmann's mother returned to Poland and emigrated with her son to America in 1949; he became a naturalized citizen in 1955.

Hoffmann was educated at Columbia and at Harvard, where he obtained his PhD in 1962. He moved to Cornell in 1965 and was appointed professor of chemistry in 1974.

In the mid-1960s Hoffmann began a research collaboration with R. B. Woodward on molecular orbital theory. Their work led to the formulation in 1965 of what are now known as the *Woodward-Hoffmann rules*. These laid down general conditions under which certain organic reactions can occur. The rules apply to pericyclic reactions. In reactions of this kind bond breaking and formation occur simultaneously without the presence of intermediates, i.e., they are said to be "concerted." The reactions also involve cyclic structures. Woodward and Hoffmann published their work in their *Conservation of Orbital Symmetry* (1969). Hoffmann's collaboration with Woodward won him a share of the 1981 Nobel Prize for chemistry with K. Fukui; Woodward's death in 1979, however, robbed him of his second Nobel Prize.

Hoffmann has also published two volumes of verse, *The Metamict State* and *Gaps and Verges*. He has also written and presented a number of television programs, *The World of Chemistry* and *The Molecular World*, in which he has attempted to introduce chemistry to a wider audience. A similar approach can be seen in his *The Same and Not the Same* (1995), in which he tries to describe for a popular audience how the world behaves at the molecular level.

Hofmann, Johann Wilhelm

(1818–1892)

GERMAN CHEMIST

Born at Giessen, Germany, Hofmann started as a law student but turned his attention to chemistry, becoming assistant to Justus von Liebig. In 1842 Liebig had visited England, where his impressive chemical knowledge drew attention to the lack of chemical skills and training in the UK. To overcome this problem a group led by Prince Albert opened the Royal College of Chemistry in London in 1845. Inevitably the college had to rely heavily on foreign staff to begin with, and Liebig recommended Hofmann as its director. He remained there until 1865, when he returned to Germany to take the chair at Berlin. His appointment in London was a great success; among his staff and pupils were William Henry Perkin, Edward Frankland, and William Odling.

It is partly owing to Hofmann that Perkin was able to develop the aniline dyes, since he was working under Hofmann's direction when he made his famous discovery of mauveine, the first synthetic dye, in 1856. Hofmann himself developed a series of violet dyes based on magenta. In theoretical chemistry he worked on type theory, showing that amines are derivatives of ammonia in which a hydrogen atom is replaced by a compound radical.

Hofmeister, Wilhelm Friedrich Benedict

(1824–1877)

GERMAN BOTANIST

> He is represented to us as one of the leading botanists in Germany, a man with the talent of a genius, highest diligence, and excellent powers of exposition...
> —Government report quoted by E. Pfitzer in *Wilhelm Hofmeister* (1903)

The father of Hofmeister (**hof**-mI-ster), a music and book publisher from Leipzig, Germany, was also a keen amateur botanist and encouraged his son's interest in botany. Wilhelm left school at 15 and served a two-year apprenticeship in a music shop before entering his father's business in 1841. He soon began to study botany seriously in his spare time and was greatly influenced by the views of Matthias Schleiden, who believed that botany could advance rapidly if researchers concentrated on studying cell structure and life histories.

Using procedures recommended by Schleiden, Hofmeister's first work was to disprove Schleiden's theory that the plant embryo develops from the tip of the pollen tube. He believed that a preexisting cell in the embryo sac gave rise to the embryo and his paper *The Genesis of the Embryo in Phanerogams* (1849) gained him an honorary doctorate from Rostock University.

Hofmeister's major discovery, however, was to demonstrate the alternation of generations between sporophyte and gametophyte in the lower plants. The work, published in 1851 as *Vergleichende Untersuchungen* (Comparative Investigations), showed the homologies between the higher seed-bearing plants (phanerogams) and the mosses and ferns (cryptogams) and demonstrated the true position of the gymnosperms between the angiosperms and the cryptogams. In 1863 Hofmeister was appointed professor at Heidelberg University and director of the botanic gardens there, and in 1872 moved to Tübingen University to succeed Hugo von Mohl.

Hofstadter, Douglas Richard

(1945–)

AMERICAN COMPUTER SCIENTIST

> Hofstadter's Law: it always takes longer than you expect, even when you take into account Hofstadter's Law.
> —*Godel, Escher, Bach* (1979)

Hofstadter (**hof**-stat-er), the son of Nobel laureate Robert Hofstadter, was born in New York and educated at Stanford and at the University of Oregon, where he completed his PhD (1976) in theoretical physics. He worked initially at the University of Indiana, Bloomington, but moved to the University of Michigan in 1984 to take up an appointment as professor of cognitive and computer science. In 1988 he returned to Bloomington as professor of computer science.

In 1979 Hofstadter published a remarkable book, *Godel, Escher, Bach*, described by him as "a metaphorical fugue on minds and machines." In the following year he was invited to succeed the much respected Martin Gardner as monthly columnist with *Scientific American*. For two and a half years Hofstadter contributed a column, *Metamagical Themas* (an anagram of Gardner's *Mathematical Games*).

Hofstadter, Robert

(1915–1990)

AMERICAN PHYSICIST

A New Yorker by birth, Hofstadter graduated from the College of the City of New York in 1935 and gained his MA and PhD at Princeton University in 1938. From 1939 he held a fellowship at the University of Pennsylvania, and in 1941 returned to the College of the City of New York as an instructor in physics. From 1943 to 1946 Hofstadter worked at the Norden Laboratory Corporation, and from there took on an assistant professorship in physics at Princeton University. In 1950 he moved to Stanford University as an associate professor and was made full professor in 1954.

His early research was in the fields of infrared spectroscopy, the hydrogen bond, and photoconductivity. One of his first notable achievements, in 1948, was the invention of a scintillation counter using sodium iodide activated with thallium. He is noted for his studies of the atomic nucleus, for which he received the 1961 Nobel Prize for physics (shared with Rudolph Mössbauer).

At Stanford, Hofstadter used the linear accelerator to study the scattering effects of high electrons fired at atomic nuclei. In many ways these experiments were similar in concept to Rutherford's original scattering experiments. He found that the distribution of charge density in the nucleus was constant in the core, and then decreased sharply at a peripheral "skin." The radial distribution of charge was found to vary in a mathematical relationship that depended upon the nuclear mass. Further, Hofstadter was able to show that nucleons (protons and neutrons) were not simply point particles, but had definite size and form. Both appeared to be composed of charged mesonic clouds (or shells) with the charges adding together in the proton, but canceling each other out in the neutral neutron. This led him to predict the existence of the rho-meson and omega-meson, which were later detected.

Hofstadter served as director of the high-energy physics laboratory at Stanford from 1967 to 1974.

Hollerith, Herman

(1860–1929)

AMERICAN ENGINEER

The father of Hollerith (**hol**-e-rith) was a German immigrant who settled in Buffalo, New York, and taught classics. Hollerith was educated at the Columbia School of Mines, New York. After graduating in 1879 he assisted his teacher, W. P. Trowbridge, working with him on the 1880 U.S. census. He also helped the head of vital statistics, John Billings, to prepare his final report.

Like many others, Hollerith and his supervisors were dismayed by the thought that, while it took only a few months to carry out the census, it would take the best part of a decade to tabulate and analyze the data collected. They might not even be finished before the 1890 census was taken. Clearly some form of mechanical aid was required. Hollerith spent the 1880s working first as an instructor at the Massachusetts Institute of Technology (1882–84) and for the rest of the decade at the Patent Office in Washington. During much of this time he worked on the census problem. He also developed a set of electrically controlled air brakes for freight trains, which he patented in 1885. His design, however, was not adopted; the Westinghouse system was preferred.

More successful was the tabulating system he invented for the 1890 census. He began with a system of punched tape, run over a metal drum and under some brushes. Whenever the brushes passed over a hole, current flowed and one bit of data was recorded. But, to retrieve an item, operators soon found, the whole tape had to be scanned. The obvious solution of turning the tape into cards was quickly introduced.

Hollerith's punched cards and related equipment operated so well in 1890 that it reduced the number of working days spent tabulating the data by two-thirds. It was quickly adopted by many other countries. By 1896 Hollerith felt sufficiently confident to set up his own company, Tabulating Machine Co., to manufacture and market machinery. The business thrived as it became apparent that Hollerith's tabulating machines could be used to record and analyze data of almost any kind. In 1911, a victim of high blood pressure, Hollerith sold out to the entrepreneur Charles Flint for $450 a share, a deal which brought Hollerith about $1.25 million. Hollerith's company thereby became the Computing-Tabulating-Recording Co. and eventually, in 1924, IBM.

Holley, Robert William

(1922–1993)

AMERICAN BIOCHEMIST

Holley was born in Urbana, Illinois. After graduating in chemistry from Illinois University in 1942, he joined the team at Cornell Medical School that achieved the first artificial synthesis of penicillin. He remained at Cornell to receive his PhD in organic chemistry in 1947.

Two years (1955–56) spent at the California Institute of Technology marked the beginning of Holley's important research on the nucleic acids. He decided that to work out the structure of a nucleic acid he first needed a very pure specimen of the molecule. Back again at Cornell, his research team spent three years isolating one gram of alanine transfer RNA (alanine tRNA) from some 90 kilograms of yeast. In March 1965 he was able to announce that they had worked out the complete sequence of 77 nucleotides in alanine tRNA. For this work Holley received the 1968 Nobel Prize for physiology or medicine, an award he shared with Marshall Nirenberg and Har Gobind Khorana.

Holmes, Arthur

(1890–1965)

BRITISH GEOLOGIST

Holmes came from a farming background in Hebburn-on-Tyne in the northeast of England. He graduated from Imperial College, London, in 1910, and went on to work with Lord Rayleigh on radioactivity. After an expedition to Mozambique in 1911 he taught at Imperial College until 1920 when he went to Burma as an oil geologist. In 1925 he returned to England to become professor of geology at Durham University, where he remained until 1943 when he moved to Edinburgh University.

Holmes conducted major work on the use of radioactive techniques to determine the age of rocks, leading to his proposal of the first quantitative geological time scale in 1913 and to his estimate of the age of the Earth being about 1.6 billion years. He continued to revise this estimate throughout his life, producing a figure in 1959 some three times larger.

Holmes also made a major contribution to the theory of continental drift proposed by Alfred Wegener in 1915. One of the early difficulties the theory faced was that geologists could not envisage a force capable of moving the continents in the way described by Wegener. In 1929 Holmes proposed the existence of convection currents in the Earth's mantle. Rocks in the Earth's interior are, according to Holmes, heated by radioactivity, causing them to rise and spread out and, when cold and dense, to sink back to the interior. It was only after World War II that hard evidence for such a view could be produced.

In 1944 Holmes published his *Principles of Physical Geology*, a major work on the subject. A substantially revised edition of this book was published in 1965, shortly before Holmes's death.

Holmes, Oliver Wendell

(1809–1894)

AMERICAN PHYSICIAN

Science is the topography of ignorance.
—*Medical Essays*

The truth is, that medicine, professedly founded on observation, is as sensitive to outside influences, political, religious, philosophical, imaginative, as is the barometer to the changes of atmospheric density.

—As above

Holmes was the son of a congregational minister and the father of the identically named jurist and Supreme Court judge. Born in Cambridge, Massachusetts, he graduated in law from Harvard in 1829 and in medicine in 1836. He was professor of anatomy and physiology at Harvard from 1847 until 1882.

In 1843 Holmes published the classic paper *The Contagiousness of Puerperal Fever* in which he repeated some of the earlier arguments of a number of notable physicians and anticipated some of the work of Ignaz Semmelweis and Joseph Lister. Puerperal (childbed) fever, a streptococcal infection of maternity wards in the early 19th century, had an average mortality of 5–10%, occasionally rising to as much as 30% in particularly virulent outbreaks. Holmes stated that puerperal fever is frequently carried from patient to patient by physicians and nurses. He advised that no doctor or nurse who had recently participated in a post-mortem should treat a patient in labor, and he also recommended that they should always wash their hands before examining patients. So little attention was paid to Holmes's paper, however, that he felt it necessary to republish it in 1855.

In addition to being a distinguished man of American letters with numerous volumes of essays, verse, and fiction to his credit, Holmes is also remembered for a letter to William Morton in 1846 concerning the condition induced by Morton's ether inhalation. In this, he wrote, "The state should, I think, be called 'Anaesthesia.' This signifies insensibility." The term had previously been employed in antiquity by Plato and Dioscorides.

Honda, Kotaro

(1870–1954)

JAPANESE METALLURGIST

Born in Aichi, Japan, Honda was educated at the Imperial University, Tokyo, graduating in 1897. After studying abroad at the universities of Göttingen and Berlin, he returned to Japan to take up an appointment at the Tohoku Imperial University. In 1922 a research institute for iron and steel was attached to the university and Honda became its director. He finally, in 1931, became president of the university.

Honda is noted for his research on magnetic alloys. In 1917 he found that an alloy of 57% iron, 35% cobalt, 2% chrome, 5% tungsten, and 1% carbon was the most highly magnetic material then known. Its use in such instruments as magnetos and dynamos permitted a marked decrease in their size.

Honda, Soichiro

(1906–1991)

JAPANESE MOTOR ENGINEER

Honda was the eldest son of a poor village blacksmith from Tenryu in the Shizuoka Prefecture, Japan. He showed an early interest in engines, although it was not until he was eight that he actually saw an automobile, an old Model-T. In 1922 he began working as an apprentice in a Tokyo car repair shop and six years later opened his own shop in Hamamatsu.

But Honda had ambitions to do more than repair vehicles; he aimed eventually to design and build them himself. After the war, during which he made piston rings, he set up the Honda Motor Company in 1947. Initially he built small engines to be fitted to bikes. Known in Japan as "bata-bata," they were very successful. Honda went on to build real motorcycles; they proved to be so effective that in 1961 his machines took the first five positions in both the 125 cc and 250 cc classes at the Tourist Trophy races on the Isle of Man.

In 1957 Honda entered the car market and within a few years had overtaken all his competitors other than Toyota and Nissan. Honda had the foresight to develop lightweight engines, which proved to be well suited to the energy crises of the 1970s. The Honda Civic of 1972, for example, was the first Japanese car to meet American pollution standards and allowed Honda to sell more cars in America than any other Japanese manufacturer apart from Toyota. In 1982 Honda established his own production lines in the United States. Honda retired in 1973.

Hood, Leroy Edward

(1938–   )

AMERICAN BIOLOGIST

Born in Missoula, Montana, Hood was educated at the California Institute of Technology, where he obtained his PhD in biochemistry in 1964, and at Johns Hopkins Medical School, Baltimore, where he qualified as an MD in 1964. He immediately joined the staff of the National Institute of Health, Bethesda, working in the area of immunology. In 1970 Hood returned to the California Institute of Technology and was appointed professor of biology in 1975.

In May 1985 at a meeting in Santa Cruz, California, plans were laid to map the human genome (the Human Genome Project). As the genome consists of 3 billion base pairs of DNA, the ability to sequence the genes rapidly would be a crucial factor.

Fortunately an automatic sequencer was almost at hand in 1985, developed by Hood and his colleague Lloyd Smith. The sequencer operates with fluorescent dyes. Each of the four DNA bases – adenine (A), cytosine (C), guanine (G), and thymine (T) – can be tagged with a different dye. Unsequenced dye-tagged DNA fragments are analyzed by gel electrophoresis, in which they migrate at different rates. The dyes are excited by an argon laser and the light emitted is turned into a digital signal by photomultiplier tubes. The digital signals can be analyzed by a computer and identified as A, T, C, or G.

Hood's automatic sequencer enabled work that once took a week or more to be carried out overnight. Later commercial models of the device can read 12,000 base pairs a day, and operate more accurately than any manual sequencing.

In 1992 Bill Gates of Microsoft presented the University of Washington Medical School, Seattle, with $12 million to establish a department of molecular biotechnology. Hood was persuaded to move to Seattle to head the new department, to work on a faster DNA sequencer, and to analyze the genes controlling the human immune response. That same year Hood, in collaboration with Ronald Cape, a former head of the biotechnology firm Cetus, founded Darwin Molecular in Seattle. Their aim is to develop new drugs utilizing processes comparable to natural selection.

Hooke, Robert

(1635–1703)

ENGLISH PHYSICIST

> The truth is, the science of Nature has been already too long made only a work of the brain and the fancy. It is now high time that it should return to the plainness and soundness of observations on material and obvious things.
> —*Micrographia* (1665; Micrography)

> He is certainly the greatest Mechanick this day in the World.
> —John Aubrey, *Brief Lives* (17th century)

Hooke, whose father was a clergyman from Freshwater on the Isle of Wight, England, was educated at Oxford University. While at Oxford he acted as assistant to Robert Boyle, constructing the air pump for him. In 1662 Boyle arranged for Hooke to become first curator of experiments to the Royal Society. There he agreed to "furnish the Society every day they meet with three or four considerable experiments." Even though the society only met once a week, the pressure on Hooke was still great and may explain why he never fully developed any of his ideas into a comprehensive treatise. He was also something of an invalid.

Hooke made numerous discoveries, perhaps the best known being his law of elasticity, which states that, within the elastic limit, the strain (fractional change in size) of an elastic material is directly proportional to the stress (force per unit area) producing that strain. He was the first to show that thermal expansion is a general property of matter. He also designed a balance spring for use in watches, built the first Gregorian (reflecting) telescope, and invented a number of scientific instruments, including the compound microscope and the wheel barometer.

In 1665 he published his main work *Micrographia* (Micrography), which was an account – fully and beautifully illustrated – of the investigations he had made with his improved version of the microscope. It also contained theories of color, and of light, which he suggested was wavelike. This led to one of the major controversies – over the nature of light and the priority of theories – that he had with Isaac Newton. The other conflict was over the discovery of universal gravitation and the inverse square law. It is true that Hooke had revealed, in a letter to Newton in 1680, that he had an intuitive understanding of the form the inverse square law must take. Newton's reply to Hooke's charge of plagiarism was to distinguish between Hooke's general intuition that may have been well founded, and his own careful mathematical treatment of the law and detailed working out of its main consequences.

Hooke was also a capable architect, having written on the theory of the arch and designed parts of London after the great fire of 1666.

Hooker, Sir Joseph Dalton

(1817–1911)

BRITISH PLANT TAXONOMIST AND EXPLORER

From my earliest childhood I nourished and cherished the desire to make a creditable journey in a new country and write such a respectable account of its natural features as should give me a niche among the scientific explorers of the globe I inhabit, and hand my name down as a useful contributor of original matter.

—Letter to Charles Darwin (1854)

Hooker was born at Halesworth in Suffolk, England, and studied medicine at Glasgow University, where his father William Hooker was professor of botany. After graduating in 1839, he joined the Antarctic expedition on HMS *Erebus* (1839–43), nominally as assistant surgeon but primarily as naturalist. Between 1844 and 1860, using collections made on the expedition, Hooker produced a six-volume flora of the Antarctic Islands, New Zealand, and Tasmania.

When he returned from the Antarctic expedition Hooker was congratulated on his work by Charles Darwin, who had been following his progress, and in 1844 Darwin confided to Hooker his theory of evolution by natural selection. This communication later proved important in establishing Darwin's precedence when his theory – together with Alfred Russel Wallace's essentially identical conclusions – was presented by Hooker and George Lyell at the famous Linnaean Society meeting of July 1858.

Following his unsuccessful application in 1845 for the botany chair at Edinburgh University, Hooker was employed to identify fossils for a geological survey, but he took time off between 1847 and 1850 to explore the Indian subcontinent. He visited Sikkim and Assam, Nepal, and Bengal, introducing the brilliant Sikkim rhododendrons into cultivation through the botanical gardens at Kew. Later (1872–97) he produced a seven-volume flora of British India.

In 1855 Hooker was appointed assistant director at Kew Gardens and in 1865 succeeded his father as director. In his 20 years as head of the institute he founded the Jodrell Laboratory and Marianne North Gallery, extended the herbarium, and developed the rock garden. His efforts established Kew as an international center for botanical research and in 1872 he successfully fought a move from the commissioner of works to relegate the gardens to a pleasure park. With George Bentham he produced a world flora, *Genera Plantarum* (1862–83; Genera of Plants) – a major work describing 7,569 genera and 97,000 species. The Kew herbarium is still arranged according to this classification.

Hooker retired from the directorship of Kew in 1885 owing to ill health but continued working until his death.

Hooker, William Jackson

(1785–1865)

BRITISH BOTANIST

> The great secret of his success was that he deemed nothing too small for his notice, if it illustrated any fact of science or economy, and nothing too difficult to be attempted.
> —William Henry Harvey

The son of a merchant's clerk, Hooker was born in Norwich in the east of England; he attended the grammar school there but had little formal education. An interest in botany led to his first voyage, in 1809, to Iceland, which was followed by an extensive study of the English flora. From 1820 until 1842 Hooker held the botany chair at Glasgow. His main interest was in ferns, mosses, and fungi but his works also include some important regional floras and he was a pioneer of economic botany. Hooker's herbarium was accessible to all scholars, and with his publications (more than 20 major books and numerous articles) and journals he became the leading British botanist of his day.

In 1841 Hooker was appointed the first director of Kew Gardens, a position he held until his death. Under his direction Kew became the world's most important botanical institution and here he founded the Museum of Economic Botany in 1847.

Hope, James

(1801–1841)

BRITISH CARDIOLOGIST

Hope, the son of a wealthy merchant from Stockport near Manchester, England, studied medicine at Edinburgh University and various London hospitals. He became assistant physician at St. George's Hospital in 1834 and in 1839, shortly before his early death from consumption (tuberculosis), was appointed full physician.

In the 1820s use of René Laennec's stethoscope became widespread in Britain. It still remained to link the sounds heard through the stethoscope and actual events in the heart, a task begun by Hope and reported in his influential *A Treatise on the Diseases of the Heart and Great Vessels* (1831), a work that went through three editions in his short life.

Hope made valuable observations on heart murmurs, valvular disease, and aneurism, and thus began the important work of transforming heart complaints from being merely a set of symptoms into identifiable and specific lesions of the heart.

Hope, Thomas Charles

(1766–1844)

BRITISH CHEMIST

Hope's father, John Hope, was a professor of botany at Edinburgh University and founder of the new Edinburgh botanic gardens. Thomas, who was born in Edinburgh, studied medicine there and became professor of chemistry at Glasgow in 1787. He returned to Edinburgh in 1795 as joint professor of chemistry with Joseph Black, succeeding Black on his death in 1799. He remained as chemistry professor until 1843.

In 1787 Hope isolated the new element strontium and named it after the town of Strontian in Scotland where it was discovered. At first it was thought to be barium carbonate and was only established as a new metal in 1791. Martin Klaproth made the same discovery independently but a little later.

Hope was also the first to show the expansion of water on freezing and demonstrated that water attains a maximum density a few degrees above its freezing point (actually 3.98°C). He published his results in his paper *Experiment on the Contraction of Water by Heat* (1805).

Hopkins, Sir Frederick Gowland

(1861–1947)

BRITISH BIOCHEMIST

Life is a dynamic equilibrium in a polyphasic system.
— Joseph Needham, *Order and Life* (1936)

Hopkins was the son of a bookseller and publisher and a distant cousin of the poet Gerard Manley Hopkins. He was born at Eastbourne on the south coast of England and, after attending the City of London School, was apprenticed as a chemist in a commercial laboratory, where for three years he performed routine analyses. An inheritance in 1881 allowed him to study chemistry at the Royal School of Mines and at University College, London. His work there brought him to the attention of Thomas Stevenson, who offered Hopkins the post of assistant in his laboratory at Guy's Hospital. Feeling the need of more formal qualifications he began to work for a medical degree at Guy's in 1889, finally qualifying in 1894. In 1898 Hopkins moved to Cambridge, where he remained for the rest of his long life and not only served as professor of biochemistry (1914–43) but also established one of the great research institutions of the century.

In 1901 Hopkins made a major contribution to protein chemistry when he discovered a new amino acid, tryptophan. He went on to show its essential role in the diet, since mice fed on the protein zein, lacking tryptophan, died within a fortnight; the same diet with the amino acid added was life-supporting. This work initiated vast research programs in biochemical laboratories.

In 1906–07 Hopkins performed a classic series of experiments by which he became convinced that mice could not survive upon a mixture of basic foodstuffs alone. This ran against the prevailing orthodoxy, which supposed that as long as an animal received sufficient calories it would thrive. He began by feeding fat, starch, casein (or milk protein), and essential salts to mice, noting that they eventually ceased to grow. Addition of a small amount of milk, however, was sufficient to restart growth. It took several years of careful experiments before, in 1912,

Hopkins was prepared to announce publicly that there was an unknown constituent of normal diets that was not represented in a synthetic diet of protein, pure carbohydrate, fats, and salts. Hopkins had in fact discovered what were soon to be called vitamins, and for this work he shared the 1929 Nobel Prize for physiology or medicine with Christiaan Eijkman.

At the same time Hopkins was working with Walter Fletcher on the chemistry of muscle contraction. In 1907 they provided the first clear proof that muscle contraction and the production of lactic acid are, as had long been suspected, causally connected. This discovery formed the basis for much of the later work done in this field. Hopkins later isolated the tripeptide glutathione, which is important as a hydrogen acceptor in a number of biochemical reactions.

In England Hopkins did more than anyone else to establish biochemistry as it is now practiced. He had to fight on many fronts to establish the discipline, since many claimed that the chemistry of life involved complex substances that defied ordinary chemical analysis. Instead he was able to demonstrate that it was a chemistry of simple substances undergoing complex reactions. Hopkins was knighted in 1925.

Hopper, Grace

(1906–1992)

AMERICAN MATHEMATICIAN AND COMPUTER SCIENTIST

Hopper, born Grace Murray, was educated at Vassar and at Yale, where she gained her PhD in 1934. She taught at Vassar until 1944, when she enlisted in the U.S. Naval Reserve and was immediately assigned to Harvard to work with Howard Aiken on the Mark I computer, the ASCC (Automatic Sequence Controled Calculator), for which she wrote the manual. Although she hoped to remain in the Navy after the war, her age prevented this and she had to be satisfied with the Naval reserve as a second choice. Consequently she remained at Harvard working on the Mark II and the Mark III computers.

In 1949 Hopper moved to Philadelphia to work with J. P. Eckhart and John Mauchly on the development of BINAC and remained with the company, despite several changes of ownership, until 1967. During this period she made a number of basic contributions to computer programming. In 1952 she devised the first compiler, a program that translated a high-level language into machine code, named A-O. She went on to produce a data-processing compiler known as Flow-matic.

It was apparent by this time to Hopper and other programmers that the business world lacked an agreed and adequate computer language. Hopper lobbied for a combined effort from the large computer companies and consequently a committee was established in 1959 under the guidance of the Defense Department to develop a common business language. Although she did not serve on the committee, the language developed by them, COBOL (Common Business Oriented Language), was derived in many respects from Flow-matic. For this reason Hopper has often been referred to as "the mother of Cobol."

Although Hopper was forced through age to resign from the U.S. Naval reserve in 1966 she was recalled a year later to work on their payroll program. She remained in the Naval reserve until 1986, having been promoted to the rank of rear admiral in 1985.

Hoppe-Seyler, (Ernst) Felix Immanuel

(1825–1895)

GERMAN BIOCHEMIST

Hoppe-Seyler (hop-e-**zI**-ler) was born in Freiberg, Germany, and early in his career became assistant to Rudolf Virchow in Berlin. He became professor of physiological chemistry (biochemistry) at Strasbourg, where he established the first exclusively biochemical laboratory, and later founded the first biochemistry journal. In 1871 Hoppe-Seyler discovered the enzyme invertase, which aids the conversion of sucrose into the simpler sugars glucose and fructose. He was also the first to prepare hemoglobin in crystalline form. He isolated the fatlike compound lecithin, one of the class of compounds called phospholipids. Hoppe-Seyler's classification of the proteins (1875) is still accepted today.

Horrocks, Jeremiah

(1619–1641)

ENGLISH ASTRONOMER

Little is known about the early life of Horrocks (or Horrox) other than that he was born into a Puritan family in Toxteth, Liverpool, and was admitted to Cambridge in 1632. Even though he died "in his twenty second year" he had made major contributions to astronomy and several original observations.

Horrocks noted that as the orbits of Venus and Mercury fall between the earth and the Sun, it would seem possible that at certain times the inner planets would appear to an observer on the Earth to cross the face of the Sun. The events, known as transits, are so rare that they are unlikely to be seen by chance. Only five transits of Venus have been observed, those of 1639, 1761, 1769, 1874, and 1882; the next is due in 2004.

At Cambridge, Horrocks had mastered the new astronomy of Kepler. From Kepler's recently published *Rudolphine Tables* (1627), he worked out that a transit of Venus was due on 24 November 1639 at 3 p.m. At this time he was probably working as a curate at Hoole near Preston in Lancashire. He prepared for the transit by directing the solar image onto a large sheet of paper in a darkened room. However, a late November afternoon in Lancashire is not the best time to observe the Sun. For Horrocks there was another problem. The predicted day was a Sunday which meant that the puritan curate could well find himself in church at the crucial moment.

Horrocks was successful in observng the transit, however, and left an account of the day in his *Venus in Sole Visa* (Venus in the Face of the Sun), published posthumously in 1662. The day was cloudy but at 3.15, "as if by divine interposition" the clouds dispersed. He noted a spot of unusual magnitude on the solar disc and began to trace its path; but, he added, "she was not visible to me longer than half an hour, on account of the Sun quickly setting."

With the aid of his observations Horrocks could establish the apparent diameter of Venus as 1′ 12″ compared with the Sun's diameter of 30′, a figure much smaller than the 11′ assigned by Kepler. Horrocks also attempted to determine the solar parallax, and derived, although with little confidence, a figure of 15″, compared with a modern value of 8″.8.

Before his death Horrocks was working on an *Astronomia Kepleriana* (Astronomy of Kepler), and essays on comets, tides, and the Moon. Unfortunately none of this was published until long after his death.

Much of his work had been lost in the chaos of the Civil War. Other material sent to a London bookseller was burned in the Great Fire of 1666. The remainder of his papers were published by John Wallis as *Opera posthuma* (1678; Posthumous Works).

Horsfall, James Gordon

(1905–　)

AMERICAN PLANT PATHOLOGIST

Born in Mountain Grove, Missouri, Horsfall graduated in soil science from the University of Arkansas and gained his PhD in plant pathology from Cornell in 1929. He remained at Cornell until 1939 when he became chief of the department of plant pathology (1939–48) and director (1948–71) of the Connecticut Agricultural Experimental Station.

A leading plant pathologist, Horsfall coedited, with A. E. Dimond, the three-volume work *Plant Pathology* (1959–60). More recently he has, with Ellis Cowling, coedited *Plant Disease: An Advanced Treatise* (5 vols. 1977–80). He had earlier published extensively on fungicides.

Hounsfield, Sir Godfrey Newbold

(1919–　)

BRITISH ENGINEER

Hounsfield was born at Newark in Nottinghamshire, England, and educated in that county before going on to the City and Guilds College, London, and the Faraday House College of Electrical Engineering in London. Having spent the war years in the RAF, he worked for Electrical and Musical Industries (EMI) from 1951 and led the design effort for Britain's first large solid-state computer. Later he worked on problems of pattern recognition. Although he had no formal university education he was granted an honorary doctorate in medicine by the City University, London (1975).

Hounsfield was awarded the 1979 Nobel Prize for medicine, together with the South-African-born physicist Allan Cormack, for his pioneering work on the application of computer techniques to x-ray examination of the human body. He was knighted in 1981. Working at the Central Research Laboratories of EMI he developed the first commercially successful machines to use computer-assisted tomography, also known as computerized axial tomography (CAT). In CAT a high-resolution x-ray picture of an imaginary slice through the body (or head) is built up from information taken from detectors rotating around the patient. These "scanners" allow delineation of very small changes in tissue density. Introduced in 1973, early machines were used to overcome obstacles in the diagnosis of diseases of the brain, but the technique has now been extended to the whole body. Although Cormack worked on essentially the same problems of CAT, the two men did not collaborate, or even meet.

New lines of research being pursued by Hounsfield include the possible use of nuclear magnetic resonance (NMR) as a diagnostic imaging technique.

Houssay, Bernardo Alberto

(1887–1971)

ARGENTINIAN PHYSIOLOGIST

Born in the Argentinian capital, Houssay (oo-**sI**) was the founder and director of the Buenos Aires Institute of Biology and Experimental Medicine. He was also professor of physiology at Buenos Aires from 1910 until 1965, apart from the years 1943–55 when he was relieved of his post by the regime of Juan Perón.

Houssay's work centered upon the role of the pituitary gland in regulating the amount of sugar in the blood, as well as its effects in aggravating or inducing diabetes. Working initially with dogs, he found that diabetic sufferers could have their condition eased by extraction of the pituitary gland, since its hormonal effect is to increase the amount of sugar in the blood and thus counter the influence of insulin. Deliberate injection of pituitary extracts actually increases the severity of diabetes or may induce it when the condition did not previously exist. He was also able to isolate at least one of the pituitary's hormones that had the reverse effect to insulin. Houssay's work on hormones led to his award, in 1947, of the Nobel Prize for physiology or medicine, which he shared with Carl and Gerty Cori. He was the author of *Human Physiology* (1951).

Hoyle, Sir Fred

(1915–   )

BRITISH ASTRONOMER

Space isn't remote at all. It's only an hour's drive away if your car could go straight upwards.
—*The Observer*, 9 September 1979

It is the true nature of mankind to learn from mistakes not from example.
—*Into Deepest Space* (1974)

[We must] recognize ourselves for what we are – the priests of a not very popular religion.
—*Physics Today*, April 1968

The son of a textile merchant from Bingley in Yorkshire, England, Hoyle was educated at Cambridge. After graduating in 1936 he remained at Cambridge as a graduate student before being elected to a fellowship at St. John's College in 1939. Hoyle spent the war working on the development of radar at the Admiralty. After the war he returned to Cambridge and was appointed Plumian Professor of Astronomy in 1958.

Hoyle first came to prominence in 1948 with his formulation of the "steady-state theory" of the universe. He was aware that cosmology at the time was inadequate in that it required a smaller age for the universe than geologists had attributed to the Earth. Hoyle's ideas about the steady-state theory were provoked one night in 1946, when he went to see a ghost film with Hermann Bondi and Thomas Gold. The film was in four parts but linked the sections together to create a circular plot in which the end of the film became its beginning. Hoyle later noted that it showed him that unchanging situations need not be static. The universe could perhaps be both unchanging and dynamic.

Hoyle worked out some of the detailed implications of this view in his 1948 paper *A New Model for the Expanding Universe*. Matter, he argued, was created continually. It arose from a field generated by the matter that already exists – that is, in the manner of the film, "Matter chases its own tail." Created matter is spread throughout the whole of space and, according to the theory, is being produced at a rate of about one atom per year in a volume equal to that of a large building. It is this creation that drives the expansion of the universe. Matter is distributed evenly through space and therefore new clusters of galaxies are forming as other galaxies are receding into the distance.

Although Hoyle's work was initially treated sympathetically, the steady-state theory failed to cope with new evidence emerging in the 1960s from radio astronomy. Counts of radio sources by Martin Ryle in the 1960s and, in particular, the discovery by Robert Wilson and Arno Penzias of the cosmic background radiation in 1964, convinced most scientists that the universe had begun with a big bang. Hoyle defended his theory strongly, objecting to the accuracy of the radio counts by arguing that they were so constructed as to allow every error to count against the theory. "Properly analyzed," Hoyle wrote in 1980, "the disproof of the theory claimed in the 1950s and early 1960s fails completely." He has also suggested that there could be alternative explanations for the background radiation.

Hoyle subsequently felt that he was not committed to the details of any cosmological orthodoxy, such as either the big bang or the steady-state theory of 1948. He spent much time exploring the implications of both theories and, in collaboration with Jayant Narlikar, developing a new theory of gravity. In 1964 they proposed, following some early arguments of Ernst Mach, that the inertia of any piece of matter derives from the rest of the matter in the universe. They also predicted that the gravitational constant changes over time.

Hoyle also worked in the 1950s on the formation of the elements. It was widely believed that carbon could be formed, along with many other elements, in the interior of stars. One reaction proposed required three helium nuclei to fuse into a carbon atom as in:

$$^{4}He + {}^{4}He + {}^{4}He \rightarrow {}^{12}C$$

Hoyle realized that the reaction would take place too infrequently to account for the abundance of carbon in the universe. Another possibility was a two-stage reaction:

$$^4He + {}^4He \rightarrow {}^8Be$$
$$^8Be + {}^4He \rightarrow {}^{12}C$$

In this, two helium nuclei first form a beryllium nucleus which fuses in turn with another helium nucleus to form carbon. As the Be has a longer life-time than the collision time of two ^4He nuclei, the reaction should make the production of carbon more likely. Something more was needed and in 1954 Hoyle predicted that there must be a resonance channel easing the two reaction steps. Hoyle's prediction was confirmed when it was shown experimentally that there was an energy level of 7.65 million electronvolts (MeV) in the ^{12}C nucleus, just above the energy of the Be + ^4He structure of 7.366 MeV.

Further work on the formation of the elements was carried out by Hoyle in collaboration with William Fowler and Geoffrey and Margaret Burbidge. In 1957 their work resulted in a paper, commonly referred to as B^2FH, that is one of the most authoritative and comprehensive works of modern science. It describes precisely how all the naturally occurring elements other than hydrogen and helium are formed in the interior of stars.

Hoyle spent much of the early 1960s working in the U.S. at the Hale Observatories and at Princeton. In 1967 he was appointed director of the newly formed Institute of Theoretical Astronomy at Cambridge. It was not a happy time. There were bitter disputes with Martin Ryle and the radio astronomers, demands for apologies, and threats of legal action. Hoyle had problems with his requests for funds from the research councils. In 1973 he resigned and since then has held no permanent post.

He has, however, continued to publish on a wide variety of topics. Much of this later work, often in collaboration with Chandra Wickramsingh of Cardiff University, stems from his claim that the blind operation of physicochemical laws would have been insufficient to shuffle an assortment of amino acids into an enzyme. The odds against this happening by chance were 1 in $10^{40,000}$, as were the chances that an atom with the properties of carbon could be produced by nature. Such considerations led Hoyle to attack the notion of evolution by natural selection.

Hoyle began his campaign with a frontal attack; he asserted that the fossil *Archaeopteryx* was a fake. Probably the most famous of all fossils, *Archaeopteryx* had been bought by the British Museum in 1862 for 700 pounds and supposedly links reptiles with birds. Hoyle published a paper in 1985 claiming that the skeleton was genuine and of a reptile, but that the feathers had been glued on. Hoyle went on to publish a book on the issue, *Archaeopteryx, the Story of a Fake* (1987) in which he identified Richard Owen as the culprit. Tests of the fossil by the British Museum have failed to detect any glue or cement.

But if enzymes, let alone organisms could not have evolved on Earth, where did they originate? In *Lifecloud* (1978), *Diseases from Space* (1979), and *Space Travellers* (1981), Hoyle argued that life must have come from space. Hoyle was partly led to this view by a longstanding interest in interstellar grains. They had long been thought to be made of ice, but, as they failed to reveal the appropriate infrared absorption bands, this view had to be ruled out. Hoyle pursued the matter and struggled for twenty years to find a particle with the observed spectral properties of the interstellar grains. In 1980 he decided to compare the grains with bacteria and found, to his great surprise, agreement so close that he was forced to conclude that "hitherto unidentified components of dust clouds were in fact bacterial cells."

Hoyle's new theory allowed him to explain not only the origin of life on Earth but also much about the spread of disease. The abrupt appearance of a new disease, such as syphilis in the 15th century, can be seen as a bacterial seeding from a passing comet. Other epidemiological problems can also be solved in this way. How, for example, Hoyle asks, did a group of Amerindians in Suriname, isolated from all alien contact until recently, become infected with the polio virus? Because, Hoyle believes, both forest and city dwellers were infected with pathogens rained on them from above.

Hoyle's numerous other publications cover such areas as the history of astronomy in his *Copernicus* (1973), an important textbook, *Astronomy and Cosmology* (1975), archeoastronomy in *From Stonehenge to Modern Cosmology* (1972), and a first volume of autobiography in his *The Small World of Fred Hoyle* (1986). He has also written fourteen science-fiction novels, the first being *The Black Cloud* (1957). In 1994 Hoyle published his long-awaited autobiography, *Home Is Where the Wind Blows: Chapters from a Cosmologist's Life.*

Hubble, Edwin Powell

(1889–1953)

AMERICAN ASTRONOMER AND COSMOLOGIST

> Equipped with his five senses, man explores the universe around him and calls the adventure Science.
>
> —*Science*

Hubble, who was born in Marshfield, Missouri, was the son of a lawyer. He was educated at the University of Chicago where he was influenced by the astronomer George Hale and, as a good athlete, was once offered the role of "Great White Hope" in a match against the world heavyweight champion, Jack Johnson. Instead he went to England, accepting a Rhodes scholarship to Oxford University where, between 1910 and 1913, he studied jurisprudence, represented Oxford in athletics, and fought the French boxer, Georges Carpentier. On his return to America he practiced law briefly before returning in 1914 to the study of astron-

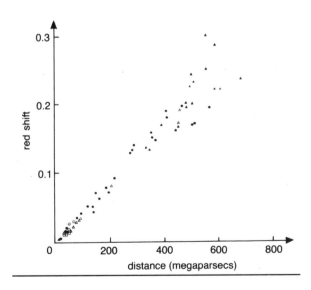

HUBBLE DIAGRAM   The variation of red shift with distance for different kinds of galaxies.

omy at the Yerkes Observatory of the University of Chicago. He obtained his PhD in 1917. After being wounded in France in World War I he took up an appointment in 1919 at the Mount Wilson Observatory in California where Hale was director and where he spent the rest of his career.

Hubble's early work involved studies of faint nebulae, which in the telescopes of the day appeared as fuzzy extended images. He considered that while some were members of our Galaxy and were clouds of luminous gas and dust, others, known as spiral nebulae, probably lay beyond the Galaxy. After the powerful 100-inch (2.5-m) telescope went into operation at Mount Wilson he produced some of the most dramatic and significant astronomy of the 20th century. In 1923 he succeeded in resolving the outer region of the Andromeda nebula into "dense swarms of images which in no way differ from those of ordinary stars." To his delight he found that several of them were Cepheids, which allowed him to use Harlow Shapley's calibration of the period-luminosity curve to determine their distance as the unexpectedly large 900,000 light-years. Although this conflicted sharply with the results of Adriaan van Maanen, Hubble continued with his observations. Between 1925 and 1929 he published three major papers showing that the spiral nebulae were at enormous distances, well outside our own Galaxy, and were in fact isolated systems of stars, now called spiral galaxies. This was in agreement with the work of Heber Curtis. In 1935 van Maanen reexamined his data and, appreciating their unsatisfactory nature, withdrew the final objection to Hubble's results.

In 1929 Hubble went on to make his most significant discovery and announced what came to be known as *Hubble's law*. Using his own determination of the distance of 18 galaxies and the measurements of radial velocities from galactic red shifts carried out by Vesto Slipher and Milton Humason, he saw that the recessional velocity of the galaxies increased proportionately with their distance from us, i.e., $v = Hd$, where v is the velocity, d the distance, and H is known as *Hubble's constant*. Further measurements made by Hubble in the 1930s seemed to confirm his earlier insight. It was this work that demonstrated to astronomers that the idea of an expanding universe, proposed earlier in the 1920s by Alexander Friedmann and Georges Lemaître, was indeed correct. The expansion of the universe is now fundamental to every cosmological model.

Hubble's law was soon seen as containing the key to the size, age, and future of the universe. Hubble's constant can be found from the mean value of v/d. Hubble himself gave it a value approximately ten times its presently accepted figure. The constant permits a calculation of the observable size of the universe to be made. The limiting value of recession must be the speed of light (*c*). If we divide this by *H* we get a "knowable" universe with a radius of about 18 billion light-years. Beyond that no signal transmitted could ever reach us, for to do so it would need to exceed the speed of light.

It is also possible to calculate the time that must have elapsed since the original highly compact state of the universe, i.e., the age of the universe. Hubble's own estimate was 2 billion years but with revisions of his constant, cosmologists now, none too precisely, assign a value of between 12 and 20 billion years.

Hubble also made a major contribution to the study of galactic evolution by producing the first significant classification of galaxies. William Herschel had simply classified them as bright or faint, large or small, while his son John Herschel introduced five categories in terms of size, brightness, roundness, condensation, and resolvability, each with five subdivisions. Hubble published his scheme in 1926. It involved dividing galaxies into two classes, elliptical and spiral. Ellipticals could be subdivided on the basis of their degree of ellipticity, ranging from the circular form (E0) to the elongated (E7). Spirals could be either barred or normal spirals which were subdivided in terms of their degree of openness. Although anomalous objects were later discovered that failed to fit it, Hubble's scheme is still used as the basis for galactic classification.

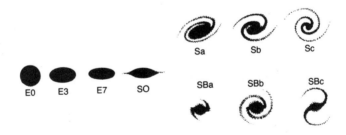

HUBBLE'S CLASSIFICATION OF GALAXIES   This is known as his "tuning-fork" diagram.

Hubel, David Hunter

(1926–   )

CANADIAN–AMERICAN
NEUROPHYSIOLOGIST

Born in Windsor, Ontario, Hubel was educated at McGill University and then worked at the Montreal Neurological Institute. He moved to America in 1954 and after working at Johns Hopkins joined the Harvard Medical School in 1959 where he was appointed professor of neurobiology from 1968 to 1982.

Beginning in the 1960s, Hubel, in collaboration with Torsten Wiesel, published a number of remarkable papers that explained for the first time the mechanism of visual perception at the cortical level.

Their work was made possible by a number of technical advances. From the early 1950s onward it became possible to use microelectrodes to monitor the activity of a single neuron. Further, the work of Louis Sokoloff allowed workers to identify precise areas of neural activity. Using this latter technique it was thus possible to identify the region known as the striate cortex, located at the back of the cortex in the occipital lobes, as one of the key centers of activity during the visual process.

The cells of the striate cortex seemed to be arranged into columns, or "hypercolumns" as they were soon described, that run the length of the cortex (3–4 millimeters) from the outer surface to the underlying white matter. Such hypercolumns were further clearly divided into distinct layers. Hubel and Weisel went on to probe the structure, function, and contents of such columns in great detail.

Above all they succeeded in establishing two crucial points. First that the retinal image was mapped in some way onto the striate cortex. That is, to each point on the retina there corresponded a group of cells in the striate cortex that would respond to a stimulation of that point and of no other.

Furthermore, the response could be evoked only by a relatively precise stimulus. Thus there were cells that would respond to a spot of light but not to a line. Cells that responded to lines would do so only to those lines with a specific tilt and if the angle of tilt was changed by as little as 10°, in either direction, the cells' ability to react would be diminished or even abolished.

As a result of such work the visual cortex has become the best known of all cortical regions. Hubel and Wiesel shared the 1981 Nobel Prize for physiology or medicine with Roger Sperry.

Huber, Robert

(1937–   )

GERMAN CHEMIST

Huber (**hoo**-ber) was educated at the Technical University in his native city of Munich where he obtained his PhD in 1972. He moved to the Max Planck Institute for Biochemistry, Munich, where he later became head of the Institute's crystallography group.

In 1982 Hartmut Michel had succeeded in crystallizing the membrane proteins of the photosynthetic reaction center. His colleague Johann Diesenhofer had managed by 1985 to work out the molecular structure of the crystals. For this work they shared the 1988 Nobel Prize for chemistry. The prize also went to Huber as head of the unit in which Michel and Diesenhofer carried out their work.

Huchra, John

(1948–   )

AMERICAN ASTRONOMER

Huchra, who was born in Jersey City, New Jersey, was educated at the Massachusetts Institute of Technology and the California Institute of Technology, where he obtained his PhD in 1976. He then moved to Harvard, serving as professor of astronomy and as a staff member at the Smithsonian Astrophysical Observatory.

In the early 1980s Huchra worked on the Tully-Fisher relation, which links the intrinsic luminosity of a spiral galaxy with the rotational velocity of its stars. He found that with regard to galaxies in the Coma cluster there was a departure of up to 20% from the supposed correlation. Huchra went on in 1982 with a number of colleagues to apply the relation to the Local Group of galaxies to see if the peculiar motion tentatively identified by Vera Rubin could be detected. The peculiar velocities of several hundred galaxies in the region of the Virgo cluster were measured. They found that velocities in the direction of Virgo steadily increased, while decreasing on the other side. The result has been interpreted by some as evidence for the existence of "The Great Attractor," a proposed massive concentration of galaxies lying beyond the Hydra-Centaurus supercluster.

In 1986 in collaboration with Margaret Geller, Huchra began a galactic survey for the Smithsonian Center for Astrophysics (CfA). They used a 1.5-meter telescope located on Mount Hopkins, Tucson, Arizona and sought to measure the red shifts of galaxies below a magnitude of 15.5 and falling within a wedge of sky 6° wide, 120° long, and out to a distance of about 300 million light years. By 1989 they had mapped the positions of 10,000 galaxies.

To their surprise, instead of producing a uniform distribution their maps revealed large voids within which huge clusters of galaxies were distributed. The largest structure they observed, dubbed "The Great Wall," stretched 500 million light years without its edge being found.

Hückel, Erich Armand Arthur Joseph

(1896–1980)

GERMAN CHEMIST

Born the son of a physician in Berlin, Germany, Hückel (**hoo**-kel) was educated at the University of Göttingen, gaining his PhD in 1921. He worked at a number of institutions, including the Zurich Technische Hochschule and in Copenhagen, Leipzig, and Stuttgart, before taking the chair of theoretical physics at Marburg in 1937.

Initially Hückel worked with Debye on electrolyte solutions. From 1930, however, he turned his attention to organic compounds. Since Friedrich Kekulé had discovered the structure of benzene (C_6H_6) in 1865, it had continued to puzzle chemists. Kekulé had shown that the six carbon atoms of benzene were formed into a ring joined by alternating single and double bonds. Organic chemists call such molecules as benzene "aromatic," thereby indicating, among other things, the molecule's great stability. Yet, double bonds normally make a molecule reactive. How, then, it was asked, can certain molecules like benzene with double bonds be so stable?

In the 1930s Hückel developed an answer to this problem based upon molecular orbital theory. Molecular orbitals are formed from overlapping atomic orbitals. Hückel proposed that the electrons of the pi-orbitals were delocalized and spread diffusely above and below the plane of the carbon ring. As this configuration was energetically more stable than placing electrons in isolated double bonds, benzene's stability followed directly from the model.

Hückel went on to generalize his model to cover other cyclic molecules containing alternating double and single bonds. Aromatic molecules were planar compounds which had precisely $4n + 2$ pi-electrons, where $n = 0, 1, 2, 3\ldots$. This is known as the *Hückel rule*. Benzene represents the case where $n = 1$; and $n = 2$ and $n = 3$ represent the 10 and 14 member aromatic rings of naphthalene and anthracene. For $n = 0$, the predicted aromaticity of a 3 member ring was confirmed in 1962 with the discovery of the cyclopropenyl cation.

Huffman, Donald Ray

(1935–   )

AMERICAN PHYSICIST

Born at Fort Worth in Texas, Huffman was educated at Texas Agricultural and Mechanical College, at Rice University, Houston, and at the University of California, Riverside, where he completed his PhD in 1966. After spending a postdoctoral year at the University of Frankfurt, Huffman moved to the University of Arizona, Tucson, in 1967 and was later appointed professor of physics in 1975.

In 1985 in the laboratory of Richard Smalley a new form of carbon had been discovered: C_{60}, known as "buckminsterfullerene." The C_{60} was produced by vaporizing a graphite target with a pulsed laser beam. The sooty carbon produced in this manner certainly contained a detectable amount of C_{60}, but all efforts to extract the substance from the residue in amounts sufficient to carry out a detailed spectroscopic study failed.

Huffman, in collaboration with Wolfgang Kratschmer of the Max Planck Institute for Physical Chemistry, Heidelberg, was involved in the discovery of the new forms of carbon known as *fullerenes*. For many years they had been interested in the nature of interstellar dust, which they believed to be mainly carbon. The interstellar matter has a characteristic broad absorption spectrum and Huffman and Kratschmer were experimenting with various forms of finely divided carbon produced in electric arcs. During this work, around 1982, they found a form of carbon with a peculiar double hump, which they called "the camel."

When, in 1985, they heard of the discovery of C_{60}, buckminsterfullerene, they suspected that this might be the cause of their camel spectrum. Huffman and Kratschmer reproduced their earlier experimental conditions, in which they had formed a carbon powder by striking an arc between graphite electrodes in a low pressure of helium.

They treated the resulting soot with benzene, from which they crystallized a light-yellow solid, which they named "fullerite." It was later found to contain about 75% of C_{60} together with 25% of another fullerene, C_{70}. The method has allowed the production of fullerenes in large quantities.

Huggins, Charles Brenton

(1901–)

CANADIAN–AMERICAN SURGEON

Huggins, who was born at Halifax in Nova Scotia, was educated at Acadia University and at the Harvard Medical School, where he obtained his MD in 1924. After graduate training at the University of Michigan he moved to the University of Chicago in 1927 where he has served as professor of surgery since 1936 and director of the May Laboratory of Cancer Research from 1951 until 1969.

In 1939 Huggins made a very simple inference that led to the development of new forms of cancer therapy. Noting that the prostate gland was under the control of androgens (male sex hormones) he concluded that cancer of the prostate might be treated by preventing the production of androgens. Admittedly his proposed treatment of orchiectomy (castration) might appear somewhat severe but it did lead to remissions in some cases and an alleviation of the condition in others.

Huggins soon appreciated however that the same results could probably be achieved by the less drastic procedure of the administration of female sex hormones to neutralize the effect of androgens produced by the testicles. Consequently in 1941 he began to inject his patients with the hormones stilbestrol and hexestrol. He was able to report later that of the first 20 patients so treated 4 were still alive after 12 years. Later workers, inspired by Huggins's work, treated women suffering from cancer of the breast with the male hormone testosterone and claimed improvement in some 20% of the cases.

It was for this work that Huggins shared the 1966 Nobel Prize for physiology or medicine with Peyton Rous.

Huggins, Sir William

(1824–1910)

BRITISH ASTRONOMER AND
ASTROPHYSICIST

It is remarkable that the elements most widely diffused through the host of stars are some of those most closely connected with the living organisms of our globe, including hydrogen, sodium, magnesium, and iron. May it not be that, at least, the brighter stars are like our Sun, the upholding and energizing centres of systems of worlds, adapted to be the abode of living beings?
—Report on his observations (1863)

Huggins, the son of a London silk merchant, attended school for a short period before being educated privately. After a few years in business he retired to devote himself exclusively to the study of science. His first interest was in microscopy but he became absorbed in the work of Gustav Kirchhoff and Robert Bunsen on spectroscopy and the solar spectrum and decided that he would try to do the same with the stars. He equipped himself with the best of instruments, including a superb 8-inch (20-cm) glass from Alvan Clark. He spent some time making maps of the terrestrial elements before moving to the stars, collaborating with William Miller, professor of chemistry at King's College, London. He then began the first major intensive spectral investigation of the stars, which lasted until he was 84 years old, when he found that he could no longer see clearly enough. In later life he was also helped by his wife, Margaret, whom he married in 1875.

Huggins's first observations, published in 1863, showed the stars to be composed of known elements occurring on the Earth and in the Sun. His next great discovery came when he obtained the spectra of those nebula that earlier astronomers had failed to resolve into stars. His excitement is apparent in his report: "I looked into the spectroscope. No spectrum such as I expected! A single bright line only!...The riddle of the nebula was solved...Not an aggregation of stars, but a luminous gas." He quickly examined the spectra of over 50 nebulae and found that a third were gaseous. In the same year he obtained the spectra of a comet and found that it contained hydrocarbons. In 1866 he showed that a nova was rich in hydrogen. He also discovered previously unidentified bright emission lines in the spectra of certain nebulae and attributed them to a new element "nebulium." The true explanation for these forbidden lines was not provided until the next century, by Ira Bowen.

In 1868 Huggins successfully employed a use of spectroscopy that has had a more profound impact on cosmology than anything else. It had been shown by Christian Doppler and Armand Fizeau that the light waves of an object leaving an observer would have a lower frequency, and the frequency of an object approaching an observer should increase. In spectral terms this means that the spectra of the former object should be shifted toward the red and the latter toward the blue. In 1868 Huggins examined the spectrum of Sirius and found a noticeable red shift. As the degree of the shift is proportional to the velocity, Huggins was able to calculate that the speed of recession of Sirius was about 25 miles (40 km) per second. He quickly determined the velocity of many other stars. He and Lady Huggins published their spectral work in its entirety as the *Atlas of Representative Stellar Spectra* in 1899. Huggins had tried to photograph Sirius but was only successful in 1876 by which time the gelatine dry plate had been developed.

Huggins was knighted in 1897, and was president of the Royal Society from 1900 to 1905.

Hughes, John Russell

(1928–)

AMERICAN NEUROPHYSIOLOGIST

Born in Du Bois, Pennsylvania, Hughes was educated at Oxford University and at Harvard, where he obtained his PhD in 1954. After some time at the National Institute of Health and the State University of New York, he moved to Northwestern University where he has served as professor of neurophysiology since 1964.

Among other problems Hughes has worked on the way in which information is transmitted within the central nervous system. In particular he has made a detailed study of the "language" used by the olfactory bulb to inform the brain of the nature of the olfactory medium. His method consisted of implanting electrodes in the olfactory bulb and recording their response to gauze soaked with a certain chemical held at a standard distance away. He found that the message transmitted essentially comprises a mixture of various frequency components.

Huisgen, Rolf

(1920–   )

GERMAN CHEMIST

Huisgen (**hoos**-gen), born the son of a surgeon in Gerolstein, Germany, studied chemistry at the universities of Bonn and Munich where he obtained his PhD in 1943. He initially taught at Tübingen before moving in 1952 to the University of Munich as professor of chemistry and director of the Institute of Physical Chemistry. He retired in 1988.

Huisgen has worked on the mechanisms of organic chemical reactions, and particularly on reactions leading to the formation of ring compounds. Many of his studies have been on reactions to which the principle of orbital symmetry, introduced by Robert Burns Woodward and Roald Hoffman, applies.

Hulse, Russell

(1950–   )

AMERICAN ASTROPHYSICIST

In 1974 Hulse was working as a graduate student at the University of Massachusetts, Amherst, under the supervision of Joseph Taylor. It was arranged that he would spend the summer in Puerto Rico using the

Arecibo Radio Telescope to search for pulsars, a type of star first observed by Jocelyn Bell Burnell in 1967. Among several pulsars detected by Hulse one particular example, named 1913+16 in the constellation Aquila, proved to be of special significance.

Hulse initially found that the pulsar had a short period of 0.059 seconds. More detailed examination, however, revealed that the pulse rate was not constant but varied by some 5 microseconds from day to day. At first Hulse suspected a computer fault. But despite writing a new program, the variability remained. Eventually Hulse spotted that the variation was cyclical, repeating itself every 7.75 hours.

Such phenomena, Hulse argued, would arise naturally if the pulsar was a binary, orbiting an undetected companion star. This would produce a Doppler effect. That is, when the pulsar travels in its orbit toward the Earth the pulses would be crowded together, giving a greater than average pulse rate; when, however, it traveled away from the Earth the pulses would be more spread out and yield a lower than average frequency.

In collaboration with Taylor, Hulse went on to establish some of the basic properties of the pulsar. It appeared to have a mass equivalent to 2.8 solar masses, was thought to be a neutron star with a diameter no more than 20–30 kilometers, and to have an approaching velocity of 300 kps (kilometers per second) and a receding velocity of 75 kps. For his work in this field Hulse shared the 1993 Nobel Prize for physics with Joseph Taylor.

After completing his work on the pulsar 1913+16 in 1977 Hulse moved to Princeton, abandoned astronomy, and began to work at the Plasma Physics Laboratory.

Humason, Milton La Salle

(1891–1972)

AMERICAN ASTRONOMER

Born in Dodge Center, Minnesota, Humason had no formal university training – in fact he began work as a donkey driver moving supplies to the Mount Wilson Observatory in southern California. Here he quickly developed an interest in astronomy and its techniques, an interest that was stimulated by the staff of the observatory. He was taken on as janitor and by 1919 he was competent enough to be appointed assistant astronomer on the staff of the Mount Wilson Observatory and, after 1948, of the Palomar Observatory, where he spent the rest of his career.

In the 1920s Edwin Hubble formulated his law that the distance of the galaxies was proportional to their recessional velocity. This work was based on the careful, painstaking, and difficult measurements of galactic red shifts made by Humason and also by Vesto Slipher. Humason developed extraordinary skill in this field. By 1936, using long photographic exposures of a day or more, he was able to measure a recessional velocity of 40,000 kilometers per second, which took him to the limits of the 100-inch (2.5-m) reflecting telescope at Mount Wilson.

With the opening of the Palomar Observatory he was able to use the 200-inch (5-m) Hale reflector and by the late 1950s was obtaining velocities of over 100,000 km per second; this corresponded to a distance, according to Hubble's law, of about six billion light-years.

Humboldt, Alexander, Baron von

(1769–1859)

GERMAN EXPLORER AND SCIENTIST

An object well worthy of research, and which has long fixed my attention, is the small number of simple substances (earthy and metallic) that enter into the composition of animated beings, and which alone appear fitted to maintain what we may call the chemical movement of vitality.
—*Personal Narrative of Travels to the Equinoctial Regions of America* (1804)

Humboldt (**hum**-bolt or **huum**-bolt) was born in Berlin, Germany. He initially showed little enthusiasm for his studies, but while taking an engineering course in Berlin suddenly became interested in botany, and a year at the University of Göttingen further increased his interest in the sciences. Geology and mineralogy particularly intrigued him and he went on to join the School of Mines in Freiberg, Saxony, staying there for two years. He then worked for the mining department in Ansbach-Bayreuth, reorganizing and supervising the mines in the region.

In 1796 Humboldt inherited enough money to finance himself as a scientific explorer, and he gave up mining to do two years' intensive preparatory studies in geological measuring methods. Initially his expeditionary plans were thwarted by the Napoleonic Wars but, in 1799, he finally managed to sail with a ship bound for Latin America.

The French botanist, Aimé Bonpland, accompanied him on the five-year journey, during which they navigated the Orinoco River and traveled widely through Peru, Venezuela, Ecuador, and Mexico, collecting scientific specimens and data and covering over 6,000 miles. Humboldt studied the Pacific coastal currents, the *Humboldt current* (now the Peru current) being named for him, and he was the first to propose building a canal through Panama. He investigated American volcanoes, noting their tendency to follow geological faults, and concluded that volcanic action had played a major part in the development of the Earth's crust, thus finally disproving the neptunist theory of Abraham Werner. He climbed the Chimborazo volcano to what was then a world record height of 19,280 feet (5,876 m), and was the first to attribute mountain sickness to oxygen deficiency. He also measured changes in temperature with altitude and noted its effect on vegetation.

On his return to Europe in 1804, Humboldt settled in Paris and began to publish the data gathered on his travels, a task that took 20 years and filled 30 volumes. He introduced isobars and isotherms on his weather maps, so pioneering the subject of comparative climatology, and also helped initiate ecological studies with his discussions on the relationship between a region's geography and its flora and fauna.

By 1827 Humboldt's finances were severely depleted and he returned to Berlin as tutor to the Prussian crown prince. Two years later he was invited by the Russian finance minister to visit Siberia, and Humboldt made use of the trip to take more geological and meteorological measurements. He also organized a series of meteorological and magnetic observatories through Russia, Asia, and the British Empire, to trace the fluctuations in the Earth's magnetic field.

Humboldt spent the last years of his life writing *Kosmos* (The Cosmos), a synthesis of the knowledge about the universe then known, of which four volumes were published during his lifetime.

Hume, David

(1711–1776)

BRITISH PHILOSOPHER

> If we take in our hand any volume, of divinity or school metaphysics, for instance, let us ask, Does it contain any abstract reasoning concerning quantity or number? No. Does it contain any experimental reasoning concerning matter of fact and existence? No. Commit it then to the flames; for it can contain nothing but sophistry and illusion.
> —*An Enquiry Concerning Human Understanding* (1748)

Hume was the younger son of a laird. Born in Edinburgh, Scotland, and educated at the university there, he intended to study law but found himself stricken with an "insurmountable aversion to everything but the pursuit of philosophy and general learning." He became a tutor, served in a variety of diplomatic posts, and spent the period 1752 to 1763 as librarian of the Edinburgh Faculty of Advocates where he wrote his *History of England* (6 vols., 1754–62). After another period of diplomatic service abroad in Paris, Hume retired to Edinburgh in 1769. In the spring of 1775 Hume contracted cancer. Shortly before his death in the summer of 1776 he was visited by James Boswell, eager to report back to Dr. Johnson that the notorious atheist, Hume, was facing death with apprehension. Instead he found Hume placid and cheerful, denying that death was to be feared and declaring survival to be "an unreasonable fancy." Boswell was most disturbed.

In 1738 Hume published his masterpiece, *A Treatise of Human Nature*, in which his aim was to do for the moral sciences, the science of man, what Newton had done for the natural sciences. In pursuing this aim Hume was lead into a profound study of causality – the idea of a "necessary connection" between two physical events when one is said to be the cause of the other – work that carried important implications for science. Against Rationalists such as Descartes, Hume argued that empirical knowledge can never be deduced a priori, thus aiding the destruction of the Cartesian tradition in science. Hume put forward the basis of modern Empiricism – that all knowledge of matters of fact (and thus scientific knowledge) is based on experience and evidence and is therefore only probable, capable of denial, and can never be logically necessary. Thus in his analysis of causation Hume argued that there is no necessary connection between physical events (e.g., when one is said to be the *cause* of the other); there is no mystical "power" in one event that "brings about" another. We merely observe that one type of event is invariably followed by another, and because of this association of ideas in our minds, when we observe an event of the first type we "predict" an event of the second.

But such a practice will only be sound if the conjunctions we have observed in the past continue to hold in the future. How can, asked Hume, this latter assumption be justified? Not by pure reason, nor from experience, for we cannot conclude from the fact that nature has behaved uniformly in the past that it will continue to do so without assuming the truth of the very principle we are examining. In this way Hume presented the classical "problem of induction" that has since been puzzled over by generations of philosophers and scientists.

Hume-Rothery, William

(1899–1968)

BRITISH METALLURGIST

The son of a lawyer, Hume-Rothery was born at Worcester Park in Surrey, England. He originally intended to pursue a military career and consequently entered the Royal Military Academy, Woolwich, on leaving school. An attack of meningitis which left him totally deaf forced him to leave the army and he turned instead to chemistry. Although refused entry to his father's college, Trinity College, Cambridge, because of his deafness, he was more graciously received by Magdalen College, Oxford. After obtaining his PhD from the Royal School of Mines in 1925, Hume-Rothery returned to Oxford where he remained for the rest of his life, being appointed in 1958 to the university's first chair of metallurgy.

With 178 published papers to his credit Hume-Rothery illuminated many areas of metallurgy. His best-known work was concerned with alloys that are solid solutions, in which atoms of the constituent metals share a common lattice. The *Hume-Rothery rules* give the conditions that have to be satisfied for metallic solid solutions to form. The first concerns the atomic size factor and claims that if the atomic diameter of the solvent differs in size from that of the solute by more than 14%, the chances of solubility are small. Secondly, the more electronegative is one component and the more electropositive the other, the more they are likely to form compounds rather than solutions. And, finally, a metal of lower valency is more likely to dissolve one of higher valency than vice versa. Much of his work in this field was published in his book *The Structure of Metals and Alloys* (1936).

Hunsaker, Jerome Clarke

(1886–1984)

AMERICAN AERONAUTICAL ENGINEER

Hunsaker was born in Cheston, Iowa, and educated at the U.S. Naval Academy, graduating in 1908. He served in the navy from 1909 until 1926, reaching the rank of commander. Selected for the Construction Corps, he studied naval architecture at the Massachusetts Institute of Technology and aeronautical engineering in Europe. In 1914 he established the first course in aeronautical engineering at MIT. Recalled by the navy (1916) to put aeronautical engineering into practice, he worked on zeppelins, producing the *Shenandoah* (1923), and flying boats. Hunsaker worked in business from 1926, initially at the Bell Telephone Laboratories and then (1928–33) at Goodyear where he built zeppelins. In 1933 Hunsaker was appointed professor of mechanical engineering at MIT, also serving concurrently as head of the department of aeronautical engineering until his retirement in 1951.

He was the author of *Aeronautics at the Mid-century* (1952), a review of the problems facing the industry and the strategies open to it.

Hunter, John

(1728–1793)

BRITISH SURGEON AND ANATOMIST

> ...A gifted interpreter of the Divine Power and Wisdom at work in the Laws of Organic Life, and...the founder of Scientific Surgery.
> —Memorial plaque to Hunter in Westminster Abbey (1859)

Hunter, who was born at Long Calderwood in Scotland, joined his elder brother William, the famous obstetrician, in London in 1748. He there assisted his brother and attended surgical classes at Chelsea Hospital. Disputes with William over their research led John to branch out on his own and in 1759 he joined the army to serve as a surgeon in Portugal during the Seven Years' War. On his return to London in 1762 he set up as a private teacher and in 1767 was appointed surgeon at St. George's Hospital, London.

As a surgeon Hunter's major innovation was in the treatment of aneurysm, a bulge appearing at a weak spot in the wall of an artery. Rather than follow the drastic procedure of amputation Hunter instead tied the artery some distance from the diseased part and found that, with the pressure of circulation removed from the aneurysmal sack, the progress of the disease is halted. He also made radical proposals, based on his military experience, for the treatment of gunshot wounds. He wisely argued in his *A Treatise on the Blood, Inflammation and Gunshot Wounds* (1794) that unless the missile in the body was actually endangering life the surgeon should leave it alone and under no circumstances enlarge the wound by opening it.

Hunter also wrote a famous work on venereal disease (1786), inadvertently producing much confusion. In the late 18th century it was still a matter of dispute whether syphilis with its chancre and gonorrhea with its purulent discharge were separate complaints. In 1767 Hunter decided to resolve the issue by inoculating himself with gonorrhea. He developed both gonorrhea and the typically hard chancre of syphilis, concluding therefore that discharge from a gonorrhea produces chancres. It seems not to have occurred to Hunter that his "gonorrhea" was also infected with syphilis.

Hunter's main claim to fame however lay in his superb anatomical collection. He was supposed to have dissected over 500 different species and at his death his collection contained over 13,000 items. Included in his museum in Leicester Square, London, was the skeleton of the Irish giant, C. Byrne, who was so keenly aware of the desire of Hunter for his 7-foot 7-inch frame that he arranged to be secretly buried at sea. Hunter was widely reported to have paid the undertakers the sum of £500 for the corpse.

His collection was purchased by the government after his death and in 1795 was presented to the Royal College of Surgeons in London where, despite some losses from bombing in World War II, it has remained ever since.

Hunter, William

(1718–1783)

BRITISH OBSTETRICIAN

> Some physiologists will have it that the stomach is a mill; – others, that it is a fermenting vat; – others again that it is a stew-pan; – but in my view of the matter, it is neither a mill, a fermenting vat, nor a stew-pan – but a stomach, gentlemen, a stomach.
> —In a lecture to medical students

A brother of John Hunter, the famous surgeon, William was born at Long Calderwood in Scotland and studied medicine at Edinburgh University before moving to London in 1740. Hunter went on to specialize in obstetrics and became an eminent practitioner, attending the royal family. He founded the Great Windmill Street School of Anatomy and his most famous work is *The Anatomy of the Human Gravid Uterus* (1774), a collation of 25 years' work, which contains 34 detailed plates produced from engravings of dissections.

Hunter built up a large and valuable collection of coins, medals, pictures, and books, which he bequeathed to Glasgow University. It is now housed in the Hunterian Museum.

Huntington, George

(1851–1916)

AMERICAN PHYSICIAN

Huntington was born in East Hampton, New York, the son and grandson of physicians. He was initially trained by his father before following a more formal course of medicine at the College of Physicians and Surgeons, Columbia University. He worked for some years with his father in East Hampton before moving to Palmyra, Ohio. Huntington returned later to Duchess County, New York.

In 1872 he published a paper, *On Chorea*, in which he described an encounter with two women near East Hampton, a mother and a daughter. They were, he noted, "tall, thin, almost cadaverous, both bowing, twisting, grimacing." The disease was common in the area and he went on to note some of its main features. The condition was invariably fatal and progressed "gradually but surely until the hapless sufferer is but a quivering wreck." He also noted that it was "an heirloom from the past" in that it was confined to a few families – if the parents contracted the chorea then so would one or more of the children. Huntington also reported that it was an adult complaint, unknown in anyone under thirty. Not much more was known about the complaint until a century later when Nancy Wexler began her search for the responsible gene. The disease, now known as Huntington's chorea, was thought to have been brought to East Hampton by a settler from Suffolk a century earlier.

Hurter, Ferdinand

(1844–1898)

SWISS CHEMIST

Born at Schaffhausen in Switzerland, Hurter (**huur**-ter) was educated at the Federal Institute of Technology, Zurich, and at Heidelberg University, where he was a pupil of Robert Bunsen. In 1867 he moved to England and became the chief chemist at Holbrook Gaskell and Henry Deacon's alkali factory in Widnes. In 1890, when the United Alkali Company was formed, Hurter was appointed its chief chemist and set up one of the first industrial research laboratories. He collaborated with Lunge in producing *The Alkali Maker's Handbook*, a work describing the Leblanc process in technical detail. Hurter also worked on photography with V. C. Driffield.

Hutchinson, George Evelyn

(1903–1991)

AMERICAN BIOLOGIST

Hutchinson was born in Cambridge, England, and graduated from the university there in 1924. He was senior lecturer at the University of Witwatersrand (1926–28) before emigrating to America where he served as Sterling Professor of Zoology at Yale from 1945 until 1971. He received American citizenship in 1941.

Hutchinson's most important work was concerned with aquatic ecosystems and the physical, chemical, meteorological, and biological conditions of lakes. He made particular studies of the classification and distribution of aquatic bugs (Hemiptera), and investigated water mixing and movement in stratified lakes, proving the circulation of phosphorus. He also studied lake sediments and investigated certain aspects of evolution. His work took him to many different regions, including the lakes of western Transvaal, Tibet, and northeastern North America. Hutchinson published much of his life's work in his *A Treatise on Limnology* (3 vols., 1957–75); a fourth volume was completed shortly before his death and published in 1993.

Hutchinson, John

(1884–1972)

BRITISH BOTANIST

Hutchinson, who was educated at the village school in Wark-on-Tyne, England, where he was born, began work in 1900 under his father, the head gardener on a large estate. In 1904 he was appointed to a junior post at the Royal Botanic Gardens, Kew, where he remained for the rest of his career. Starting as an assistant in the herbarium he was in charge of the Africa section from 1919 until 1936 when he became keeper of the Museum of Economic Botany, a post he occupied until his retirement in 1948.

Hutchinson's most significant work was his *Families of Flowering Plants* (2 vols. 1926–34; 2nd edition 1959), which contains details of 342 dicotyledon and 168 monocotyledon families. Hutchinson drew most of the illustrations for this work himself. In it he concentrated on the different plant families that various workers had considered the most primitive. He concluded that bisexual flowers with free petals, sepals, etc., as seen in the magnolia and buttercup families, are more ancient than the generally unisexual catkinlike flowers found in the nettle and beech families, which lack these parts. This conclusion supported the classification of George Bentham and Joseph Hooker and added weight to arguments against the system of Adolf Engler. Furthermore Hutchinson stated that families with apparently more simple flowers are in fact more advanced, and have evolved by reduction from more complex structures; that is, the families show retrograde evolution. In this, the now generally accepted view, Hutchinson was developing the earlier ideas of the German botanist, Alexander Braun.

An enormously prolific and industrious worker, Hutchinson also published, with John Dalziel, the standard work, *Flora of West Tropical Africa* (1927–36) and at the time of his death was engaged in a revision of the *Genera Plantarum* (Genera of Plants) of Bentham and Hooker.

Hutton, James

(1726–1797)

BRITISH GEOLOGIST

> There is presently laying at the bottom of the ocean the foundation of a future land, which is to appear after an indefinite space of time.
> —*Concerning the System of the Earth, its Duration, and Stability* (1788)

It is scarcely more difficult to procure the secrets of science from Nature herself, than to dig them from the writings of this philosopher.
—Thomas Thomson (1801)

Hutton was born in Edinburgh, Scotland, the son of a merchant who became the city treasurer. He was educated at Edinburgh University, which he left in 1743 to be apprenticed to a lawyer. This did not retain his interest long for, in 1744, he returned to the university to read medicine. He studied in Paris for two years and finally gained his MD from Leiden in 1749. He next devoted several years to agriculture and industry, farming in Berwickshire and commercially producing sal ammoniac. In 1768 he returned to Edinburgh, financially independent, and devoted himself to scientific studies, especially of geology, for the rest of his life.

Hutton's uniformitarian theories were first published as a paper in 1788 and later extended into a two-volume work, *Theory of the Earth* (1795). This work proved difficult to read and it only reached a wide audience when his friend John Playfair edited and summarized it as *Illustrations of the Huttonian Theory* (1802). It marked a turning point in geology. The prevailing theory of the day, the neptunism of Abraham Werner, was that rocks had been laid down as mineral deposits in the oceans. However, Hutton maintained that water could not be the only answer for it was mainly erosive. The water could not account for the nonconformities caused by the foldings and intrusions characteristic of the Earth's strata. Hutton showed that the geological processes that had formed the Earth's features could be observed continuing at the present day. The heat of the Earth was the productive power, according to Hutton, that caused sedimentary rocks to fuse into the granites and flints, which could be produced in no other way. It could also produce the upheaval of strata, their folding and twisting, and the creation of mountains.

A long time scale is essential to Hutton's theory of uniformitarianism as the forces of erosion and combustion work, in general, only slowly, as demonstrated by the presence of visible Roman roads. He concluded that on the face of the Earth "we find no vestige of a beginning – no prospect of an end."

Hutton's work was accepted with little delay by most geologists, including the leading Edinburgh neptunist, Robert Jameson. In the 19th century Charles Lyell expanded the theories of uniformitarianism and these were to influence Charles Darwin in his theory of evolution.

Huxley, Sir Andrew Fielding

(1917–   )

BRITISH PHYSIOLOGIST

Huxley, a grandson of T. H. Huxley, was born in London and graduated in 1938 from Cambridge University, receiving his MA there three years later. He is best known for his collaboration with Alan Hodgkin in elucidating the "sodium pump" mechanism by which nerve impulses are transmitted, for which they were awarded, with John Eccles, the Nobel Prize for physiology or medicine (1963). He has also done important work on muscular contraction theory and has been involved in the development of the interference microscope and ultramicrotome. Huxley was reader in experimental biophysics at Cambridge (1959–60), and from 1960 to 1969 was Jodrell Professor of Physiology at University College, London. In 1969 he was elected research professor becoming emeritus professor in 1983. In 1980 he succeeded Alexander Todd as president of the Royal Society, a position he held until 1985. He also served as master of Trinity College, Cambridge, from 1984 to 1990 and was knighted in 1974.

Huxley, Hugh Esmor

(1924–)

BRITISH MOLECULAR BIOLOGIST

Huxley (no relation to T. H. Huxley or any of his descendants) was born at Birkenhead in northwest England. He studied physics at Cambridge University where he obtained his PhD in 1952 after wartime research on the development of radar. Like many other physicists after the war Huxley was interested in applying physics to biological problems. After two years in America at the Massachusetts Institute of Technology and the period 1956–61 at the biophysics unit of the University of London, he returned to Cambridge to join the staff of the Medical Research Council's molecular biology laboratory, where he remained until 1987. In 1988 he became director and professor of biology at Brandeis University, Boston. He also served from 1988 to 1994 as director of the Rosenstiel Basic Medical Sciences Research Centre.

In 1953, in collaboration with Jean Hanson, Huxley proposed the sliding-filament theory of muscle contraction. This was based on his earlier study of myofibrils, the contractile apparatus of muscle, with the electron microscope. He found that myofibrils are made of two kinds of filament, one type about twice the width of the other. Each filament is aligned with other filaments of the same kind to form a band across the myofibril, and the bands of thick and thin filaments overlap for part of their length. The bands are also linked by an elaborate system of crossbridges. When the muscle changes length the two sets of filaments slide past each other. Further, the two sorts of filaments can be identified with the two chief proteins of muscle, myosin in the thick filament and actin in the thin. This made possible an elegant solution to how muscles contract at the molecular level.

In the areas where both kinds of protein are in contact, Huxley suggested that one, most probably myosin, serves as an enzyme, splitting a phosphate from ATP and so releasing the energy required for contraction. He concluded that the evidence of the combination of actin and myosin is seen in the bridges between the two kinds of filaments.

The theory has since been much enlarged and taken to deeper levels of molecular understanding. Despite this, the basic insight of Huxley and Hanson has remained intact.

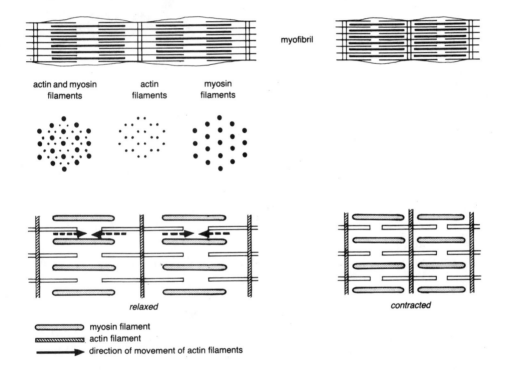

myofibril

actin and myosin
filaments

actin
filaments

myosin
filaments

relaxed

contracted

myosin filament
actin filament
direction of movement of actin filaments

MUSCLE CONTRACTION   The sliding filament theory proposed by Hugh Huxley and Jean Hanson.

Huxley, Sir Julian Sorell

(1887–1975)

BRITISH BIOLOGIST

Operationally, God is beginning to resemble not a ruler but the last fading smile of a cosmic Cheshire cat.
— *Religion without Revelation* (1927)

A grandson of T. H. Huxley, Julian Huxley was born in London and graduated in zoology from Oxford University in 1909. He did research on sponges (Porifera) at the Naples Zoological Station (1909–10) before taking up the post of lecturer in biology at Oxford (1910–12). From 1912 until 1916 he worked at the Rice Institute, Houston, Texas, where he met the famous American geneticist Hermann Muller. Before returning to Oxford to take up the post of senior demonstrator in zoology (1919–25) he saw war service in Italy. He was next appointed professor of zoology at King's College, London (1925–27), resigning from this post to devote more time to writing and research.

Huxley was a keen ornithologist and published, in 1914, a classic paper on the courtship of the great crested grebe. In the 1930s he was involved in the production of natural-history films, the most notable of which was the highly praised *Private Life of the Gannet* (1934), which he produced with the help of R. M. Lockley. One of the leading popularizers of science of modern times (especially the years before and just after World War II), Huxley spent much of his life explaining advances in natural science to the layman and in advocating the application of science to the benefit of mankind. To many he is best remembered as a most capable and lucid educationalist, but Huxley was also eminent in many other fields.

In 1946 he was appointed the first director-general of UNESCO, a post he held for two years. As an administrator, he also did much to transform the Zoological Society's collections at Regent's Park (London Zoo). Viewing man as "the sole agent of further evolutionary advance on this planet," he caused considerable controversy by advocating the deliberate physical and mental improvement of the human race through eugenics. Huxley's biological research was also extensive, carrying out work on animal hormones, physiology, ecology, and animal (especially bird) behavior as it relates to evolution. He was president of the Institute of Animal Behaviour and the originator of the term "ethology," now in general use to define the science of animal behavior. He also introduced several other scientific terms, such as cline and clade.

Huxley's publications are extensive and include *Evolution: the Modern Synthesis* (1942, 1963). He was knighted in 1958.

Huxley, Thomas Henry

(1825–1895)

BRITISH BIOLOGIST

The great tragedy of science – the slaying of a beautiful hypothesis by an ugly fact.
—"Biogenesis and Abiogenesis,"
Collected Essays, Vol. VIII

Huxley, the seventh child of a school teacher, was born in Ealing in southeast England and received only two years' schooling. From the age of 10 he educated himself, doing sufficiently well to be admitted to Charing Cross Hospital to study medicine. He graduated in 1845 and the following year was employed as surgeon on HMS *Rattlesnake*, which was due to survey the Torres Strait between Australia and Papua. During the voyage Huxley studied the marine life of tropical waters and wrote an important paper on the medusae (jellyfish) and related species, naming a new phylum, the Coelenterata, into which these were placed. Recognizing the value of this work, the Royal Society elected Huxley a member in 1851. In 1854 he became lecturer in natural history at the Royal School of Mines (later the Royal College of Science) and while there gave a lecture on "The Theory of the Vertebrate Skull," which disproved the idea that the skull originates from the vertebrae.

Huxley is best remembered as the main advocate of Charles Darwin's theory of evolution, and in 1860 – the year following the publication of *The Origin of Species* – he took part in the famous debate with the bishop of Oxford, Samuel Wilberforce, at the Oxford meeting of the

British Association for the Advancement of Science. During the discussion Wilberforce asked whether Huxley traced his ancestry to the apes on his mother's or father's side of the family. Huxley answered witheringly that given the choice of a miserable ape and a man who could make such a remark at a serious scientific gathering, he would select the ape. The meeting resulted in a triumph for science, and after it Huxley continued to gain the better of many other distinguished theologians in long academic wrangles. He introduced the term "agnosticism" to describe his own view that since knowledge rested on scientific evidence and reasoning (and not blind faith) knowledge of the nature and certainty about the very existence of God was impossible.

Huxley worked hard to better educational standards for the working classes and spoke out against the traditional method of learning by rote. He opened Josiah Mason College (later Birmingham University), Owens College Medical School (later part of Manchester University), and Johns Hopkins University, Baltimore. Huxley was the grandfather of the author Aldous Huxley, the Nobel Prize winner Andrew Huxley, and the biologist Sir Julian Huxley.

Huygens, Christiaan

(1629–1695)

DUTCH PHYSICIST AND ASTRONOMER

A man that is of Copernicus's opinion, that this earth of ours is a Planet, carry'd round and enlightn'd by the Sun, like the rest of them, cannot but sometimes have a fancy...that the rest of the Planets have their Dress and Furniture, nay and their Inhabitants too...
—*New Conjectures Concerning the Planetary Worlds, Their Inhabitants, and Productions* (c. 1690)

Huygens (**hI**-genz or **hoi**-gens), whose father was the famous Renaissance poet Constantin Huygens, was born in The Hague and studied at the University of Leiden and the College of Breda. He worked in Paris as one of the founding members of the French Academy of Sciences from 1666 to 1681 when, as a Protestant, he found the growing religious intolerance threatening, and returned to The Hague. His first work was in mathematics, but his greatest achievements were in physical optics and dynamics, and his importance to 17th-century science is second only to that of Newton.

Huygens's first great success was the invention of the pendulum clock. Galileo had noted in 1581 that a pendulum would keep the same time whatever its amplitude. Many, including Galileo himself, had tried unsuccessfully to use this insight to construct a more reliable clock. Huygens showed that a pendulum that moves in the arc of a circle does not move with an exactly equal swing. To produce an isochronous (equal-timed) swing it would need to move in a curve called a cycloid. It should be emphasized that Huygens worked this out largely from first principles. He also showed how the pendulum could be constructed so to move in a cycloidal path and how to make the connection to the escapement. The first clock was made to his design by Salomon Coster in 1657 and was described in Huygens's book *Horologium* (1658; The Clock). The pendulum became one of the basic tools of 17th-century scientific investigation.

Huygens also made major contributions to astronomy as a designer of improved telescopes and as an observer of Saturn. He discovered Titan, Saturn's largest satellite, in 1655 and after prolonged observation was able to describe Saturn's rings correctly.

In 1673 Huygens published *Horologium oscillatorium* (The Clock Pendulum), a brilliant mathematical analysis of dynamics, including discussions of the relationship between the length of a pendulum and its period of oscillation, and the laws of centrifugal force. It also included an early formulation of Newton's first law of motion: that without some external force, such as gravity, a body once set in motion would continue in a straight line. His views on gravity were worked out in *Discours de la cause de la pesanteur* (1690; Discourse on the Cause of Gravity). As a Cartesian (a follower of René Descartes) he could not accept Newtonian action at a distance or, in fact, any talk of forces. Instead he would only accept a mechanical explanation, which meant a return to some kind of vortex theory. That is, bodies can only be heavy not because they are attracted by another body but because they are pushed by other bodies.

Huygens's greatest achievement was his development of the wave theory of light, described fully in his *Traité de la lumière* (1690; Treatise on Light). He assumed that space was pervaded by ether formed of particles, the disturbance of which constituted the radiation of light with the disturbance of one particle being passed on to its neighbor and so on.

The disturbances can be considered as waves spreading in a regular spherical form from the point of origin – the particles disturbed in phase constituting a wave front. Each point on a wave front may be regarded as a source of new secondary wavelets and a surface tangent joining such wavelets (i.e., the envelope of the secondary wavelets) can be considered as a new wave front. This method of treating light waves is known as the *Huygens construction*. Using it, Huygens dealt with reflection and refraction and predicted – as Newtonian theory did not – that light should travel more slowly in a denser medium. But as Huygens considered the waves to be longitudinal, the theory could not explain polarization.

Newton's *Opticks* (1704) presented a corpuscular (particle) theory of light, and the wave theory lay dormant until it was taken up by Thomas Young and his contemporaries.

Hyman, Libbie Henrietta

(1888–1969)

AMERICAN ZOOLOGIST

Born in Des Moines, Iowa, and educated at the University of Chicago, Hyman also held a research post there from 1916 until 1931 where, under Charles Manning Child, she worked on the physiology and morphology of the lower invertebrates, particularly the planarians (flatworms). She published a number of works on invertebrate and vertebrate zoology, anatomy, physiology, and embryology, but her major compilation is *The Invertebrates*, a monumental work, six volumes of which had been published (1940–68) at the time of her death.

Hypatia

(*c.* 370–415)

GREEK MATHEMATICIAN

He who influences the thought of his times, influences all the times that follow.
He has made his impress on eternity.
—Quoted by Elbert Hubbard in *Little Journeys to the Homes of Great Teachers*

Hypatia (hI-**pay**-sha), who was born in Alexandria, Egypt, was the daughter of Theon of Alexandria, the author of a well-known commentary on Ptolemy. In 400 she was reported to be head of the Neoplatonic school in Alexandria. None of her work has survived, although some information about her comes from the letters of her pupil Synesius of Cyrene. To her have been attributed commentaries on Ptolemy's *Almagest*, Diophantus's *Arithmetic*, and Apollonius's *Conics*. She also designed several scientific instruments including an astrolabe, a hydrometer, and a still.

Learning and science came to a violent conclusion in Alexandria and in the West, as did Hypatia. In conflict with Cyril, bishop of Alexandria, through her friendship with Orestes, the Roman prefect of the city, she was killed by a Christian mob. The circumstances of her death in March 415 have been described by the fifth-century historian Socrates Scholasticus:

"All men did both reverence and had her in admiration for the singular modesty of her mind. Wherefore she had great spite and envy owed unto her, and because she conferred oft, and had great familiarity with Orestes, the people charged her that she was the cause why the bishop and Orestes were not become friends. To be short, certain heady and rash cockbrains whose guide and captain was Peter, a reader of that Church, watched this woman coming home from some place or other, they pull her out of her chariot: they hail her into the Church called Caesarium: they strip her stark naked: they raze the skin and rend the flesh of her body with sharp shells, until the breath departed out of her body: they quarter her body: they bring her quarters unto a place called Cinaron and burn them to ashes."

The manner of her death and reports of her intellect and beauty have made her a romantic figure. For many centuries, with the possible exception of the alchemist Marie the Jewess, she was regarded as the only woman scientist of the Ancient World.

I-Hsing

(*c.* 681–*c.* 727)

CHINESE MATHEMATICIAN AND ASTRONOMER

I-Hsing (I-**shing**) was a Buddhist monk around whom many legends have grown. Only a small portion of his work has survived so it is difficult to appreciate it in detail. There is, however, no reason to doubt his involvement in two major astronomical achievements. In the period 723–26, in collaboration with the Astronomer Royal, Nankung Yueh, expeditions were organized to measure, astronomically, the length of a meridional line. Over a distance of 1,553 miles (2,500 km) along this line, simultaneous measurements of the Sun's solstitial shadow were made at nine stations. The estimated length of a degree, on the basis of their measurements, was far too large and it must be supposed that some systematic error in the method of observation was taking place. However, when it is appreciated that research expeditions to determine the length of a meridional degree were not organized in Europe until the 17th century, the amazing nature of I-Hsing's work can be appreciated. He also probably anticipated Su Sung in the use of an escapement in an astronomical clock. It was described in a 13th-century encyclopedia: "Water, flowing into scoops, turned a wheel automatically, rotating it one complete revolution in one day and one night." This turned various rings representing the motion of the celestial bodies. It was soon reported to be corroded, relegated to a museum, and to have fallen into disuse.

Imbrie, John

(1925–)

AMERICAN GEOLOGIST

Imbrie was born at Penn Yan, New York and educated at Princeton and Yale, where he obtained his PhD in 1951. He joined the Columbia faculty in 1952 and, after serving as professor of geology (1961–66), he moved to Brown University where he was professor of geology until 1975. He was then appointed to the chair of oceanography.

In his 1956 paper *Biometrical Methods in the Study of Invertebrate Fossils* Imbrie showed how statistical techniques could be applied to the analysis of variation in fossil assemblies. He has also worked on the paleoecology of the Great Bahamas Bank and in his *Ice Ages* (1979) produced a comprehensive and popular survey of the subject.

Ingenhousz, Jan

(1730–1799)

DUTCH PLANT PHYSIOLOGIST
AND PHYSICIAN

Ingenhousz (**ing**-en-hows), who was born at Breda in the Netherlands, studied medicine, chemistry, and physics at the universities of Louvain and Leiden, receiving his MD from Louvain in 1752. In 1765 he visited London and became expert at administering smallpox inoculations using Edward Jenner's method. News of his expertise spread and he was invited to Vienna in 1768 by the Empress Maria Theresa to inoculate her family and to become court physician.

In 1779 Ingenhousz returned to England and published his work on gaseous exchange in plants. His experiments demonstrated that plants absorb carbon dioxide and give off oxygen (in his words, "purify the air") only in the light, and that the reverse process occurs in the dark. The light process later became known as photosynthesis. Ingenhousz also conducted research on soils and on plant nutrition, improved apparatus for generating static electricity, and studied heat conduction in metals.

Ingold, Sir Christopher Kelk

(1893–1970)

BRITISH CHEMIST

The calculations must have been dreadful...but one structure like this brings more certainty into organic chemistry than generations of activity by us professionals.

—On the structures of hexamethyl benzene and hexachlor benzene as revealed by x-ray crystallography. *Nature*, 1928

Ingold, a Londoner, was educated at the University of Southampton and at Imperial College, London. After serving as professor of organic chemistry at the University of Leeds from 1924 until 1930, he moved to the chair of chemistry at University College, London, where he remained until his retirement in 1961.

With over 400 papers to his credit and as the author of the classic text *Structure and Mechanism in Organic Chemistry* (1953), Ingold was one of the leading figures in British chemistry. The basic aim running through all his work was to understand the mechanism of organic reactions, particularly the kinetics of elimination and substitution reactions. In 1926 he introduced the idea of mesomerism, fully explained in his paper *Principles of an Electronic Theory of Organic Reactions* (1934). This was similar to the concept of resonance proposed by Linus Pauling in the early 1930s. The basic idea was that if a molecule could exist in two electronic structures then its normal state was neither one nor the other but some "hybrid" form. This theory was substantiated by measuring bond lengths in appropriate molecules.

Ingram, Vernon Martin

(1924–)

GERMAN–BRITISH–AMERICAN
BIOCHEMIST

Ingram, born Immerwahr (**im**-er-var) in Breslau (now Wrocław in Poland), was brought to Britain as a refugee from Nazi Germany as a child. He was educated at Birkbeck College, London, where he obtained his PhD in 1949. After working briefly at Rockefeller and Yale he returned to England and joined the staff of the Medical Research Council's molecular biology unit at the Cavendish Laboratory, Cambridge, in 1952. In 1958 however he moved to the Massachusetts Institute of Technology where he has served as professor of biochemistry since 1961 and as John and Dorothy Wilson Professor of Biology since 1988.

By the mid 1950s it was clear to Francis Crick that it should be possible, and was indeed essential, for molecular biology to be able to show that mutant genes produced changes in the amino acid sequences of proteins. Although such a claim was central to the supposed revolution in molecular biology, there was, as Crick realized in 1955, no direct evidence that proteins are in fact coded by genes.

Consequently Crick and Ingram attempted to reveal such a change in the lysozyme of fowl eggs. However, although they succeeded in distinguishing differences between lysozymes from such different birds as duck and pheasant, they failed to find any difference in lysozymes between two hens of the same species. At this point, however, Max Perutz gave Ingram some sickle-cell hemoglobin (hemoglobin S) to work with. (Hemoglobin S, possessed by sufferers of a crippling anemia, had been distinguished from normal hemoglobin A by Linus Pauling and his student Harvey Itano in 1949.) Ingram split the hemoglobin into smaller units by using the enzyme trypsin to break the peptide bonds. He then separated these units by electrophoresis and paper chromatography. This allowed him to show that hemoglobin S differs from normal hemoglobin at just one site where the amino acid valine replaces the glutamic acid of the A form. Although it came as a surprise that the alteration of one amino acid in over 500 could produce such major effects, it also dramatically established that molecular biology was not just an abstract and remote branch of structural chemistry.

Ingram went on to show that this and other point mutations of hemoglobin could be used to trace the evolutionary history of vertebrates, work reported in his *The Hemoglobins in Genetics and Evolution* (1963).

Ipatieff, Vladimir Nikolayevich

(1867–1952)

RUSSIAN–AMERICAN CHEMIST

Ipatieff (i-**pa**-tyef), a Muscovite by birth, became an officer in the Imperial Russian Army in 1887 and was educated at the Mikhail Artillery Academy (1889–92) in St. Petersburg. After further study in Germany and France he returned to the academy in 1898 and became professor of chemistry until 1906.

While in Munich (1897) Ipatieff achieved the synthesis of isoprene, the basic unit of the rubber molecule. On his return to Russia he carried out important work on high-pressure catalytic reactions. The first breakthrough in organic catalysis had been due to Paul Sabatier who had demonstrated the use of finely ground nickel to catalyze hydrogenation of unsaturated hydrocarbons (1897). Ipatieff greatly extended this work. He showed how it could be applied to liquids and demonstrated that the process became much more powerful and adaptable at high pressures. To this end he designed the so-called *Ipatieff bomb* – an autoclave that permitted the heating of substances under pressure to above their boiling point. Thus before World War I Ipatieff had synthesized isooctane, and had polymerized ethylene.

During World War I and after the revolutionary years in Russia Ipatieff held a number of important advisory posts, in addition to continuing with his own research, despite his anti-Communist feelings. In 1930, worried for his own safety, he traveled to America. Despite being 64 when he arrived in America Ipatieff still had much to offer, publishing over 150 papers in this last phase of his career. He was appointed professor of chemistry at Northwestern University, Illinois (1931–35) and also acted as a consultant to the Universal Oil Products Company of Chicago which, in 1938, established at Northwestern University the Ipatieff High Pressure Laboratory, which he directed. With the growth of the petrochemical industry after 1918, Ipatieff's techniques became widely used. Working in America he showed how low-octane gasolines could be converted to high-octane gasoline by "cracking" hydrocarbons at high temperatures.

Irvine, Sir James Colquhoun

(1877–1952)

BRITISH CHEMIST

Irvine studied chemistry at the Royal Technical College in his native Glasgow and at Leipzig. His father was a manufacturer of light iron castings and appears to have been a capable mathematician. Irvine's whole career was spent at St. Andrews beginning in 1901 as a lecturer, being appointed professor of chemistry in 1909, and finally, in 1921, becoming vice-chancellor of the university. Under Irvine the tradition of carbohydrate studies established by Thomas Purdie was to continue. Irvine's work involved the application of Purdie's methylation technique to carbohydrates. He realized that the constitution of disaccharides and other compound carbohydrates might be found by methylating them and he isolated the first methylated sugars, trimethyl and tetramethyl glucose.

Irvine's fruitful line of research was to be continued at St. Andrews and later at Birmingham by Norman Haworth.

Isaacs, Alick

(1921–1967)

BRITISH VIROLOGIST AND BIOLOGIST

Isaacs, who was born in Glasgow, Scotland, graduated in medicine from the university there in 1944. After three years' work in the department of bacteriology he moved to Sheffield University for a year and then spent two years in Australia at the Hall Institute for Medical Research, Melbourne. During this time he studied influenza, in particular the genetic variation of the various strains of the virus and also the response of the body to attack by the virus. He continued with this work from 1950 at the National Institute for Medical Research in London, where he was director of the World Influenza Centre.

In 1957, together with the Swiss virologist Jean Lindenmann, Isaacs reported that a specific low-molecular-weight protein, which interfered with the multiplication of viruses, was produced by animal cells when under viral attack. This was interferon, which he studied closely for the rest of his life, investigating problems associated with its production and isolation, its mechanism of action, and its chemical and physical properties. Isaacs's work formed the basis for all present-day research on this potentially important drug, the full effects of which are still being closely studied.

In the early 1960s his health began to deteriorate but he continued work as head of the Laboratory for Research on Interferon at the National Institute.

Ivanovsky, Dmitri Iosifovich

(1864–1920)

RUSSIAN BOTANIST

Ivanovsky (i-van-**of**-skee) was born in Gdov, Russia, and studied natural sciences at St. Petersburg University, graduating in 1888. He obtained his master's degree in botany in 1895 and worked (1896–1901) as an instructor in plant anatomy and physiology at the Technological Institute, St. Petersburg. In 1908 he was appointed professor at the University of Warsaw.

In 1892, following his investigations of tobacco mosaic disease in the Crimea, he demonstrated that a filtrate of the sap from infected tobacco plants had the ability to transmit the disease to healthy plants. Ivanovsky showed that minute crystalline particles were present in the filtrate and asserted that they were somehow linked to the disease. However, he wrongly attributed the cause of the disease to minute bacteria. Ivanovsky's work was confirmed in a publication by the Dutch bacteriologist Martinus Beijerinck in 1898. It was Beijerinck who stated that such infective agents are not bacterial and coined the term "virus." This, together with the work of the French bacteriologist Charles Chamberland on rabies, was one of the earliest pieces of evidence for the existence of viruses although it was not until 1935 that Wendell Stanley confirmed this.

J

Jackson, Charles Thomas

(1805–1880)

AMERICAN CHEMIST

Chas. T Jackson

No true man of science will ever disgrace himself by asking for a patent; and if he should, might not know what to do with it any more than the man did who drew an elephant at a raffle. He cannot and will not leave his scientific pursuits to turn showman, mechanic, or merchant.

—Address to the American Institute (1851)

Born in Plymouth, Massachusetts, Jackson studied medicine at Harvard and continued his education at the Sorbonne in Paris, working on chemistry and geology. He returned to America and set up a practice in Boston. Jackson's professional career consisted of a series of spectacular claims to the work of others. These started on his homeward voyage and were to persist until he finally became insane in 1873.

While sailing from France to America in 1832 Jackson befriended a fellow American, the portrait painter Samuel Morse, with whom he discussed the possibilities of electric telegraphy. When Morse exhibited his telegraph to Congress in 1837 he found that he had to establish a right to his own invention against Jackson's claim that Morse had stolen it from him. It took Morse seven years to prove the validity of his claim.

In July 1844 Jackson recommended to William Morton, a young dentist lodging with him, that he should try treating his patients using ether, which was commonly used by medical students as a joke. Morton took up his suggestion and found it promising. He experimented on himself, gave up his practice to work on dosages and systems of inhalation, and introduced the anesthetic to the medical profession. Nothing was heard from Jackson until it was clear that money and fame were going to be awarded to someone. When Morton went to Congress to ask for compensation for yielding his patent to the U.S. government he found some senators who took him for a thief. When he went to Paris in 1847 to lecture on his discovery he found that Jackson had already lodged a sealed envelope with the Académie claiming a priority going back to 1842. Committees were set up by governments, states, academies, and professional bodies but Jackson managed to so confuse the issue that when Morton collapsed and died in 1868 he was still fighting his claim and still penniless.

Jackson became obsessive about his "discovery," ignored his other work, took to drink, and spent the last seven years of his life in a lunatic asylum. He even wrote a book on the subject, *A Manual of Etherisation* (1861). Curiously, both Morton and Jackson have monuments in the same cemetery, both proudly proclaiming their triumph in alleviating the misery of mankind.

Jackson, John Hughlings

(1835–1911)

BRITISH NEUROLOGIST

Jackson was born at Green Hammerton in England and educated at York Hospital and St. Bartholomew's Hospital, London. He received his MD from St. Andrews University in 1860. He served on the staff of the

London Hospital as assistant physician (1863) and physician (1874–94) and in 1862 began his long association with the National Hospital for the Paralysed and Epileptic, London. Here he specialized in neurology and ultimately exercised a profound influence on the development of clinical neurology. Through his work with epileptics, he described the condition, now called *Jacksonian seizure* or *Jacksonian epilepsy*, in which part of the leg, arm, or face undergoes spasmodic contraction due to local disease of the cerebral cortex in the brain.

Jackson's work supported the findings of Paul Broca and others – that different bodily functions are controlled by different regions of the cerebral cortex. Jackson also described a local paralysis of the tongue and throat caused by disease of the corresponding cranial nerves. This is now known as *Jackson's syndrome*.

Jacob, François

(1920–   )

FRENCH BIOLOGIST

> Myths and science fulfill a similar function: they both provide human beings with a representation of the world and of the forces that are supposed to govern it. They both fix limits of what is considered as possible.
> —*The Possible and the Actual* (1981)

Born at Nancy in France, Jacob (zha-**kob**) served with the Free French forces during World War II. Although badly wounded, he resumed his medical studies in 1945, obtaining his MD from the University of Paris in 1947. In 1950 he became André Lwoff's assistant at the Pasteur Institute, Paris, and, with Elie Wollman, began working on the bacteria, discovered by Lwoff, that carry a nonvirulent virus incorporated in their genetic material. In 1961 they introduced the term "episomes" for genetic elements that become established in bacterial cells. Jacob and Wollman also studied conjugation in bacteria, the process by which genetic material is transferred from one cell to another. They found that the genes of the donor cell enter the recipient cell in a specific order and by interrupting the process, the position of given genes on the chromosome could be determined.

In 1958 Jacob began collaborating with Jacques Monod and Arthur Pardee on the control of bacterial enzyme production, research that culminated in a greatly increased understanding of the regulation of gene activity. In 1960 Jacob and Monod proposed the existence of the operon, consisting of an operator gene and structural genes that code for the enzymes needed in a given biosynthetic pathway. When the enzymes are not required another gene outside the operon, the regulator gene, produces a protein that binds with the operator and renders the operon ineffective. Jacob and Monod received the 1965 Nobel Prize for physiology or medicine for this research, sharing the award with Lwoff.

Since 1964, Jacob has occupied the chair of cellular genetics at the Collège de France; the chair was created in his honor. He became a foreign member of the Royal Society in 1973 and a member of the Academy of Sciences, Paris, in 1977. He has also written on some of the wider implications of biology in *The Possible and the Actual* (1981) and has published an autobiography, *The Statue Within* (1987).

Jacobi, Karl Gustav Jacob

(1804–1851)

GERMAN MATHEMATICIAN

Mathematics is the science of things that are self-evident.
—Describing the nature of mathematics

Jacobi (yah-**koh**-bee) was born at Potsdam, in Germany. After studying in Berlin, he became a lecturer at Königsberg where he managed to attract the favorable attention of Karl Friedrich Gauss. He was a superb teacher and had an astonishing manipulative skill with formulae. He made a brief but disastrous foray into politics that resulted in his losing a pension he had been granted by the king of Prussia.

Jacobi's most important contributions to mathematics were in the field of elliptic functions. Niels Hendrik Abel had partially anticipated some of Jacobi's work, but the two were equally important in the creation of this subject. Jacobi also worked on Abelian functions and discovered the hyperelliptic functions. He applied his work in elliptic functions to number theory.

Jacobi worked in many other areas of mathematics as well as the theory of functions. He was a pioneer in the study of determinants and a certain type of determinant arising in connection with partial differential equations is known as the *Jacobian* in his honor. This work was the result of his interest in dynamics, in which field he continued and developed the work of William Hamilton, and produced results that are important in quantum mechanics.

Jansky, Karl Guthe

(1905–1950)

AMERICAN RADIO ENGINEER

Born in Norman, Oklahoma, Jansky was educated at the University of Wisconsin and started his career with the Bell Telephone Laboratories in 1928. He was given the task of investigating factors that could interfere with radio waves used for long-distance communication. He designed a linear directional antenna, which, mounted on wheels from a Model T Ford, could scan the sky. He identified all the sources of interference, such as thunderstorms, except for one weak emission. This he found to be unconnected with the Sun and in 1931 he discovered that the radio interference came from the stars.

Jansky published his findings in the *Proceedings of the Institute of Radio Engineers* in December 1932, the date that marks precisely the beginnings of radio astronomy. In his paper Jansky made two astute comments: he suggested that the radio emission was somehow connected with the Milky Way and that it originated not from the stars but from interstellar ionized gas. He did not pursue his suggestions and it was left to Grote Reber, the amateur astronomer, to keep the subject alive until it developed into a major research field after 1945.

The unit of radio-wave emission strength was named the *jansky* in his honor.

Janssen, Pierre Jules César

(1824–1907)

FRENCH ASTRONOMER

The 20th century...will see...the terrestrial atmosphere navigated by apparatuses that will take possession of it to make a daily and systematic study of it, or to establish among nations communications...that will take continents, seas, and oceans in their stride.

—On the future role of aviation. Address to the International Aeronautical Congress, Paris (1889)

Janssen (zhahn-**sen**) studied mathematics and physics at Paris University before becoming professor of general science at the school of architecture. In 1857 he went to Peru to determine the magnetic equator. He observed the transits of Venus of 1874 and 1882 in Japan and Algeria and went on all the major eclipse expeditions. So eager was he to witness the 1870 eclipse in Algeria that he had to escape from the siege of Paris by balloon. While in India in 1868, observing the solar eclipse spectroscopically, he noticed the hydrogen lines visible in the solar prominences and wondered if they could still be detected after the eclipse. The next day he found them still visible. This meant that while photography and observation would still depend on eclipse work the spectroscope could be used almost anywhere anytime. Janssen made one further important discovery on the same trip; he discovered lines in the solar spectrum that he could not identify. He sent his results to Norman Lockyer who suggested that they were produced by some element found only on the Sun, which Lockyer called "helium." In 1895 William Ramsay discovered a substance on Earth that matched exactly with Janssen's spectral lines.

In later life Janssen arranged for an observatory to be built on Mont Blanc in order to avoid as much atmospheric interference as possible. Using data from observations made there, he showed that absorption lines in the solar spectrum are caused by elements in the Earth's atmosphere.

Janssen, Zacharias

(1580–*c.* 1638)

DUTCH INSTRUMENT MAKER

Zacharias Janssen (**yahn**-sen) was born in Middelburg, now in the Netherlands. Together with his father, Hans, he is believed to have invented the first compound microscope in 1590. He is also credited with having made the first telescope in 1608, although Hans Lippershey, who also lived in Middelburg, and Jacobus Metius share claims to this invention.

Jeans, Sir James Hopwood

(1877–1946)

BRITISH MATHEMATICIAN, PHYSICIST, AND ASTRONOMER

> Life exists in the universe only because the carbon atom possesses certain exceptional properties.
>
> —*The Mysterious Universe* (1930)

Jeans, the son of a London journalist, graduated from Cambridge University in 1900 and obtained his MA in 1903. After lecturing at Cambridge (1904–05) he became professor of applied mathematics at Princeton University (1905–09), and, back in England, Stokes Lecturer in applied mathematics at Cambridge (1910–12). There followed a period of writing and research during which his interest turned to astronomy. In 1923 he became a research assistant at the Mount Wilson Observatory, Pasadena, California, where he worked until 1944. Jeans was also professor of astronomy at the Royal Institution in London from 1935 until his death. He was knighted in 1928.

Jeans is best known as an astronomer and as a writer both of popular books on science and of several excellent textbooks. His earlier books were devoted to physics and included *Dynamical Theory of Gases* (1904) and *Mathematical Theory of Electricity and Magnetism* (1908). His serious astronomical works included *Problems of Cosmogony and Stellar Dynamics* (1919) and *Astronomy and Cosmogony* (1928) while among his popular books were *The Universe Around Us* (1929) and *The Mysterious Universe* (1930).

Jeans pioneered various ideas in astronomy and astrophysics. He showed that Pierre Simon Laplace's theory of the origin of the solar system, in which the Sun and planets condensed from a contracting cloud of gas and dust, was untenable. In collaboration with Harold Jeffreys he proposed a new view in its place. According to this "tidal theory" a star had passed close by the newly formed Sun and the planets had been formed from the cigar-shaped filament of material drawn away from this star. Jeans and Jeffreys based their theory on a similar idea proposed earlier by Thomas Chamberlin and Forest Ray Moulton. The tidal theory was eventually superseded in the 1940s by revamped versions of Laplace's nebular theory.

Jeans also investigated other astronomical phenomena, among them spiral nebulae, binary and multiple star systems, and the source of energy in stars, which he concluded involved radioactivity.

Jeffreys, Sir Alec John

(1950–)

BRITISH GENETICIST

Jeffreys was born at Luton in Bedforshire, England, and educated at Oxford, where he completed his PhD in 1975. After spending two years at the University of Amsterdam as a research fellow he joined the genetics department of the University of Leicester. He was appointed professor of genetics in 1987 and knighted in 1994.

Jeffreys is noted as the discoverer of the technique known as "genetic (or DNA) fingerprinting." In 1984 he was working on the gene that codes for the protein, myoglobin. Part of the gene consisted of short sequences repeated a number of times. The number of repeats was found to vary between individuals and became known as VNTRs ("variable number tandem repeats"). Initially Jeffreys saw the VNTRs as no more than useful gene markers of the myoglobin gene. Later he came to the conclusion that they were unique to the individual – they could act like a fingerprint.

The marker sequences can be identified by cleaving the DNA with restriction enzymes and using a gene probe – a single-strand fragment of DNA or RNA with a base sequence complementary to that of the marker. If the bases are labeled with a radioactive tracer, they can be identified on separation by electrophoresis.

Very small samples of DNA can be used, obtained, for example, from blood, semen, saliva, etc., and the technique has been exploited in forensic science and in investigating paternity and other family relationships.

Jeffreys, Sir Harold

(1891–1989)

BRITISH ASTRONOMER AND
GEOPHYSICIST

Jeffreys was born in Birtley in the northeast of England and educated in Newcastle upon Tyne and at Cambridge University. After graduating in 1913 he was made a fellow of his college. He was reader in geophysics from 1931 to 1946 before being elected to the Plumian Professorship of Astronomy and Experimental Philosophy where he remained until his retirement in 1958.

In 1924 Jeffreys produced one of the fundamental works in geophysics of the first half of the 20th century, *The Earth: Its Origin, History, and Physical Constitution*. In this he argued forcibly against Alfred Wegener's proposed theory of continental drift. He demonstrated that the forces proposed by Wegener were inadequate. This did much to inhibit interest and research into drift theory for a while but much new evidence in its favor has since been uncovered.

Jeffreys was also joint author, with Keith Bullen, of the *Seismological Tables* (1935). These, more frequently known as the *JB Tables*, were revised in 1940 and are the present standard tables of travel times of earthquake waves. They allow observers to determine from the elapsed time between the arrival of the primary (P) waves and the secondary (S) waves the distance between the observer and the earthquake.

Jeffreys's work in astronomy included studies on the origins of the universe. He developed James Jeans's theory of tidal evolution. He also devised models for the planetary structure of Jupiter, Saturn, Uranus, and Neptune. He was knighted in 1953.

Jemison, Mae Carol

(1956–)

AMERICAN PHYSICIAN AND ASTRONAUT

Jemison studied chemical engineering at Stanford and then medicine at Cornell, where she gained her MD in 1981. After serving her internship in Los Angeles, she joined the Peace Corps and spent the period from 1983 until 1985 working as area medical officer for Liberia and Sierra Leone.

Following her return to the United States in 1985 Jemison applied to join NASA as an astronaut. However, following the 1986 *Challenger* disaster, NASA had stopped recruiting at all levels, and it was not until 1987 that Jemison was accepted into the program. She was assigned in 1989 to Mission STS-47 Spacelab J, a joint U.S.–Japanese project during which it was proposed to study space sickness and the effects of weightlessness on the development of several species of animal.

On 12 September 1992 Jemison became the first black woman in space when the *Endeavor* was successfully launched. Accompanying the crew of seven on the *Endeavor*'s eight-day flight were two fish, four frogs, 180 hornets, and 7,600 flies.

Jemison left NASA in 1993 to accept a position on the faculty at Dartmouth College, New Hampshire.

Jenner, Edward

(1749–1823)

BRITISH PHYSICIAN

The scepticism that appeared, even among the most enlightened of medical men when my sentiments on the important subject of the cow-pox were first promulgated, was highly laudable. To have admitted the truth of a doctrine, at once so novel and so unlike anything that ever appeared in the annals of medicine, without the test of the most rigid scrutiny, would have bordered on temerity.
—*A Continuation of Facts and Observations Relative to the Variolae Vaccinae*

Jenner, born a vicar's son at Berkeley in Gloucestershire, England, was apprenticed to the London surgeon John Hunter from 1770 to 1772. He then returned to country practice and established a reputation as a field naturalist. In 1787 Jenner observed that the newly hatched cuckoo, rather than the adult cuckoo, was responsible for removing the other eggs from the nest. He was elected a fellow of the Royal Society in 1789 partly on the basis of this work. Jenner's lasting contribution to science, however is his investigations into the disease smallpox.

In 17th-century London some 10% of all deaths were due to smallpox. In response to this the practice of variolation – inoculation with material taken from fresh smallpox sores – was widely adopted. This was first described in England in 1713. However variolation suffered from two major defects for, if too virulent a dose was given, a lethal case of smallpox would develop and, secondly, the subject inoculated, unless isolated, was only too likely to start an epidemic among those in contact with him.

Jenner had heard reports that milkmaids once infected with cowpox developed a lifelong immunity to smallpox. On 14 May 1796 he made the crucial experiment and took an eight-year-old boy and injected him with cowpox. He followed this on 1 July with injections taken from smallpox pustules, repeating the procedure several months later. On both occasions the boy did not develop smallpox and the same happy result was later observed with other experimental subjects. Jenner's conclusion that cowpox infection protects people from smallpox infection was first published in *An Inquiry into the Causes and Effects of the Variolae Vaccinae* (1798).

General acceptance of Jenner's work was almost immediate. In 1802 he was awarded £10,000 by a grateful House of Commons and in 1804 he was honored by Napoleon who made vaccination compulsory in the French army. Variolation was made illegal in England in 1840 and in 1853 further legislation made the vaccination of infants compulsory. As a consequence of this deaths from smallpox, running at a rate of 40 per 10,000 at the beginning of the 19th century, fell to 1 in 10,000 by the end.

Jensen, Johannes Hans Daniel

(1907–1973)

GERMAN PHYSICIST

Jensen (**yen**-zen) was educated at the university in his native city of Hamburg and at Freiburg, where he obtained his doctorate in 1932. He worked at Hamburg and Hannover before his appointment in 1949 as professor of physics at Heidelberg. In 1963 Jensen was awarded the Nobel Prize for physics with Maria Goeppert-Mayer for their independent publication of the "shell" theory of the nucleus.

Jerne, Niels Kaj

(1911–1994)

DANISH IMMUNOLOGIST

London-born Jerne (**yairn**-e) was educated at the University of Copenhagen, where he gained his doctorate in medicine in 1951 while working as a researcher at the Danish State Serum Institute (1943–54). After a period of research at the California Institute of Technology (1954–55), he was appointed chief medical officer with the World Health Organization in Geneva (1956–62) and also professor of biophysics at the University of Geneva (1960–62). He returned to America in 1962 to become head of the department of microbiology at the University of Pittsburgh. Subsequently he served for three years (1966–69) as director of the Paul Ehrlich Institute, Frankfurt, before leaving to found the Basel Institute for Immunology, where he served as director until 1980.

Jerne is noted for his theories concerning the diversity and production of antibodies. In 1955 he proposed the *clonal selection theory* of antibody formation to account for how the body's white blood cells (lymphocytes) are able, potentially, to manufacture such a huge range of different antibodies. He refuted the idea that antibodies are formed from scratch as and when required. Instead, Jerne proposed that different cells, each capable of producing a particular antibody, are present in the body from birth. When an agent such as a virus or bacteria enters the body, its chemical components (antigens) activate the relevant lymphocytes and cause them to divide repeatedly, thereby producing a clone of cells and enhancing manufacture of the appropriate antibody. The theory has since been shown to be correct.

The immense diversity of antibodies presents the problem of how the genome accommodates all the genetic information. Jerne was one of the first to advance the notion that some form of somatic mutation may be involved, an idea that led to the theory of so-called "jumping genes" and its demonstration in mouse cells by Jerne's colleague, Susumu Tonegawa.

Jerne also constructed a model of immune-system self-regulation based on the interactions of antibodies. Although a valuable contribution, the model does not anticipate the great complexity of control mechanisms revealed by recent discoveries of numerous chemical modulators of the immune system.

For his work, which helped to inspire a whole generation of immunologists, Jerne received the 1984 Nobel Prize for physiology or medicine. The prize was shared with César Milstein and Georges Köhler, another colleague of Jerne's working at Basel.

Jobs, Steven Paul

(1955–   )

AMERICAN COMPUTER ENGINEER
AND ENTREPRENEUR

An orphan, Jobs was adopted by a machinist working for a company manufacturing scanners. In 1960 the family moved to Palo Alto, where Jobs showed little interest in school but an early attraction to electronics. After graduating from high school in 1972 and a single term at the liberal arts college Reed, in Portland, Oregon, Jobs began to explore a number of alternative lifestyles before joining the computer-game manufacturer Atari in 1974.

He had already joined the Homebrew Computer Club, a meeting ground for computer enthusiasts, and had collaborated with Steve Wozniak to make the so-called "blue boxes" – electronic devices used to make free telephone calls. They began making simple computers and in April 1976 they had the Apple ready to be exhibited at a Homebrew meeting. They sold 150 devices for $666 each and suddenly found investors willing to back them.

Apple II was the first recognizable personal computer by later standards. It had a keyboard, memory, expansion slots, video terminal, and color graphics. When fully assembled it sold at an affordable price of $1,350. A disk drive was added in 1978, and in 1979 the first spreadsheet,

VisCalc, could be installed for an extra $100. Sales soared with 2 million models sold by 1984. Apple went public in 1980, and Jobs became a multimillionaire.

The problem was, however, to sustain Apple's success against competition, firstly from IBM, which entered the personal-computer market in 1982, and later from the clones that quickly followed. Apple III could sell no more than 90,000 models. Jobs himself took over the production of the next model, the Apple Macintosh (named after a variety of eating apple), which was notable for its user-friendly graphical user interface (GUI) employing a mouse and icons.

Jobs resigned from the company in 1985 to pursue other interests. He set up a new company, NeXT, financed by the sale of $100 million of his own Apple stock, to develop educational computers. He also acquired Pixar, a computer graphics firm.

Johannsen, Wilhelm Ludwig

(1857–1927)

DANISH BOTANIST AND GENETICIST

It is a pure waste of time to lose oneself in such an author's...views; they are just not worth a bean.
—On the vitalist theories of the French philosopher Henri Bergson.
Falske Analogier (1914; False Analogies)

Johannsen (yoh-**han**-sen) was born in the Danish capital Copenhagen. On leaving school in 1872 he became apprenticed to a pharmacist as his father could not afford university fees. From his work in Danish and German pharmacies, Johannsen taught himself chemistry and developed an interest in botany. In 1881 he began work under Johan Kjeldahl in the chemistry department of the Carlsberg laboratories, investigating dormancy in seeds, tubers, and buds.

In 1892 Johannsen became lecturer at the Copenhagen Agricultural College. On reading Francis Galton's *Theory of Heredity* he was impressed by experiments demonstrating that selection is ineffective if applied to the progeny of self-fertilizing plants. Johannsen repeated this work using the Princess bean, but found that selection did work on the offspring of a mixed population of self-fertilizing beans. It was only when plants were derived from a single parent that selection had no effect. He called the descendants of a single parent a "pure line" and argued that individuals in a pure line are genetically identical: any variation among them is due to environmental effects, which are not heritable. In 1905 he coined the terms "genotype" to describe the genetic constitution of an individual and "phenotype" to describe the visible result of the interaction between genotype and environment.

Johannsen explained his ideas in *On Heredity and Variation* (1896), which he revised and lengthened with the rediscovery of Gregor Mendel's laws and reissued as *Elements of Heredity* in 1905. The enlarged German edition of this work became available in 1909 and proved the most influential book on genetics in Europe. In the same year Johannsen proposed the term "genes" to describe Mendel's factors of inheritance. Johannsen's research, with its emphasis on the quantitative variation of characters in populations and the application of statistical methods, played a major role in the development of modern genetics from 19th-century ideas.

In 1905 Johannsen became professor of plant physiology at Copenhagen University and was made rector of the University in 1917. He spent his later years writing on the history of science.

Johanson, Donald Carl

(1943–)

AMERICAN PALEOANTHROPOLOGIST

It's clear from these fossils [found at Hadar] that upright walking happened long before brain expansion. Hominid brains don't show any striking signs of getting particularly big until two to two-and-a-half million years ago, and yet these creatures were bipedal at least a million years before that.
—Quoted by Richard Leakey in *The Making of Mankind* (1981)

Johanson, who was born in Chicago, gained his BA in anthropology from the University of Illinois in 1966; he received an MA from the University of Chicago in 1970 and a PhD in 1972. Two years later he was appointed professor of anthropology at Case Western Reserve University, Cleveland, and was also made associate curator of anthropology at the Cleveland Museum of Natural History. He was later given the position of curator of physical anthropology and director of scientific research at the Museum. In 1981 he moved to California as director of the newly founded Institute of Human Origins at Berkeley, and later became professor of anthropology at Stanford University (1983–89).

In 1973 Johanson led his first expedition to Hadar about 100 miles northeast of Addis Ababa. Here he found a hominid knee joint. The following year he discovered further remains of a new species of fossil primate that challenged the existing theories of the evolution of modern man (*Homo sapiens*) and other hominids. The remains were reconstructed to form, remarkably, a 40% complete skeleton, revealing a female hominid about three and a half feet tall with a bipedal stance and a relatively small brain. The fossil proved to be some 3 million years old, making it the oldest known fossil member of the human tribe. Johanson named it *Australopithecus afarensis*, after the Afar triangle of northeast Ethiopia where the find was made. The skeleton is popularly called "Lucy," prompted by the Beatles' song "Lucy in the sky with diamonds," which was playing in the camp site of Johanson's team on the evening following their momentous discovery.

During the 1975 season Johanson's team made another dramatic find. Scattered in a single hillside were more than 350 fossil pieces from a group of thirteen men, women, and children, all dating from the same time as Lucy. The "first family," as it was later called, was Johanson's last major find at Hadar. Following the 1976 expedition a series of military coups, civil wars, and famines closed Ethiopia to scientific expeditions.

Johanson's analysis of the "Lucy" skeleton showed it to belong to an upright chimpanzeelike creature with an apelike face, a slightly bow-legged gait, and curved toe and finger bones. According to Johanson, Lucy demonstrated that bipedalism preceded enlarged brain capacity, rather than vice versa, and marked a crucial step toward the evolution of all other antecedents of modern man, as well as the later australopithecines identified by Raymond Dart.

The findings of Johanson's team were published in 1979, and sparked controversy among other workers in the field, notably Richard Leakey. He maintained that the genus *Homo* could be traced back to an age comparable with the Lucy skeleton, and was descended not from an australopithecine ancestor, such as Lucy, but from some earlier, hypothetical, hominid, perhaps some 4–5 million years old.

Although the precise relationship of *A. afarensis* to the early human ancestors remains in doubt, the significance of Johanson's discovery is unquestioned. His account of the discovery of Lucy was published as *Lucy: The Beginnings of Humankind* (with Maitland A. Edey; 1981). Johanson and Edey have also written *Blueprints: Solving the Mystery of Evolution* (1989).

Joliot-Curie, Frédéric

(1900–1958)

FRENCH PHYSICIST

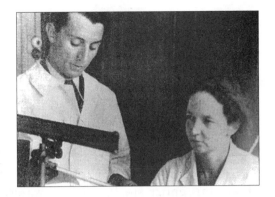

> I have always attached great importance to the manner in which an experiment is set up and conducted...the experiment should be set up to open as many windows as possible on the unforeseen.
>
> —Describing research in physics

Frédéric Joliot (zho-**lyoh**), the son of a prosperous Paris tradesman, was educated at the School of Industrial Physics and Chemistry. In 1923 he began his research career at the Radium Institute under Marie Curie, where he obtained his doctorate in 1930. He was appointed to a new chair of nuclear chemistry at the Collège de France in 1937 and, after World War II in which he played an important part in the French Resistance, was head of the new Commissariat à l'Energie Atomique (1946–50. In 1956 he became head of the Radium Institute.

In 1926 Joliot married the daughter of Marie Curie, Irène, and changed his name to Joliot-Curie. In 1931 they began research that was to win them the Nobel Prize for chemistry in 1935 for their fundamental discovery of artificial radioactivity (1934). His description of the crucial experiment is as follows: "We bombarded aluminum with alpha rays [the heavy nucleus of a helium atom, made of two protons and two neutrons]...then after a certain period of irradiation, we removed the source of alpha rays. We now observed that the sheet of aluminum continued to emit positive electrons over a period of several minutes." What had happened was that the stable aluminum atom had absorbed an alpha-particle and transmuted into an (until then) unknown isotope of silicon, which was radioactive with a half-life of about 3.5 minutes. The significance of this was that it produced the first clear chemical evidence for transmutation and opened the door to a virtually new discipline. Soon large numbers of radioisotopes were created, and they became an indispensable tool in various branches of science. Dramatic confirmation of the Joliot-Curies' discovery was provided when Frédéric realized that the cyclotron at the laboratory of Ernest Lawrence in California would have been producing artificial elements unwittingly. He cabled them to switch off their cyclotron and listen. To their surprise the Geiger counter continued clicking away, registering for the first time the radioactivity of nitrogen–13.

In 1939 Joliot-Curie was quick to see the significance of the discovery of nuclear fission by Otto Hahn. He confirmed Hahn's work and saw the likelihood of a chain reaction. He further realized that the chain reaction could only be produced in the presence of a moderator to slow the neutrons down. A good moderator was the heavy water that was produced on a large scale only in Norway at Telemark. With considerable foresight Joliot-Curie managed to persuade the French government to obtain this entire stock of heavy water, 185 kilograms in all, and to arrange for its shipment to England out of the reach of the advancing German army.

Joliot-Curie, Irène

(1897–1956)

FRENCH PHYSICIST

> That one must do some work seriously and must be independent and not merely amuse oneself in life – this our mother has told us always, but never that science was the only career worth following.
> —Recalling the advice of her mother, Marie Curie. Quoted in Mary Margaret McBride, *A Long Way from Missouri*

Irène Curie was born in Paris, the daughter of Pierre and Marie Curie, the discoverers of radium. She received little formal schooling, attending instead informal classes where she was taught physics by her mother, mathematics by Paul Langevin, and chemistry by Jean Baptiste Perrin. She later attended the Sorbonne although she first served as a radiologist at the front during World War I. In 1921 she began work at her mother's Radium Institute with which she maintained her connection for the rest of her life, becoming its director in 1946. She was also, from 1937, a professor at the Sorbonne.

In 1926 Irène Curie married Frédéric Joliot and took the name Joliot-Curie. As in so many other things she followed her mother in being awarded the Nobel Prize for distinguished work done in collaboration with her husband. Thus in 1935 the Joliot-Curies won the chemistry prize for their discovery in 1934 of artificial radioactivity.

Irène later almost anticipated Otto Hahn's discovery of nuclear fission but like many other physicists at that time found it too difficult to accept the simple hypothesis that heavy elements like uranium could split into lighter elements when bombarded with neutrons. Instead she tried to find heavier elements produced by the decay of uranium.

Like her mother, Irène Joliot-Curie produced a further generation of scientists. Her daughter, Hélène, married the son of Marie Curie's old companion, Paul Langevin, and, together with her brother, Paul, became a distinguished physicist.

Joly, John

(1857–1933)

IRISH GEOLOGIST AND PHYSICIST

Joly was the son of a clergyman from Hollywood, now in the Republic of Ireland. He entered Trinity College, Dublin, in 1876 where he studied literature and engineering. He taught in the engineering school from 1883 and was appointed professor of geology and mineralogy in 1897, a post he held until his death.

Joly's major geological work was in the field of geochronology. He first tried to estimate the age of the Earth by using Edmond Halley's method of measuring the degree of salinity of the oceans, and then by examining the radioactive decay in rocks. In 1898 he assigned an age of 80–90 million years to the Earth, later revising this figure to 100 million years. He published *Radioactivity and Geology* in 1909 in which he demonstrated that the rate of radioactive decay has been more or less constant through time.

Joly also carried out important work on radium extraction (1914) and pioneered its use for the treatment of cancer. His inventions in physics included a constant-volume gas thermometer, a photometer, and a differential steam calorimeter for measuring the specific heat capacity of gases at constant volume.

Jones, Sir Ewart Ray Herbert

(1911–)

BRITISH CHEMIST

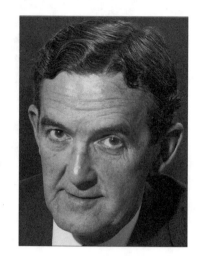

Born in Wrexham, North Wales, Jones was educated at the University College of Wales at Bangor and at Manchester University. He taught at Imperial College, London, from 1938 until 1947 when he returned to Manchester as professor of chemistry. In 1955 he moved to a similar chair at Oxford, in which post he remained until his retirement in 1978.

Jones worked mainly on the structure, synthesis, and biogenesis of natural products, particularly the steroids, terpenes, and vitamins.

Jordan, (Marie-Ennemond) Camille

(1838–1922)

FRENCH MATHEMATICIAN

> I shall never forget the astonishment with which I read that remarkable work [Jordan's *Cours d'analyse* (A Course of Analysis)], the first inspiration for so many mathematicians of my generation, and learnt for the first time as I read it what mathematics really meant.
> —Godfrey Harold Hardy, *A Mathematician's Apology* (1940)

Born at Lyons in France, Jordan (zhor-**dahn**) studied in Paris at the Ecole Polytechnique, where he trained as an engineer. Later he taught at both the Ecole Polytechnique and the Collège de France until his retirement in 1912. His interests lay chiefly in pure mathematics, although he made contributions to a wide range of mathematical subjects.

Jordan's most important and enduring work was in group theory and analysis. He was especially interested in groups of permutations and grasped the intimate connection of this subject with questions about the solvability of polynomial equations. This basic insight was one of the fundamental achievements of the seminal work of Evariste Galois, and Jordan was the first mathematician to draw attention to Galois's work, which had until then been almost entirely ignored. Jordan played a major role in starting the systematic investigation of the areas of research opened up by Galois. He also introduced the idea of an *infinite* group.

Jordan also passed on his interest in group theory to two of his most outstanding pupils, Felix Klein and Sophus Lie, both of whom were to develop the subject in novel and important ways.

Jordan, Ernst Pascual

(1902–1980)

GERMAN THEORETICAL PHYSICIST AND MATHEMATICIAN

Jordan (**yor**-dahn) was educated at the Institute of Technology in his native city of Hannover and at the University of Göttingen, where he obtained his doctorate in 1924. He left Göttingen in 1929 for the University of Rostock and after being appointed professor of physics there in 1935, later held chairs of theoretical physics at Berlin from 1944 to 1952 and at Hamburg from 1951 until his retirement in 1970.

Jordan was one of the founders of the modern quantum theory. In 1925 he collaborated with Max Born and in 1926 with Werner Heisenberg in the formulation of quantum mechanics. He also did early work on quantum electrodynamics. He developed a new theory of gravitation at the same time as Carl Brans and Robert Dicke.

Josephson, Brian David

(1940–   )

BRITISH PHYSICIST

Josephson was born in Cardiff and educated at Cambridge University, where he obtained his PhD in 1964. He remained at Cambridge and in 1974 was appointed to a professorship of physics.

His name is associated with the *Josephson effects* described in 1962 while still a graduate student. The work came out of theoretical speculations on electrons in semiconductors involving the exchange of electrons between two superconducting regions separated by a thin insulating layer (a *Josephson junction*). He showed theoretically that a current can flow across the junction in the absence of an applied voltage. Furthermore, a small direct voltage across the junction produces an alternating current with a frequency that is inversely proportional to the voltage. The effects have been verified experimentally, thus supporting the BCS theory of superconductivity of John Bardeen and his colleagues. They have been used in making accurate physical measurements and in measuring weak magnetic fields. Josephson junctions can also be used as very fast switching devices in computers. For this work Josephson shared the 1973 Nobel Prize for physics with Leo Eskai and Ivar Giaevar.

More recently, Josephson has turned his attention to the study of the mind and has argued strongly for a connection between parapsychology and quantum mechanics.

Joule, James Prescott

(1818–1889)

BRITISH PHYSICIST

The phenomena of nature, whether mechanical, chemical, or vital, consist almost entirely in continual conversion of attraction through space, living force, and heat into one another. Thus it is that order is maintained in the universe – nothing is destroyed, nothing ever lost, but the entire machinery, complicated as it is, works smoothly and harmoniously.

—*Manchester Courier*, 12 May 1847

Joule, the son of a brewer from Salford in England, received little formal education, was never appointed to an academic post, and remained a brewer all his life. He began work in a private laboratory that his father built near the brewery.

His first major research was concerned with determining the quantity of heat produced by an electric current and, in 1840, Joule discovered a simple law connecting the current and resistance with the heat generated. For the next few years he carried out a series of experiments in which he investigated the conversion of electrical and mechanical work into heat. In 1849 he read his paper *On the Mechanical Equivalent of Heat* to the Royal Society. Joule's work (unlike that of Julius Mayer) was instantly recognized.

In 1848 Joule published a paper on the kinetic theory of gases, in which he estimated the speed of gas molecules. From 1852 he worked with William Thomson (later Lord Kelvin) on experiments on thermodynamics. Their best known result is the *Joule–Kelvin effect* – the effect in which an expanding gas, under certain conditions, is cooled by the expansion. The SI unit of work and energy, the *joule*, was named in his honor.

Julian, Percy Lavon

(1899–1975)

AMERICAN ORGANIC CHEMIST

Julian's mother and father were a railway clerk and schoolteacher respectively. His grandfather had been born into slavery and had been punished for daring to learn to write by having two right-hand fingers amputated. Julian was educated at DePauw University, Indiana, and at Harvard, where he gained his MA in 1923. Despite his obvious talents, he found it difficult to find either funding or an appropriate position. Consequently he decided in 1929 to move to the University of Vienna to acquire further experience in the synthesis of complex organic molecules and to work for his PhD, which he finally received in 1931. He returned soon after to the United States and was appointed professor of chemistry at Howard University, Washington DC.

Julian's first major success came in 1934, when he announced that he had worked out the structure of, and synthesized, physostigmine, an alkaloid derived from the Calabar bean and used in the treatment of glaucoma. At this time Julian had a dispute with the Howard administration. As no suitably senior academic posts were open elsewhere to a black chemist, he turned to industry. In 1936 he was appointed chief chemist at the Glidden Company, Chicago.

While in Vienna Julian had been made aware that the soya bean was a useful source for producing many valuable and biologically active molecules. He began to investigate whether sex hormones, such as progesterone and testosterone, could be derived from soya beans. He also worked out ways to synthesize a cheap and active substitute for cortisone using soya as a starting point.

In 1954 Julian decided to leave Glidden and establish his own business, Julian Laboratories Inc., which was based in Chicago and Mexico City and specialized in deriving drugs and hormones from soya beans and wild yam. In 1961 he sold his business to Smith, Kline and French and went on to establish the Julian Research Institute in Franklin Park, Illinois.

Jung, Carl Gustav

(1875–1961)

SWISS PSYCHOLOGIST AND PSYCHIATRIST

> Show me a sane man and I will cure him for you.
> —*Modern Man in Search of a Soul*

The separation of psychology from the premises of biology is purely artificial, because the human psyche lives in indissoluble union with the body.
> —*Factors Determining Human Behavior*

Born the son of a pastor in Kesswil, Switzerland, Jung (yuung) studied medicine at the universities of Basel (1895–1900) and Zurich, where he obtained his MD in 1902. From 1902 until 1909 he worked under the direction of Eugen Bleuler at the Burghölzi Psychiatric Clinic, Zurich, while at the same time lecturing in psychiatry at the University of Zurich (1905–13). In 1907 Jung met Sigmund Freud, whose chief collaborator he became. Following the formation of the International Psycho-Analytical Association (1910) he served as its first president from 1911 until his break with Freud in 1912.

Jung continued to practice in Zurich and to develop his own system of analytical psychology. He became professor of psychology at the Federal Institute of Technology in Zurich (1933–41) and was appointed professor of medical psychology at the University of Basel in 1943 but was forced to resign almost immediately for health reasons. He continued however to write, hold regular seminars, and take patients until well over 80.

Like Alfred Adler, who had broken away from Freudian orthodoxy earlier, Jung minimized the sexual cause of neuroses but, unlike Adler, he continued to emphasize the role of the unconscious. His final break with Freud followed publication of his *Wandlungen und Symbole de Libido* (1912) translated into English in 1916 as *Psychology of the Unconscious.* To the "personal" unconscious of the Freudian he added the "collective unconscious" stocked with a number of "congenital conditions of intuition" or archetypes. In search of such archetypes Jung spent long periods with the Pueblo of Arizona, and visited Kenya, North

Africa, and India, and also sought for them in dreams, folklore, and the literature of alchemy.

Jung also emphasized the importance of personality and in his *Psychologische Typen* (1921; Psychological Types) introduced his distinction between introverts and extroverts.

Jussieu, Antoine-Laurent de

(1748–1836)

FRENCH PLANT TAXONOMIST

Jussieu (zhoo-**syu(r)**) was born into a family of eminent botanists from Lyons in France. His uncles Antoine, Bernard, and Joseph de Jussieu all made important contributions to botany and his son, Adrien, subsequently continued the family tradition.

After graduating from the Jardin du Roi in 1770, Jussieu continued to work there, becoming subdemonstrator of botany in 1778. In his first publication in 1773, which reexamined the taxonomy of the Ranunculaceae, he advanced the idea of relative values of characters; the following year he applied this principle to other plant families.

Jussieu is remembered for introducing a natural classification system that distinguishes relationships between plants by considering a large number of characters, unlike the artificial Linnean system, which relies on only a few. In producing the famous *Genera Plantarum* (1789; Genera of Plants) Jussieu had access to a number of collections, including Linnaeus's herbarium and some of Joseph Banks's Australian specimens. He was also able to include many tropical angiosperm families thanks to the collection made by Philibert Commesson. From all this material he distinguished 15 classes and 100 families, and the value of his work can be seen in the fact that 76 of his 100 families remain in botanical nomenclature today. Both Georges Cuvier and Augustin de Candolle built on Jussieu's system.

Jussieu was in charge of the hospital of Paris during the French Revolution and was professor of botany at the National Natural History Museum (formerly the Jardin du Roi) from 1793 to 1826.

Just, Ernest Everett

(1883–1941)

AMERICAN BIOLOGIST

> Few investigators subscribe to the naive but seriously meant comparison that the experimenter on an egg seeks to know its development by wrecking it...The days of experimental embryology as a punitive expedition against the egg, let us hope, have passed.
> —*American Naturalist* (1933)

The grandson of a freed slave and the son of an alcoholic, Just was brought up by his mother, a teacher. He was educated at school in Vermont and at Dartmouth College, where he was the only black student. He graduated in biology in 1907 and took up a post at the leading black college, Howard University, Washington DC.

Just had ambitions to work as a research scientist. In 1909 he was given a summer assistantship at the Marine Biological Laboratory (MBL), at Woods Hole, Massachusetts. Here he was encouraged to pursue his research interests and work for his doctorate, which he finally gained in 1916 from the University of Chicago. He also continued to work each summer at the MBL and published his results.

In an early paper Just demonstrated that in the eggs of marine invertebrates the initial plane of cleavage was determined simply by the point of fertilization, which could occur anywhere on the egg's surface – a result strongly suggesting that the embryo was not preformed. Just also came to realize that the cell surface did more than enclose an all-powerful nucleus; it too was biologically active. His ideas were put forward in his most important work, *The Biology of the Cell Surface* (1938).

Despite Just's skills as an experimental embryologist, which were widely recognized, his numerous applications for full-time research posts were all rejected. Finally realizing that he would never receive proper recognition at home, Just left the United States in 1929 and settled in Europe. For the next decade he worked in Berlin at the Kaiser Wilhelm Institute for Biology, at the Naples Marine Institute, and at the Sorbonne in Paris. After the fall of France in 1940, Just returned to Howard but died soon after from pancreatic cancer.

Kaluza, Theodor Franz Eduard

(1885–1954)

GERMAN MATHEMATICAL PHYSICIST

> Your idea of determining electromagnetic fields through a five-dimensional mani-
> fold has never occurred to me and is, I believe, thoroughly original. This notion
> of yours pleases me enormously.
> —Albert Einstein, letter to Kaluza, 21 April 1919

The son of a phonetician, Kaluza (kah-**loot**-sa) was born at Ratibor in
Germany and educated at the University of Königsberg where he served
(1902–29) as a privatdocent (a largely unpaid teaching assistant). On
Einstein's recommendation he was appointed in 1929 to a professorship
in physics at the University of Kiel. He remained there until 1935, when
he moved to a similar appointment at Göttingen University.

In Einstein's theory of general relativity, space and time are joined together into a four-dimensional space–time. In 1921 Kaluza decided to
supplement Einstein's model with a fifth spatial dimension. Within this
model it proved possible to derive Einstein's four-dimensional gravitational equations as well as the equations for the electromagnetic field.
Thus in a world of five dimensions gravity and electromagnetism were
not distinct forces.

There were, however, two major defects in Kaluza's theory. Firstly,
he could give no indication of the nature of this fifth dimension. Moreover, his theory assumed that bodies behave classically and quantum-
mechanical effects were not considered. An attempt to remedy these de-

fects was made in 1926 by Oskar Klein. This revised form, known as the *Kaluza–Klein theory*, has proved to be of considerable interest to string theorists such as Ed Witten.

Kamen, Martin David

(1913–   )

AMERICAN BIOCHEMIST

The father of Kamen (**kah**-men) arrived in Canada in 1906 as a Russian political exile with a forged passport. He moved to Chicago in 1911 where he worked as a photographer. Kamen himself was born in Toronto, Canada, and was educated at the University of Chicago. After completing his PhD in 1936 on nuclear chemistry, he moved to the Radiation Laboratory at the University of California, Berkeley.

Kamen had a number of early successes. In 1940, in collaboration with Sam Ruben, he discovered the isotope carbon-14. Soon after, Kamen, working with Ruben, used oxygen-18 to show that the oxygen liberated in the photosynthetic process came from water and not from CO_2.

Soon after Kamen became part of the Manhattan project. He worked at the Radiation Laboratory on uranium-235 separation. In July 1944, however, Kamen was dismissed from the project without notice; the only ground given was that of security. Many colleagues stood by Kamen and in 1945 he was invited to join the Medical School at Washington University, St. Louis.

Kamen retained his productivity. Working with Sol Spiegelman in 1947, he proposed a process in which nucleic genes produced partial copies that transferred genetic information to the cytoplasm; an anticipation, perhaps, of messenger RNA. At about the same time he established that certain nitrogen-fixing bacteria evolve hydrogen in the light. In the 1950s Kamen worked on the respiratory pigment, cytochrome c.

At the same time Kamen was under intense pressure from the security services and the media, so intense that at one point he even attempted suicide. His passport was taken away and colleagues felt it wiser not to be seen with him. In 1947 he was called to Washington to testify before the House Committee on UnAmerican Activities (HUAC). Leaks from HUAC appeared in the *Chicago Times* linking Kamen with a Soviet "atom-spy ring."

Kamen fought back by suing the *Times* for libel and the Federal Government for withholding his passport. The processes were lengthy, expensive, and involved several severe setbacks. Kamen persisted and in 1955 he finally received his passport and won $7,500 compensatory damages from the *Times*. During the trial the HUAC file on Kamen was produced. It contained no more than the charges that Kamen had discussed "atoms" at the Berkeley Faculty Club, and that, with his sister, he had been a member in the 1930s of the American Student Union. It contained no reference to Soviet agents and left Kamen bitterly wondering how such innocuous data could impose upon him such a monstrous burden. Kamen published a vivid account of both aspects of his life in his *Radiant Science, Dark Politics* (1985).

Following the resolutions of Kamen's political troubles he moved to Brandeis University, Massachusetts, in 1957 to establish a new postgraduate school of biochemistry. He undertook a similar task in 1961 when he joined Roger Revelle to build a new campus of the University of California at La Jolla.

Kamerlingh-Onnes, Heike

(1853–1926)

DUTCH PHYSICIST

I should like to write *"Door meten tot weten"* ["Through measuring to knowing"] as a motto above each physics laboratory.
— Inaugural address on appointment to the chair of physics, University of Leiden (1882)

Born at Groningen in the Netherlands, Kamerlingh-Onnes (kah-mer-ling-o-nes) was educated at the university there, obtaining his doctorate in 1879. In 1882 he was appointed professor of physics at Leiden, where he remained for the rest of his career. There he started the study of low-temperature physics, at first in order to gather experimental evidence for the atomic theory of matter. However, his interest turned to the problems involved in reaching extremely low temperatures and, in 1908, he became the first to succeed in liquefying helium. Matter at low temperatures – only a few degrees above absolute zero – has such strange properties that a completely new field of cryogenic physics was opened up. The first of these properties to be studied was superconductivity, which

Kamerlingh-Onnes discovered in 1911. This phenomenon involves the total loss of resistance by certain metals at low temperatures.

Kamerlingh-Onnes was elected to the Royal Academy of Sciences in Amsterdam for this research and, in 1913, was awarded the Nobel Prize for physics.

Kamin, Leon

(1927–)

AMERICAN PSYCHOLOGIST

Kamin, who was born in Taunton, Massachusetts, has served since 1968 as professor of psychology at Princeton.

Psychologists have devoted much effort to the notion of intelligence. They have introduced a measure of intelligence, namely the intelligence quotient (IQ), and have claimed that they have worked out how to determine it accurately and reliably. In the process a vast amount of material has been gathered about the IQs of peoples of all ages and races and how they relate to occupations, wealth, marriages, health, etc. Although much of this material was controversial, and some of it implausible, it was claimed that IQ research met the highest scientific and statistical standards.

In the 1970s Kamin began to challenge many of these claims. In his *The Science and Politics of I.Q.* he surveyed much of the literature on the subject and found it far from rigorous. Not only did he expose the dubious nature of much of the material collected for separated identical twins by Sir Cyril Burt, but he also found flaws in other twin studies. Repeatedly he claimed to find evidence slanted toward a hereditarian position. When Kamin came to examine the early history of IQ testing he claimed that the evidence shows how it was linked with bogus racist theories and a confused eugenics lobby. This led him to conclude that the IQ test "has served as an instrument of oppression against the poor dressed in the trappings of science, rather than politics."

Kammerer, Paul

(1880–1926)

AUSTRIAN ZOOLOGIST

Kammerer (**kam**-e-rer), the son of a prosperous factory owner, was educated at the university in his native city of Vienna, where he obtained his PhD. He then joined the staff of the university's recently opened Institute of Experimental Biology, where he worked until the end of 1922 and soon established a reputation as a skilled experimentalist. Much of his work appeared to support the unorthodox doctrine of the inheritance of acquired characteristics associated with Jean Lamarck. The most famous of Kammerer's experiments concerned the breeding behavior of *Alytes obstetricans*, the midwife toad. Unlike most other toads this species mates on land; the male consequently lacks the nuptial pads, blackish swellings on the hand, possessed by water-breeding males in the mating season to enable them to grasp the female during copulation.

Kammerer undertook the experiment of inducing several generations of *Alytes* to copulate in water to see what changes resulted. This involved overcoming the difficult task of rearing the eggs in water and ensuring the developing tadpoles were kept free of fungal infection. After almost ten years following this line he noted that in the F_3 generation (the great grandchildren of the original parents) grayish-black swellings, resembling rudimentary nuptial pads, could be seen on the upper, outer, and palmar sides of the first finger.

In 1923 Kammerer visited Britain in the hope of resolving a controversy that had arisen between himself and the leading Cambridge geneticist William Bateson. As virtually all his animals had been destroyed in the war, he brought with him as evidence one preserved specimen and slides of the nuptial pads from the F_5 generation made some ten years earlier. His lectures at Cambridge and to the Linnean Society were successful and none of the eminent biologists who examined Kammerer's specimen noticed anything suspect.

However, when, early in 1926, G. Noble of the American Museum of Natural History came to examine the specimen in Vienna he found no nuptial pads, only blackened areas caused by the injection of ink. Despite the support of the institute's director, Hans Przibram, several possible explanations of the obvious fraud, and a still-open invitation from Moscow to establish an experimental institute there, Kammerer shot himself some six months after Noble's visit.

Kammerer had in fact carried out a whole series of experiments of which the work with *Alytes* was but a part, and for him not the most important part. In 1909 he claimed to have induced inherited color adaptation in salamander, and by cutting the siphons of the sea squirt *Ciona intestinalis*, to have induced hereditary elongations. The few people who attempted to repeat Kammerer's results were unsuccessful although in certain cases Kammerer was able to claim, with some justification, that his protocols had not been scrupulously followed.

Kane, Sir Robert John

(1809–1890)

IRISH CHEMIST AND
EDUCATIONALIST

Kane, born the son of a manufacturing chemist in Dublin, studied medicine at Trinity College there and became professor of chemistry in 1831. The following year he founded the *Dublin Journal of Medical Science*. He was president of Queen's College, Cork, from 1845 until 1873 and president of the Royal Irish Academy in 1877. In 1873 he was appointed the commissioner of national education and in 1880 he became vice-chancellor of Queen's University, Belfast. He was knighted in 1846.

In his books Kane did much to try and spread the new chemistry and show its relevance to industrial Ireland. After his early work *Elements of Practical Pharmacy*, he published his *Elements of Practical Chemistry* (1841–43). His most famous work, however, was his *Industrial Resources of Ireland* (1844), which caught the attention of Peel and led to his becoming an adviser to the government on the development of industry and education in Ireland and his sitting on the commission in 1846 to investigate the potato blight.

Kane's main work was that of administering and encouraging institutions rather than that of a creative scientist. His attempts to stimulate Irish industry and science were unfortunately held back by the famine and its consequences.

Kant, Immanuel

(1724–1804)

GERMAN PHILOSOPHER

> Two things fill the mind with ever new and increasing wonder and awe, the more often and more seriously reflection concentrates upon them: the starry heaven above me and the moral law within me.
> —*Critique of Practical Reason* (1788)

The son of a saddle maker and the grandson of a Scottish immigrant, Kant (kant or kahnt) was born in Königsberg (now Kaliningrad in Russia) and educated at the university there. Owing to interruptions necessary to fulfill family obligations it was not until 1755 that Kant, who had studied mathematics and physics, received his doctorate. He remained on the university staff, as a *Privatdozent* until 1770 when he was appointed to the chair of logic and metaphysics, a post he occupied until his retirement in 1797.

Apart from his influential philosophical works, Kant's first significant scientific publication was his *The Theory of the Heavens* (1755), which contained the first statement of the nebular hypothesis, an account of the origin of solar systems perhaps better known in the later version of Pierre Simon Laplace.

A more pervasive influence was exerted by Kant however in his *Metaphysische Angfangsgründe der Naturwissenschaft* (1786; Metaphysical Foundations of Natural Science). Here he squarely faced the problem of action at a distance arising from Newtonian mechanics. How could gravity act over the vast distances of space once the idea that causes act continuously in space had been rejected? He answered that there were two basic forces, attractive or gravitational and repulsive or elastic. While the latter requires physical contact to operate, the former is "possible without a medium," acts immediately at a distance, and "penetrates space without filling it."

Such ideas, together with his rejection of classical atomism in favor of the infinite divisibility of matter, were not just idle philosophical speculations. They were to exercise much influence over Michael Faraday in his later development of field theory, one of the great ideas of modern science.

Kapitza, Pyotr Leonidovich

(1894–1984)

RUSSIAN PHYSICIST

Theory is a good thing but a good experiment lasts forever.
—*Experiments, Theory, Practice* (1980)

The year that Rutherford died (1938) there disappeared forever the happy days of free scientific work, which gave us such delight in our youth. Science has lost her freedom. Science has become a productive force. She has become rich but she has become enslaved and part of her is veiled in secrecy. I do not know whether Rutherford would continue to joke and laugh as he used to.
—*Science Policy News*, No. 2 (1969)

Pyotr (or Peter) Kapitza (kah-**pyi**-tsa or ka-**pit**-sa) was born in Kronstadt, Russia, and educated (1918–21) at the Polytechnic Institute and the Physical and Technical Institute in Petrograd (now St. Petersburg). He lectured at the Polytechnic Institute from 1919 to 1921. From 1921 to 1924 he was involved in magnetic research at the Cavendish Laboratory of Cambridge University, England, under Ernest Rutherford and gained his PhD there in 1923. He was made director of the Royal Society Mond Laboratory at Cambridge in 1930. In 1934 he paid a visit to his homeland but was detained by the Soviet authorities. The next year Kapitza was made director of a newly founded research institute in Moscow – the Institute for Physical Problems – and was able to continue the line of his Cambridge research through the purchase of his original equipment. He worked there until 1946 when, apparently, he fell into disfavor with Stalin for declining to work on nuclear weapons. He was held under house arrest until 1955, when he was able to resume his work at the Institute. Kapitza had shown similar courage earlier in 1938 when he had intervened on behalf of his colleague Lev Landau who had been arrested as a supposed German spy. Without Landau, Kapitza insisted, he would be unable to complete work considered to be important by the authorities. Soon after, Landau was released.

Kapitza's most significant work in low-temperature physics was on the viscosity of the form of liquid helium known as He–II. This he (and, independently, J. F. Allen and A. D. Misener) found to exist in a "superfluid" state – escaping from tightly sealed vessels and exhibiting unusual flow behavior. Kapitza found that He–II is in a macroscopic quantum state with perfect atomic order. In a series of experiments, he found also that a novel form of internal convection occurs in this form of helium.

Besides work on the unusual properties of helium, Kapitza also devised a liquefaction technique for the gas, which is the basis of present-day helium liquefiers, and was able to produce large quantities of liquid hydrogen, helium, and oxygen. The availability of liquid helium has led to the production of electric superconductors and enabled much other work at extremely low temperatures to proceed. Kapitza also created very high magnetic fields for his experiments, and his record of 500 kilogauss in 1924 was not surpassed until 1956. Kapitza's low-temperature work was honored after almost forty years by the award of the 1978 Nobel Prize for physics.

From 1955 Kapitza headed the Soviet Committee for Interplanetary Flight and played an important part in the preparations for the first Soviet satellite launchings. In his career Kapitza collected many awards from scientific institutions of both East and West, including the Order of Lenin on six occasions. In 1965 he was finally allowed to travel outside the Soviet Union. He first visited Copenhagen and in 1966 he spent some time in Cambridge, England, with his colleagues of the 1930s, John Cockroft and Paul Dirac.

Kapoor, Mitchell David

(1950–)

AMERICAN COMPUTER SCIENTIST

Kapoor was educated at Yale and MIT. He worked initially at a variety of odd jobs before setting up as a freelance consultant in the software business in 1978. He worked as product manager with VisiCorp from 1980 until 1982, when he began the Lotus Development Corporation in Cambridge, Massachusetts, serving as its president from 1982 until 1986.

The major product of the company was Lotus 1-2-3, comprising spreadsheet, graphics, and database in one software package. This was a major competitor to VisiCalc – the spreadsheet program invented by Dan Bricklin. Lotus 1-2-3 was a highly successful product designed to run on an IBM PC. Its availability increased the sale of IBM machines significantly.

Kapoor went on to develop further products. These included Symphony, a word processing package to add onto 1-2-3, and Jazz, an integrated package for Apple. Neither was particularly successful. By this time Kapoor was beginning to tire of running a big company. Consequently he resigned from Lotus in 1986. He went on in 1990 to set up the Electronic Frontier Foundation to explore more original forms of software.

Kapteyn, Jacobus Cornelius

(1851–1922)

DUTCH ASTRONOMER

Born at Barneveld in the Netherlands, Kapteyn (kahp-**tIn**) studied at Utrecht University and became professor of astronomy at the University of Groningen in 1878. He was a very careful stellar observer and using David Gill's photographs of the southern hemisphere skies, he published in 1904 a catalog of over 450,000 stars within 19 degrees of the south celestial pole. He repeated William Herschel's count of the stars by sampling various parts of the heavens and supported Herschel's view that the Galaxy was lens-shaped with the Sun near the center; but his estimate of its size was different from Herschel's – 55,000 light-years long and 11,000 light-years thick. He pioneered new methods for investigating the distribution of stars in space.

Kapteyn also discovered the star, now called *Kapteyn's star*, with the second greatest proper motion – 8.73 seconds annual motion compared to the 10″.3 of Barnard's star. He found this as part of a wider study of the general distribution of the motions of stars in the sky. To his surprise he found, in 1904, that they could be divided into two clear streams: about 3/5 of all stars seem to be heading in one direction and the other 2/5 in the opposite direction. The first stream is directed toward Orion and the second to Scutum, and a line joining them would be parallel to the Milky Way. Kapteyn was unable to explain this phenomenon; it was left to his pupil Jan Oort to point out that this is a straightforward consequence of galactic rotation.

Karle, Isabella Helen

(1921–   )

AMERICAN CRYSTALLOGRAPHER

Karle was born Isabella Lugoski (loo-**gos**-kee) in Detroit, Michigan, the daughter of Polish immigrants; her father was a house painter and her mother a seamstress. She first heard English spoken only when she began school. She was educated at the University of Michigan, where she obtained her PhD in 1943. Here she met Jerome Karle, a physicist who would win the 1985 Nobel Prize for chemistry for work in x-ray crystallography. They married in 1942 and worked together during the war on the Manhattan Project in Chicago. After the war they moved in 1946 to the Naval Research Laboratory in Washington D.C.

With over 200 papers to her credit Karle has made a number of major contributions to the development of x-ray crystallography. In the 1950s, Jerome Karle and Herb Hauptman had developed new and powerful techniques to enable the phase of diffracted x-rays to be calculated directly. Isabella Karle was one of the first to deploy the new method successfully, and thereby to draw the attention of other workers to its potential.

In her first major success in 1969 she established the structure of venom extracted from South American frogs. This was followed in 1975 with the structure of valinomycin, a polypeptide that transports potassium ions across biological membranes. At the time it was the largest molecule to be worked out directly. In 1979 the structure of another peptide, antamanide, was solved. More recently she has determined the structure of the natural opiate, enkephalin.

Karle, Jerome

(1918–)

AMERICAN PHYSICIST

Born in Brooklyn, New York, Karle was educated at the City College there and at the University of Michigan, where he obtained his PhD in 1943. After working on the Manhattan Project in Chicago, Karle moved in 1946 to the Naval Research Laboratory, Washington D.C., becoming chief scientist in the lab for the structure of matter in 1968.

While in Washington Karle began an important collaboration with Herb Hauptman exploring new ways to determine the structure of crystals using x-ray diffraction techniques. Before their work the structure of anything but the simplest molecule was usually worked out with the so-called "heavy-atom" technique. This involved substituting a heavy atom, such as mercury, in a definite position in the structure. The changes produced in the intensities of the diffraction patterns allowed the phases to be inferred. The method, however, is limited and time consuming.

In 1953 Karle and Hauptman published a monograph, *The Phases and Magnitudes of the Structure Factors*, in which they demonstrated how phase structures could be inferred directly from diffraction patterns. For their work in this field Hauptman and Karle shared the 1985 Nobel Prize for chemistry.

In 1942 Karle had married Isabella Lugoski, also a crystallographer. She was one of the earliest workers to apply the new direct method to a number of important molecules.

Karrer, Paul

(1889–1971)

SWISS CHEMIST

Karrer (**kar**-er), the son of a Moscow dentist, was educated at the University of Zurich where he obtained his PhD. After working in Frankfurt he returned to the University of Zurich in 1918, where he served as professor of chemistry until his retirement in 1959.

He began his research career working on the chemistry of plant pigments. Although Karrer tackled a wide variety of such pigments his most significant result was his determination, by 1930, of the structure of carotene, the yellow pigment found in such vegetables as carrots. By 1931 he had also worked out the structure of vitamin A and synthesized it. The similarity between the two molecules did not escape Karrer's attention and it was later shown that vitamin A is derived from the breakdown of carotene in the liver. Karrer went on to synthesize vitamin B_2 (riboflavin) in 1935 and vitamin E (tocopherol) in 1938.

In 1937 Karrer was awarded, with Norman Haworth, the Nobel Prize for chemistry for his work on the "constitution of carotenoids, flavins, and vitamins A and B." Karrer was also the author of a much respected textbook, *Lehrbuch der organischen Chemie* (1927; Textbook of Organic Chemistry).

Kastler, Alfred

(1902–1984)

FRENCH PHYSICIST

Kastler (kast-**lair**), who was born in Gebweiler (now Guebwiller in France) was educated at the Ecole Normale Supérieure. He then taught at the University of Bordeaux where he became professor of physics in 1938. He moved to the University of Paris in 1941 where he remained until his retirement in 1972.

He worked on double-resonance techniques of spectroscopy, using absorption by both optical and radiofrequency radiation to study energy levels in atoms. He also introduced the technique known as "optical pumping" – a method of exciting atoms to a different energy state. In practical terms Kastler's work led to new frequency standards and new methods for the measurement of weak magnetic fields. Kastler received the 1966 Nobel Prize for physics for his work on double resonance.

Katz, Bernard

(1911–)

GERMAN–BRITISH
NEUROPHYSIOLOGIST

Born at Leipzig in Germany, Katz (kats) received his MD from the university there in 1934 and his PhD, under Archibald Hill, from the University of London in 1938. He spent the war in Australia first working with John Eccles and later in the Royal Australian Air Force as a radar operator. Katz returned to London in 1946 to University College and in 1952 became professor of biophysics, a post he retained until he retired in 1978.

In 1936 Henry Dale demonstrated that peripheral nerves act by releasing the chemical acetylcholine in response to a nerve impulse. To find how this secretion takes place Katz, working in collaboration with the British biophysicist Paul Fatt, inserted a micropipette at a neuromuscular junction to record the "end-plate potential" or EPP. He noted a random deflection on the oscilloscope with an amplitude of about 0.5 millivolt even in the absence of all stimulation. At first he assumed such a reading to be interference arising from the machine but the application of curare, an acetylcholine antagonist, by abolishing the apparently random EPPs, showed the activity in the nerves is real.

Consequently Katz proposed his quantum hypothesis. He suggested that nerve endings secrete small amounts of acetylcholine in a random manner in specific amounts (or quanta). When a nerve is stimulated it does not begin secreting but instead enormously increases the number of quanta of acetylcholine released. Katz was able to produce a good deal of evidence for this hypothesis, which he later presented in his important work *Nerve, Muscle and Synapse* (1966).

It was mainly for this work that Katz shared the 1970 Nobel Prize for physiology or medicine with Julius Axelrod and Ulf von Euler.

Keeler, James Edward

(1857–1900)

AMERICAN ASTRONOMER

Born in La Salle, Illinois, Keeler graduated from Johns Hopkins University in 1881, becoming an assistant at the Allegheny Observatory. In 1888 he moved to the Lick Observatory at Mount Hamilton, California, for a short period but returned as director to Allegheny in 1891, being appointed professor of astrophysics in the Western University of Pennsylvania in the same year. He became director of Lick in 1898.

Using spectroscopic methods Keeler made several important discoveries. In 1895 he showed that the rings of Saturn do not rotate uniformly but that the inner border is rotating much faster than the outer. The difference is quite striking, as the innermost edge revolves in about 4 hours while the system's outermost edge needs over 14 hours. This is only possible if the rings are not solid but made from numerous small particles. He also worked on nebulae, photographing and taking the spectra of hundreds. He showed that about 3/4 of them had a spiral structure and demonstrated that their line-of-sight motion showed that they are receding and advancing like the stars. He further studied the spectra of the Orion Nebula and showed that the bright lines in its spectra correspond to the dark lines in the stellar spectra. He was one of the growing band of astronomers who failed to see the supposed canals on Mars despite using a new 36-inch (91-cm) refractor at Allegheny. He died when only 42.

Keenan, Philip Childs

(1908–)

AMERICAN ASTRONOMER

Keenan, who was born in Bellevue, Pennsylvania, graduated in 1929 from the University of Arizona and obtained his PhD from the University of Chicago in 1932. He worked initially at Chicago's Yerkes Observatory from 1929 until 1942 when he joined the Bureau of Ordnance. With the return of peace, Keenan was appointed to the staff of the Perkins Observatory of Ohio State University, becoming professor of astronomy in 1956.

Keenan is best known for his work with William Morgan and Edith Kellman on their *Atlas of Stellar Spectra with an Outline of Spectral Classification* (1943). It was this work that formed the basis for the MKK system of classifying stars by their luminosity in addition to their spectral type.

Keilin, David

(1887–1963)

BRITISH BIOLOGIST AND ENTOMOLOGIST

Keilin was born in Moscow, Russia, and educated at Cambridge University, England. He was subsequently professor of biology at Cambridge from 1931 until 1952 and also director of the Cambridge Moltena

Institute. His most important research was the discovery of the respiratory pigment cytochrome, which, he demonstrated, is present in animal, yeast, and higher plant cells. He also studied the biochemistry of the Diptera (true flies), and investigated the respiratory systems and adaptations of certain dipterous larvae and pupae.

Keir, James

(1735–1820)

BRITISH CHEMIST AND
INDUSTRIALIST

Keir was the youngest of 18 children. He came from a prosperous Edinburgh family and was educated at the high school and the university there, where he started a lifelong friendship with Erasmus Darwin. He left the university without graduating to join the army and served in the West Indies, reaching the rank of captain before resigning in 1768.

Keir settled near Birmingham and became a leading member of the famous Lunar society, an organization founded to promote interest in science and its applications. At this time he translated Pierre Macquer's *Dictionary of Chemistry* (1776), which was one of the key volumes whereby chemical knowledge was transmitted to mechanics and engineers. He served as an assistant to Joseph Priestley during his stay in Birmingham. In 1778 he acted as general manager for the firm of Boulton and Watt.

Together with James Watt and Matthew Boulton, Keir started a venture to obtain soda from nonvegetable sources. He tried to extract it from potassium and sodium sulfates, which were waste products of the vitriol industry. He passed these waste products slowly through a sludge of lime, producing an insoluble calcium sulfate and a weak solution of alkali. He then used this in soap production. By 1801 Keir's alkali factory, which he founded in 1780, was paying excise duty on the production of £10,000 worth of soap. As a pure producer of alkali the venture was not a success; the future was to lie with the Leblanc process.

Keith, Sir Arthur

(1866–1955)

BRITISH ANATOMIST

Keith, the son of a farmer from Old Machan in Scotland, was educated at the University of Aberdeen, where he qualified as a doctor in 1888. He served as a medical officer in Siam (now Thailand) from 1889 until 1892, when his interest in the comparative anatomy of the primates was first aroused. On his return to Europe he studied anatomy in Leipzig and London before being appointed (1895) demonstrator in anatomy at the London Hospital. In 1908 Keith moved to the Royal College of Surgeons, where he served as curator of the Hunterian Museum until his retirement in 1933.

On 18 December 1912, Arthur Woodward and Charles Dawson announced to the Geological Society the discovery at Piltdown in Sussex of a remarkable skull, which apparently combined the mandible of an ape with the cranium of a man. Here at last, it was felt, was solid evidence for the antiquity of man. Although some at the meeting were skeptical of the find, suggesting that the skull and jaw must have come from two different individuals, Keith was not among them. It thus appeared that a man with a cranial capacity of 1,500 cubic centimeters (as estimated by Keith) and with the jaw of an ape had coexisted with the mastodon. Keith, in the first edition of his *Antiquity of Man* (1915), dated Piltdown man to the beginning of the Pliocene, which was then assumed to be about a million years ago. With the change in geological fashion Keith was forced to halve the date of Piltdown man in the second edition of his book (1925).

In 1915 Keith estimated the actual separation of man from the apes to have taken place in the lower Miocene, then considered to be some 2–4 million years ago. This meant that Keith was unable to accommodate the discovery of the famous Taung skull by Raymond Dart in 1924, and consequently he denied that Dart's *Australopithecus* was either man or a link between ape and man, considering it to be a pure ape having affinities with two living apes, the gorilla and the chimpanzee.

Keith lived long enough to witness the exposure of Piltdown man by Kenneth Oakley in 1949, using modern fluorine dating techniques. These showed the fossil to date back only as far as the Pleistocene, while later work (1953) revealed its fraudulent nature by assigning markedly different dates to the skull and jaw. When Oakley made a special journey to the 87-year-old Keith to inform him of his results, Keith commented "I think you are probably right, but it will take me some time to adjust myself to the new view."

Kekulé von Stradonitz, Friedrich August

(1829–1896)

GERMAN CHEMIST

Kekulé (**kay**-koo-lay) was born in Darmstadt, Germany. As a youth he showed considerable skill in drawing and was consequently encouraged to be an architect. Although he began as a student of architecture at Giessen he soon switched, despite family opposition, to the study of chemistry, which he continued abroad. He first went to Paris in the period 1851–52 where he studied under Jean Dumas and Charles Gerhardt who influenced him greatly. He worked in Switzerland for a while before taking a post in England in 1854–55 as a laboratory assistant at St. Bartholomew's Hospital, London. While in London he met and was influenced by Alexander Williamson and William Odling. He accepted an unsalaried post at the University of Heidelberg before his appointment to the chair of chemistry at Ghent in 1858. He then moved to the chemistry chair at the University of Bonn in 1867, where he remained for the rest of his life.

Kekulé's main work was done on the structure of the carbon atom and its compounds. It has often been claimed that he had changed his career from the architecture of buildings to the architecture of molecules. Certainly, after Kekulé it was much easier to visualize the form of atoms and their combinations. In 1852 Edward Frankland had pointed out that each kind of atom can combine with only so many other atoms. Thus hydrogen can combine with only one other atom at a time, oxygen could combine with two, nitrogen with three, and carbon with four. Such combining power soon became known as the valency (valence) of an atom. Each atom would be either uni-, bi-, tri-, quadrivalent, or some higher figure.

In 1858 both Kekulé and Archibald Couper saw how to use this insight of Frankland to revolutionize organic chemistry. They both assumed that carbon was quadrivalent and that one of the four bonds of the carbon atom could be used to join with another carbon atom. The idea came to him, he later claimed, while traveling on a London bus to Clapham Road. He fell into a reverie, "and lo, the atoms were gamboling before my eyes...I saw frequently how two smaller atoms united to form a pair; how a larger one embraced two smaller ones; how still larger ones kept hold of three or even four of the smaller...I saw how the longer ones formed a chain...(and then) the cry of the conductor 'Clapham Road' awakened me from my dreaming; but I spent part of the night in putting on paper at least sketches of these dream forms." He published his results in 1858 in his paper *The Constitution and the Metamorphoses of Chemical Compounds and the Chemical Nature of Carbon* and in the first volume of his *Lehrbuch der organische Chemie* (1859; Textbook of Organic Chemistry).

The diagrams of carbon compounds used today come not from Kekulé but from Alexander Crum Brown in 1865. Kekulé's own notation, known as "Kekulé sausages," in which atoms were represented by a cumbersome system of circles, was soon dropped. The gains from such representations were immediate. It can be seen why two molecules could have the same number of atoms of each element and yet differ in properties. Thus C_2H_6O represents both ethanol and dimethyl ether. If the rules of valence are observed these are the only two ways in which two carbon, six hydrogen, and

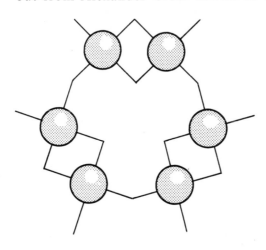

BENZENE   *Kekulé's structure of the benzene molecule.*

one oxygen atom can be combined and indeed these are the only two compounds of the formula ever observed.

While Kekulé had dramatic success demonstrating how organic compounds could be constructed from carbon chains, one set of compounds, the aromatics, resisted all such treatment. Benzene, discovered by Michael Faraday in 1825, had the formula C_6H_6, which, on the assumption of a quadrivalent carbon atom, just could not be represented as any kind of chain. The best that could be done with alternating single and double carbon bonds would still violate the valence rules, for at the end of the chain the carbon atoms will both have an unfilled bond. Kekulé once more has left a description of how the solution of the puzzle came to him. In 1890 he recalled that while working on his textbook in 1865, "I dozed off. Again the atoms danced before my eyes. This time the smaller groups remained in the background. My inner eye...now distinguished bigger forms of manifold configurations. Long rows, more densely joined; everything in motion, contorting and turning like snakes. And behold what was that? One of the snakes took hold of its own tail and whirled derisively before my eyes. I woke up as though I had been struck by lightning; again I spent the rest of the night working out the consequences."

The snake with its tail in its mouth is in fact an ancient alchemical symbol and is named Ouroboros but, to Kekulé, it meant a more prosaic image, that of a ring. For if the two ends of the benzene chain are joined to each other then benzene will have been shown to have a ring structure in which the valence rules have all been observed. Again the rewards in understanding were immediate. It was now obvious why substitution for one of benzene's hydrogen atoms always produced the same compound. The mono-substituted derivative C_6H_5X was completely symmetrical whichever H atom it replaced. Each of the hydrogen atoms was replaced by NH_2 and in each case the same compound, aniline $C_6H_5.NH_2$, was obtained.

Such was the revolution in organic chemistry initiated by Kekulé. Together with new methods introduced by Stanislao Cannizzaro at Karlsruhe in 1860 for the determination of atomic weight, a new age of chemistry was about to dawn in which the conflicts and uncertainties of the first half of the 19th century would be replaced by a unified chemical theory, notation, and practice. After this it comes as something of a shock to discover that Kekulé had no firm belief in the existence of atoms. Whether they exist, he argued in 1867, "has but little significance from a chemical point of view; its discussion belongs rather to metaphysics. In chemistry we have only to decide whether the assumption of atoms is an hypothesis adapted to the explanation of chemical phenomena."

Kellner, Karl

(1851–1905)

AUSTRIAN CHEMICAL ENGINEER

Kellner (**kel**-ner) worked as an engineer in his native city of Vienna. In 1894 he took out a patent on the manufacture of caustic soda from the electrolysis of brine and founded the Konsortium für Electrochemische Industrie at Salzburg for its exploitation. The same discovery had also been made quite independently by the American, Hamilton Castner. To avoid costly litigation the two inventors exchanged patents, and plants using the *Castner–Kellner process* were opened at Niagara Falls in 1896 and in England in 1897 at Runcorn in Cheshire.

Kelvin, William Thomson, Baron

(1824–1907)

BRITISH THEORETICAL AND EXPERIMENTAL PHYSICIST

> When thermal energy is spent in conducting heat through a solid, what becomes of the mechanical effect it might produce? Nothing can be lost in the operations of nature – no energy can be destroyed.
> —*Account of Carnot's Theory* (1849)

Born in Belfast, Northern Ireland, William Thomson was an extremely precocious child intellectually and matriculated at Glasgow University at the astonishingly early age of 10. He went on to Cambridge, after which he returned to Glasgow to become professor of natural philosophy. He was to occupy this chair for 53 years. It was in Glasgow that he organized and ran one of Britain's first adequately equipped physical laboratories. In 1892 in recognition of his contributions to science he was raised to the British peerage as Baron Kelvin of Largs. He was also a devout member of the Scottish Free Church.

Kelvin's work on electromagnetism is second only to that of Michael Faraday and James Clerk Maxwell. Together with Faraday he was responsible for the introduction of the concept of an electromagnetic field. Kelvin was of a much more mathematical turn of mind than Faraday, but it was left to Maxwell to weld the ideas of Faraday and Kelvin together into a powerful, elegant, and succinct mathematical theory. But Maxwell's work would have been greatly hampered without some of the penetrating suggestions made by Kelvin. Particularly important is a fundamental paper of 1847 in which Kelvin drew an analogy between an electrostatic field and an incompressible elastic solid. Kelvin made many other innovations, including the introduction of the use of vectors to represent magnetic induction and magnetic force. He also put his knowledge of electromagnetism to use in many practical inventions of which the transatlantic electric telegraph cable and the mirror galvanometer were among the most important.

Kelvin's other great area of work was thermodynamics. He was one of the first to understand and appreciate the importance of James Joule's seminal work in the field. In his 1852 paper on the *Dissipation of Mechanical Energy* Kelvin set out the fundamentally important law of conservation of energy that was to be so important in the physics of the second half of the 19th century. In his work on thermodynamics Kelvin assimilated and developed the work of the great pioneers of the subject, Nicolas Carnot and James Joule. He also collaborated with Joule in experimental work. One of the important results of Kelvin's work was his introduction of the concept of *absolute zero* and his recognition of the theoretical importance of the absolute scale of temperature, which is named in his honor. Kelvin was able to calculate the value of absolute zero from theoretical considerations. One of the first formulations of the second law of thermodynamics was given by Kelvin. With Joule he first demonstrated the *Joule–Kelvin effect*. He also made important contributions to the theory of elasticity and some basic contributions to hydrodynamics in which he collaborated with George Stokes.

Kemeny, John George

(1926–1992)

HUNGARIAN–AMERICAN MATHEMATICIAN

Kemeny was born in Budapest, Hungary. In 1938 his father was so alarmed by the Nazi annexation of Austria that he moved to the United States. The family followed in 1940 and Kemeny entered Princeton in 1943 to study mathematics. A year later he was drafted onto the Manhattan Project and sent to Los Alamos where he operated an IBM calculator. He returned to Princeton in 1946, completed his PhD in 1949, and moved to Dartmouth in 1953, serving as professor of mathematics from 1956 until 1968, as president of the college from 1970 until 1981, and once more, from 1981 until his retirement in 1990, as professor of mathematics.

Between 1963 and 1964 Kemeny, working with a Dartmouth colleague, Thomas Kurtz, developed BASIC (Beginner's All Purpose Symbolic Instruction Code), probably the best known of all computer languages. Previously the large computers could only be approached through specialized computer programmers. BASIC was conceived initially as something for Dartmouth students to use on Dartmouth computers. With a few simple self-evident commands and an equally simple syntax and vocabulary, it proved remarkably easy to use.

As it was meant to be freely available to students, the software was placed in the public domain. Subsequently it became the most widely used computer language of the 1970s and 1980s.

Kemeny himself became something of a public figure. It was during his presidency that Dartmouth became coeducational and he did much to open up the college to minorities. He also campaigned against the Vietnam War. Kemeny was one of the main campaigners for the not altogether successful "new math" introduced into America in the 1970s. In 1979 he was invited by President Carter to chair the committee set up to investigate the nuclear accident at Three Mile Island.

Kendall, Edward Calvin

(1886–1972)

AMERICAN BIOCHEMIST

Kendall, a dentist's son from South Norwalk, Connecticut, studied chemistry at Columbia University where he obtained his PhD in 1910. After working briefly at St. Luke's Hospital in New York from 1911 to 1914, Kendall moved to the Mayo Foundation in Rochester, Minnesota, where from 1921 to 1951 he served as professor of physiological chemistry.

In 1914 Kendall achieved an early success by isolating the active constituent of the thyroid gland. The importance of hormones in the physiology of the body had become apparent through the work of William Bayliss and Ernest Starling on the pancreas. Kendall was able to demonstrate the presence of a physiologically active compound of the amino acid tyrosine and iodine, which he named thyroxin.

Kendall was led from this to investigate the more complex activity of the adrenal gland. This gland secretes a large number of steroids, many of which he succeeded in isolating. Four compounds, labeled A, B, E, and F, seemed to possess significant physiological activity. They were shown to affect the metabolism of proteins and carbohydrates and in their absence animals seemed to lose the ability to deal with toxic substances. It was therefore hoped that some of these compounds might turn out to be therapeutically useful. After much effort sufficient compound A was obtained but, to Kendall's surprise and disappointment, it was shown to have little effect on Addison's disease, a complaint caused by a deficient secretion from the adrenal cortex. Kendall was more successful with his compound E – later known as cortisone to avoid confusion with vitamin E – when in 1947 a practical method for its production was established. Clinical trials showed it to be effective against rheumatoid arthritis. It was for this work that Kendall shared the 1950 Nobel Prize for physiology or medicine with Tadeus Reichstein and Philip Hench.

Kendall, Henry Way

(1926–   )

AMERICAN PHYSICIST

Kendall, who was born in Boston, Massachusetts, was educated at Amherst College and the Massachusetts Institute of Technology, where he gained his PhD in 1955. After a four-year spell in California at Stanford, Kendall returned to MIT in 1961 and was appointed to the chair of physics in 1967.

In a series of experiments at Stanford in 1967, Kendall and his collaborators, Richard Taylor and Jerome Friedman, provided the first experimental evidence that the proton has an inner structure, and that it could indeed contain the quarks first described by Murray Gell-Mann in 1964. The Stanford experiment won for Kendall a share of the 1990 Nobel Prize for physics along with Taylor and Friedman.

Kendrew, Sir John Cowdery

(1917–   )

BRITISH BIOCHEMIST

Kendrew, who was born at Oxford in England, graduated in natural science from Cambridge University in 1939. He spent the war years working for the Ministry of Aircraft Production, becoming an honorary wing commander in 1944. In 1946 he joined Max Perutz at Cambridge and, like Perutz, used x-ray diffraction techniques to study the crystalline structure of proteins, particularly that of the muscle protein myoglobin. X-ray diffraction, or crystallography, involves placing a crystal in front of a photographic plate and rotating the crystal in a beam of x-rays. The pattern of dots that is formed on the plate by the x-rays can be analyzed to find the positions of the atoms in the crystal. The technique had been used successfully to show the structures of small molecules but Kendrew's progress with the much larger myoglobin structure was slow, especially since diffraction patterns yield no information on the phases of the directed x-rays. However, in 1953 Perutz made a breakthrough by incorporating atoms of heavy elements into the protein crystals. Kendrew modified this new method and applied it successfully in his myoglobin studies, so that four years later he had built up a rough model of the three-dimensional structure of myoglobin. By 1959 he had greatly clarified the structure and could pinpoint most of the atoms.

Kendrew and Perutz received the 1962 Nobel Prize for chemistry for their work on protein structure. Kendrew was knighted in 1974 and served as director general of the European Molecular Biology Laboratory in Heidelberg from 1975 to 1982.

Kennelly, Arthur Edwin

(1861–1939)

BRITISH–AMERICAN ELECTRICAL ENGINEER

Kennelly, the son of an Irish-born employee of the East India Company, was born near Bombay in India and was educated in Europe. He left school at the age of 14 to become office boy to the London Society of Telegraph Engineers. From 1876 to 1886 he worked for the Eastern Telegraph Company, acquiring an engineering education through practice and independent study. He emigrated to America in 1887 and became an assistant to Thomas Edison and a consulting engineer. In 1894, together with E. J. Houston, he founded his own consulting firm. Kennelly was professor of electrical engineering at Harvard University from 1902 to his retirement in 1930; between 1913 and 1925 he held a second appointment as professor of electrical communication at the Massachusetts Institute of Technology.

Kennelly made many contributions to the theory and practice of electrical engineering. These included the representation of quantities by complex variables, a mathematical treatment that helped in understanding the behavior of electrical circuits. In 1902 he explained the Atlantic transmission of radio waves by suggesting that they were reflected back to Earth by some layer of electrically charged particles in the upper atmosphere (suggested independently by Oliver Heaviside and called the *Kennelly–Heaviside layer*). Kennelly was a great scientific administrator and made contributions to the development of electrical units and standards.

Kepler, Johannes

(1571–1630)

GERMAN ASTRONOMER

Oh God, I am thinking Thy thoughts after Thee.
—On his studies of astronomy

It may well wait a century for a reader, as God has waited 6,000 years for an observer.
—On the publication of his astronomical observations. Quoted by David Brewster in *Martyrs of Science* (1841)

The grandfather of Kepler (**kep**-ler) had been the local burgomaster but his father seems to have been a humble soldier away on military service for most of Kepler's early youth. His mother was described by Kepler as "quarrelsome, of a bad disposition." She was later to be accused of witchcraft. Kepler was born at Würtenburg, in Germany, and was originally intended for the Church; he graduated from the University of Tübingen in 1591 and went on to study in the theological faculty. In 1594 he was offered a teaching post in mathematics in the seminary at Gratz in Styria. It was from his teacher, Mästlin, who was one of the earliest scholars fully to comprehend and accept the work of Nicolaus Copernicus, that the young Kepler acquired his early Copernicanism. In addition to his teaching at Gratz and such usual duties as mathematicians were expected to do in those days Kepler published his first book – *Mysterium cosmographicum* (1596; Mystery of Cosmography). The book expresses very clearly the belief in a mathematical harmony underlying the universe, a harmony he was to spend the rest of his life searching for. In this work he tried to show that the universe was structured on the model of Plato's five regular solids. Although the work verges on the cranky and obsessive it shows that Kepler was already searching for some more general mathematical relationship than could be found in Copernicus.

He married in 1597 shortly before he was forced to leave Gratz when, in 1598, all Lutheran teachers and preachers were ordered to leave the city immediately. Fortunately for Kepler, he had an invitation to work with Tycho Brahe who had recently become the Imperial Mathematician in Prague. Tycho was the greatest observational astronomer of the century and he had with him the results of his last 20 years' observations. Kepler joined him in 1600 and although their relationship was not an easy one it was certainly profitable. Tycho assigned him the task of working out the orbit of Mars. Somewhat rashly Kepler boasted he would solve it in a week – it took him eight years of unremitting effort. Not only did Kepler lack the computing assistance now taken for granted but he was also working before the invention of logarithms. It was during this period that he discovered his first two laws and thus, with Galileo, began to offer an alternative physics to that of Aristotle. The first law asserts that planets describe elliptic orbits with the Sun at one focus while the second law asserts that the line joining the Sun to a planet sweeps out equal areas in equal times. The laws were published in his magnum opus *Astronomia nova* (1610; New Astronomy).

Tycho had died in 1601 leaving Kepler with his post, his observations, and a strong obligation to complete and publish his tables under the patronage of their master, the emperor Rudolph II. This obligation was to prove even more onerous and time consuming than the orbit of Mars. It involved dealing with

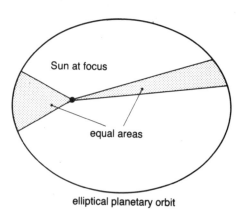

KEPLER'S SECOND LAW *The planet moves such that equal areas are swept out in equal times.*

Tycho's predatory kin, attempting, vainly, to extract money from the emperor to pay for the work, which he ended up financing himself, and trying to find a suitable printer. All this, it must be realized, was done against the background of the Thirty Years' War, marauding soldiery, and numerous epidemics. His work, the *Tabulae Rudolphinae* (Rudolphine Tables), was not completed until 1627 but remained the standard work for the best part of a century.

While serving the emperor in Prague, Kepler had also produced a major work, *Optics* (1604), which included a good approximation of Snell's law, improved refraction tables, and discussion of the pinhole camera. In the same year he observed only the second new star visible to the naked eye since antiquity. He showed, as Tycho had done with the new star of 1572, that it exhibited no parallax and must therefore be situated far beyond the solar system. He studied and wrote upon the bright comet of 1607 – later to be called Halley's comet – and those of 1618 in his *Three Tracts on Comets* (1619). His final work in Prague, the *Dioptrics* (1611), has been called the first work of geometrical optics.

In 1611 Kepler's wife and son died, civil war broke out in Prague, and Rudolph was forced to abdicate. Kepler moved to Linz in the following year to take up a post as a mathematics teacher and surveyor. Here he stayed for 14 years. He married again in 1613. While in Linz he produced a work that, starting from the simple problem of measuring the volume of his wine cask, moved on to more general problems of mensuration – *Nova stereometria* (1615; New Measurements of Volume). One further crisis he had to face was his mother's trial for witchcraft in Würtemburg. The trial dragged on for three years before she was finally freed. His greatest work of this period, *Harmonices mundi* (1619; Harmonics of the World), returns to the search for the underlying mathematical harmony expressed in his first work of 1596. It is here that he stated his third law: the squares of the periods of any two planets are proportional to the cubes of their mean distance from the Sun. After the completion of the Rudolphine tables Kepler took service under a new patron, the Imperial General Wallenstein. He settled at Sagan in Silesia. In return for the horoscopes Wallenstein expected from him, Kepler was provided with a press, a generous salary, and the peace to publish his ephemerides and to prepare his work of science fiction – *A Dream, or Astronomy of the Moon* (1634). He left Sagan in 1630 to see the emperor in Ratisbon, hoping for a payment of the 12,000 florins still owed him. He died there of a fever a few days later.

As a scientist Kepler is of immense importance. Copernicus was in many ways a traditional thinker, still passionately committed to circles. Kepler broke away from this mode of thought and in so doing posed questions of planetary motion that it took a Newton to answer.

Kerr, John

(1824–1907)

BRITISH PHYSICIST

Born at Ardrossan in Scotland, Kerr studied at Glasgow University and carried out research work under Lord Kelvin. He taught mathematics at a training college in Glasgow. He is remembered for his work on polarized light, in which he discovered that certain substances placed in a strong electric field exhibit birefringence (the *Kerr effect*). Kerr also described the behavior of polarized light when reflected from the polished pole of an electromagnet (the *Faraday effect*).

Kerst, Donald William

(1911–1993)

AMERICAN PHYSICIST

Kerst's name is primarily associated with the development of the betatron, a machine capable of accelerating beta particles (electrons) to speeds approaching that of light. Born at Galena, Illinois, Kerst graduated from the University of Wisconsin in 1937, going on to be assistant professor at the University of Illinois, becoming full professor in 1943. In 1939 he developed the idea of the cyclotron particle accelerator a stage further. He circulated electrons in a doughnut-shaped vacuum tube, guiding them round the circle in a magnetic field similar to that of a toroidal electrical transformer. The electrons are accelerated, but are kept in their circular orbits by increasing the magnetic field. Kerst was responsible for the building of the largest such machine (the betatron), completed at the University of Illinois in 1950, in which electrons attained energies of up to 310 MeV (million electronvolts).

Kerst's work on the betatron, and other nuclear physics work primarily with the Van der Graaf generator, led to his involvement during World War II in the Los Alamos thermonuclear (atom-bomb) project, after which he returned to Illinois. He returned to the University of Wisconsin as professor of physics in 1962.

Kettlewell, Henry Bernard Davis

(1907–1979)

BRITISH GENETICIST AND LEPIDOPTERIST

Kettlewell was educated at Cambridge University and St. Bartholomew's Hospital, London, where he gained his medical qualification in 1933. He practiced in Cranleigh and then worked as an anesthetist in Surrey. After the war he worked in South Africa at the International Locust Control Centre in Cape Town before returning to Britain in 1952 as research fellow in genetics at Oxford, a post he continued to hold until his retirement in 1974.

Kettlewell is best known for his work on the occurrence of melanism – black pigmentation in the epidermis of animals. In 1953 he set out to explain why, in the mid-19th century, certain moth species had a light coloration, which camouflaged them on such backgrounds as light tree trunks where they sat motionless during the day. However, by the 1950s, of 760 species of larger moths in Britain 70 had changed their light color and markings for dark or even totally black coloration.

Kettlewell suspected that the success of the melanic form was linked with the industrial revolution and the consequent darkening of the trees by the vast amounts of smoke produced by the 19th-century factories. To test his hypothesis he released large numbers of the dark and light forms of the peppered moth, *Biston betularia*, in the polluted woods around Birmingham and in a distant unpolluted forest. As many of the released moths as possible were recaptured and when the results were analyzed it was found that the light form had a clear advantage over the dark in the unpolluted forest but in the polluted Birmingham woods the result was just the opposite. From this Kettlewell concluded that if the environment of a moth changes so that it is conspicuous by day, then the species is ruthlessly hunted by predators until it mutates to a form better suited to its new environment. His work was seen as a convincing and dramatic confirmation of the Darwinian hypothesis of natural selection.

Kety, Seymour Solomon

(1915–   )

AMERICAN NEUROPHYSIOLOGIST

Kety was born in Philadelphia and educated at the University of Pennsylvania where he obtained his MD in 1940. He continued working there and was appointed professor of clinical physiology in 1948. In 1951 he also took on the directorship of the National Institute of Health. From 1967 to 1980 he was professor of psychiatry at Harvard, becoming professor of neuroscience in 1980 and emeritus professor in 1983.

Kety's first major success was his development of a treatment for lead poisoning using the lead-citrate complex. He later concentrated on measuring the blood flow and energy metabolism of the brain. One of the most interesting results arising from this was his demonstration that the brain's energy consumption during sleep is the same as in the conscious state.

Kety later worked mainly on the role of biological mechanisms in mental illness. He pointed out that both schizophrenia and manic depression run in families. This led him to conclude that because genes can only express themselves through biochemical mechanisms, the hereditary nature of mental disorders suggests the involvement of biochemical substrates. However, although he started to examine the blood and urine of schizophrenics as early as 1957 for such biochemical substrates, none has yet been specifically identified.

Khorana, Har Gobind

(1922–   )

INDIAN–AMERICAN CHEMIST

Khorana (koh-**rah**-na), who was born at Raipur (now in Pakistan), gained his BSc (1943) and MSc (1945) from the University of Punjab. He then traveled to Liverpool University to work for his doctorate. On receiving his PhD in 1948, he did two years postdoctoral research in Switzerland before taking up a Nuffield Fellowship at Cambridge University. There he worked with Alexander Todd, who fired his interest in nucleic acid research – the field in which Khorana later made his name.

Shortly after Khorana joined Wisconsin University in 1960 he became interested in unraveling the genetic code. He synthesized each of the 64 nucleotide triplets that make up the code, and for this work received the Nobel Prize for physiology or medicine in 1968, sharing the award with Marshall Nirenberg and Robert Holley.

Khorana's next major achievement came in 1970, when he announced the synthesis of the first artificial gene. The same year he moved to the Massachusetts Institute of Technology, where, by 1976, his team had made a second gene, which (unlike the first) was capable of functioning in a living cell. Such work has far-reaching possibilities, bringing scientists a step nearer to understanding gene action. The future could see artificial genes being used to make valuable proteins (e.g., insulin) and perhaps to cure human hereditary diseases.

Kidd, John

(1775–1851)

BRITISH CHEMIST

Kidd was the son of a London merchant captain. He was educated at Oxford University, where he graduated in 1797, spending the next four years at Guy's Hospital in London. In 1803 he became the first Aldrichian Professor of Chemistry at Oxford. He stayed in this chair until 1822, when he became professor of physics.

In 1819 Kidd obtained naphthalene from coal tar. This aromatic hydrocarbon, which is used in mothballs, played an important role in the development of aniline dyes by Sir William Perkin 40 years later. Kidd also published in 1809 *Outlines of Mineralogy*. In 1833 he contributed to the "Bridgewater Treatises" – a series commissioned by the Earl of Bridgewater in his will in which eight scientists selected by the Royal Society would demonstrate "the Power, Wisdom, and Goodness of God, as manifested in the creation." Kidd's treatise was on *The Adaptation of External Nature to the Physical Condition of Man*.

Kiddinu

(about 379 BC)

BABYLONIAN ASTRONOMER

Almost nothing is known about Kiddinu (**kid**-i-noo), although he was head of the astronomical school in the Babylonian city of Sippar, and some late classical writers such as Pliny refer to him as Kidenas. There are references to some lunar eclipse tables that Kiddinu had prepared and he is credited with a new method of construction of ephemerides (tables of planetary motion), the so-called "System B." He is also thought to have discovered the precession of the equinoxes – the slow westward motion of the equinoctial points that is caused by the rotation of the Earth's axis.

Kilby, Jack St. Clair

(1923–)

AMERICAN ELECTRONICS ENGINEER

The son of an electrical engineer from Jefferson City, Missouri, Kilby failed his entrance to the Massachusetts Institute of Technology. He was drafted into the army, spending most of his time attempting to reduce the size of radio sets for jungle-warfare units. After demobilization, he was admitted to the University of Illinois. After graduating in 1947 he began work for Centralab, Milwaukee, Wisconsin, producing parts for television sets and hearing aids.

In 1952 Centralab decided to use the transistors recently developed by William Shockley and Kilby was sent to Bell Laboratories at Murray Hill, New Jersey, to learn about the new device. In 1958 he moved to Texas Instruments, Dallas, the firm that had had the foresight in 1954 to switch from germanium to silicon transistors. Engineers at TI, and elsewhere, had come up against the difficulty of fitting on a transistor the number of parts and connections demanded by their designs. It was here in July 1958, while the rest of the laboratory was on holiday, that Kilby came up with what was later termed "the Monolithic Idea."

His basic intuition was that silicon alone could fill most electronic demands. It is possible to modify the semiconductor properties of silicon by adding different amounts of impurities – a process known as "doping." It should be possible to build a whole circuit out of a single piece of material by using different doping levels; no connections would be called for. He built a test circuit and it worked. It was, in fact, the first integrated circuit. Kilby was awarded patent rights in 1967, having first fought off a challenge from Robert Noyce. On appeal the decision was reversed and, in 1968, the patent was awarded to Noyce.

Kilby also worked for Texas Instruments on the development of what was the first pocket calculator, the Pocketronic. It was launched on 14 April 1971, weighed 2.5 pounds, was very expensive, and could only perform the four main arithmetical functions. By this time Kilby had left TI in 1970 to work in Dallas as a self-employed inventor. He also served as a distinguished professor of electrical engineering at the University of Texas from 1978 to 1985.

Kildall, Gary

(1942–1995)

AMERICAN COMPUTER SCIENTIST

Kildall was educated at the University of Washington where he gained his PhD in 1972. Rather than be drafted to Vietnam, he opted to teach computer science at the Naval Postgraduate School, Monterey, California.

With the emergence of the personal computer in the 1970s, operating systems were needed in order to run the various machines coming onto the market. One of the first and most successful of these early systems was Kildall's CP/M (Control Program for Microcomputers). It was flexible enough to work on most computers with 16K of memory and an 8080 Intel chip; it would also, unlike any other system at that time, control floppy disks. In 1976 Kildall resigned from the Naval School to found Digital Research to develop and market CP/M. The system sold well in its various versions, with about 200 million copies produced.

The software could have been even more successful for, in 1980, Kildall was approached by IBM, which was looking for a system to operate its new 16-bit PC. In the event, IBM elected to work with Bill Gates of Microsoft and MS-DOS, rather than CP/M, became the industry-standard operating system for personal computers.

Kildall continued to develop software. He produced, for example, one of the earliest multitask operating systems, Concurrent CP/M, in 1983, bringing out a DOS compatible version in 1984. Later work was more concerned with CD ROMs.

Kimura, Doreen

(*c.* 1935–   )

CANADIAN PSYCHOLOGIST

Kimura (ki-**muur**-a) was born at Winnipeg, Manitoba, and educated at McGill University, Montreal, where she obtained her PhD in 1961. After working briefly at the University of California, Los Angeles, and at McMaster University, Hamilton (1964–67), Kimura moved to the University of Western Ontario, London, and was later appointed professor of psychology in 1974.

Kimura's early work was concerned with possible differences in function between the left and right sides of the brain. Different series of numbers were played simultaneously into the left and right ears of her experimental subjects. The subjects could more easily remember numbers that were fed into their right ear – i.e., the ear connected directly with the left side of the brain. When melodies were substituted for numbers, subjects recognized tunes more easily with the left ear and, accordingly, the right side of the brain. Kimura's work thus supported a slowly emerging hypothesis that there was a functional asymmetry to be found in the cerebral hemispheres. More precisely, the left side was thought to process verbal data, while the right side handled such nonverbal data as music and spatial relationships.

In the 1970s Kimura extended her work to cover differences between the sexes. Among other differences, she found women better at matching items and arithmetical calculation, and that they also had a greater verbal fluency. Men seemed to perform better at certain spatial tasks, at mathematical reasoning, and at disembedding tests.

Kimura proposed that the answer may well lie in the level of sex hormones such as estrogen and testosterone. She found, for example, that women's spatial skills increased when they had low estrogen levels; similarly, men's skills improved when testosterone levels were low.

More recently Kimura has begun to study body asymmetry. She has found that men tend to be larger on the right side and women larger on the left. Much to her surprise Kimura found that body differences might correlate with intellectual skills. Thus mathematical problems are handled better by right-larger individuals, be they male or female.

Kimura, Hisashi

(1870–1943)

JAPANESE ASTRONOMER

Kimura, who was born at Kanazawa in Japan, graduated from Tokyo University in 1892. He worked mainly on latitude variation at the Mizusawa Latitude Observatory, where he served as director from 1899 onward. The International Geodetic Association had organized an International Latitude Service in 1899 provided by six latitude observatories set up on the line of latitude 39°08′ N; Mizusawa was one of the six observatories.

Variations in latitude had been identified first by Leonhard Euler in 1765. A perfectly symmetrical sphere will have a stable spin. The earth's mass, however, is not distributed uniformly about its axis of rotation. Consequently the axis of rotation and the axis of figure, also known as the axis of the moment of inertia, do not coincide. This will lead to a slight wobble with a periodicity of about 14 months. The distances are small and over a fourteen month period the poles will drift no more than 72 feet (22 m). The variation was first detected in 1891 when observations made from Berlin and, 180° away in Waikiki, found that an increase in Berlin's latitude was matched by a decrease in that of Waikiki. Knowledge of the variation is important when very precise and accurate astronomical measurements need to be made.

In 1902 Kimura announced the discovery of a new annual term in the variation of latitude, independent of the components of the pole's motion.

Kimura, Motoo

(1924–1994)

JAPANESE POPULATION GENETICIST

Kimura was born in Okazaki, Japan, and educated at Kyoto University and the University of Wisconsin, where he gained his PhD in 1956. He joined the research staff of the National Institute of Genetics, Mishima, and served from 1964 as head of the population genetics department.

From 1968 Kimura developed a cogent alternative to the neo-Darwinian synthesis as it emerged in the 1930s in the works of such scholars as J. B. S. Haldane. He gathered evidence to show that certain mutations can increase in a population without necessarily having any selective advantage. He examined a number of mutant genes whose effects were not apparent in the phenotype and could only be detected by advanced chemical techniques. He found that adaptively they were neither better nor worse than the genes they replaced, concluding that, at the molecular level, most evolutionary changes are the result of "random drift" of selectively equivalent mutant genes.

Kimura allowed that at the level of the phenotype evolution is basically Darwinian but insisted that the laws governing molecular evolution are clearly different. Such views have met with much opposition from Darwinians. They have argued that many of the apparently neutral mutations are, on closer examination, found to be selective; also many cases, such as human hemoglobin, do not seem to show the variants expected from Kimura's theory.

King, Charles Glen

(1896–1986)

AMERICAN BIOCHEMIST

Born in Entiat, Washington, King was educated at Washington State University and the University of Pittsburg, where he obtained his PhD in 1923 and became professor of chemistry in 1930. He later moved to Columbia University in New York, where he held the chair of chemistry from 1946 until his retirement in 1962.

In 1928 Albert Szent-Györgyi isolated from the adrenal gland a substance that he named "hexuronic acid"; he had in fact discovered vitamin C. It was left to King in 1932 to complete the work. He isolated from lemon juice and cabbages a substance, identical to Szent-Györgyi's hexuronic acid, that possessed powerful antiscorbutic properties. It was vitamin C, later called ascorbic acid. In the following year King determined its formula ($C_6H_8O_6$).

Kinsey, Alfred Charles

(1894–1956)

AMERICAN ZOOLOGIST

There were wives and husbands in the older generation, who did not even know that orgasm was possible for a female; or if they knew that it was possible, they did not comprehend that it could be desirable.
—Alfred Kinsey, *Sexual Behavior in the Human Female* (1953)

Kinsey was born in Hoboken, New Jersey, and educated at Bowdoin College and Harvard. He was professor of zoology (from 1920) and director of the Institute for Sex Research, Indiana University, which he helped found, from 1942 until his death.

Kinsey's researches on human sexual behavior, published as *Sexual Behavior in the Human Male* (1948) and *Sexual Behavior in the Human Female* (1953), have attracted much interest and some controversy. His work demonstrated that there was considerable variation in behavior in all social classes and helped to dispose of certain erroneous ideas, for example, with regard to juvenile sexual activity and homosexuality. Even though based on many (about 18,500) carefully conducted personal interviews, Kinsey's findings have been criticized for sampling limitations and the general unreliability of personal communication in this sphere of human activity.

Kipping, Frederic Stanley

(1863–1949)

BRITISH CHEMIST

> The prospect of any immediate and important advance in this section of organic chemistry [silicone polymer synthesis] does not seem to be very hopeful.
> —*Proceedings of the Royal Society* (1937)

Kipping, a banker's son from Manchester in England, was educated at Owens College, the forerunner of Manchester University. After a period as chemist at the Manchester gas plant and postgraduate work in Munich, Kipping took up his first academic appointment at Heriot-Watt College in Edinburgh in 1885. From 1890 to 1897 he was chief demonstrator at the City and Guilds College in London and in 1897 was appointed to the chair of chemistry at Nottingham University, where he remained until his retirement in 1936.

Kipping is best known as the author, with William Perkin, Jr., of *Organic Chemistry* (1894). This was one of the first works to be devoted to organic chemistry alone, and was the basic textbook for organic chemists for over fifty years.

One of the burning issues of the day when Kipping was an undergraduate was that of stereoisomerism, which had earlier been demonstrated in carbon compounds by Jacobus Van't Hoff. Working with William Pope, Kipping showed that such isomerism was not exclusive to carbon but was detectable in compounds of nitrogen and other atoms. Thus Kipping went on to show the same effect in silicon, discovering between 1905 and 1907 a number of asymmetric silicon compounds. This was the beginning of Kipping's exhaustive study of the chemistry of silicon, on which he published 51 papers.

Kirchhoff, Gustav Robert

(1824–1887)

GERMAN PHYSICIST

Kirchhoff (**keerk**-hof) studied in his native city of Königsberg (now Kaliningrad in Russia), graduating in 1847. Three years later he was appointed a professor at Breslau. He moved to Heidelberg, where Robert Bunsen was professor of chemistry, in 1854.

Kirchhoff was one of the foremost physicists of the 19th century and is remembered as one of the founders of the science of spectroscopy. He is also known for *Kirchhoff's laws*, formulated in 1845 while he was still a student, which refer to the currents and electromotive forces in electrical networks.

In 1859 he published an explanation of the dark lines in the solar spectrum discovered by Josef von Fraunhofer, in which he suggested that they are due to absorption of certain wavelengths by substances in the Sun's atmosphere. He later formulated *Kirchhoff's law of radiation*, which concerns the emission and absorption of radiation by a hot body. It states that the rate of emission of energy by a body is equal to the rate at which the body absorbs energy (both emission and absorption being in a given direction at a given wavelength). Kirchhoff gave a final proof of this in 1861.

In about 1860 Bunsen was analyzing the colors given off by heating chemicals to incandescence, using colored glass to distinguish between similar shades. Kirchhoff joined this research when he suggested that the observation of spectral lines, by dispersing the light with a prism, would be a more precise way of testing the color of the light. Kirchhoff and Bunsen found that each substance emitted light that had its own unique pattern of spectral lines – a discovery that began the spectroscopic method of chemical analysis. In 1860, a few months after publishing these results, they discovered a new metal, which they called cesium and the next year found rubidium. Kirchhoff and Bunsen also constructed improved forms of the spectroscope for such work and Kirchhoff showed that, if a gas emitted certain wavelengths of light then it would absorb those wavelengths from light passing through it.

Kirchhoff was crippled by an accident in mid-life but remained in good spirits and, when his health forced him to stop experimental work in 1875, he was offered the chair of theoretical physics in Berlin. He remained there until his death 12 years later.

Kirkwood, Daniel

(1814–1895)

AMERICAN ASTRONOMER

> Planets and comets have not formed from rings but rings from planets and comets.
>
> —*The Divisions in Saturn's Rings* (1883)

Born in Harford County, Maryland, Kirkwood became professor of mathematics at the University of Delaware in 1851, moving to the University of Indiana in 1856. In 1857 he noted that the asteroids (planetoids) are not evenly distributed in between the orbits of Mars and Jupiter but that there are areas in which no – or very few – asteroids orbit. He showed that these gaps in the asteroid belt – since known as *Kirkwood gaps* – occur where the period of revolution of an asteroid would have been an exact simple fraction of the Jovian period. Kirkwood explained that any asteroids in these areas would eventually be forced into other orbits by perturbations caused by Jupiter. Similarly he was able to explain gaps in the rings of Saturn (the Cassini division) as being caused by the satellite Mimas. Kirkwood published his findings in *The Asteroids* (1887).

Kirwan, Richard

(1733–1812)

IRISH CHEMIST AND
MINERALOGIST

Born in Galway, now in the Republic of Ireland, Kirwan studied in France to become a Jesuit but returned to Ireland after only a year. There he inherited the family estates following his brother's death in a duel in 1755. He was called to the Irish bar in 1766 but gave up law just two years later to devote himself to science. He was made a fellow of the Royal Society in 1780 and won the Copley medal in 1782 for his work on chemical affinity. In 1787 he settled in Dublin, where he remained until his death. In 1799 he was elected president of the Royal Irish Academy.

Kirwan was at first a staunch supporter of the phlogiston theory and in 1787 he wrote his *Essay on Phlogiston*, which was translated into French. He conceded to Antoine Lavoisier's criticism of this and Lavoisier's subsequent evidence of oxygen by giving up his support of the theory in 1791.

Kirwan was also an eminent mineralogist and published, in 1784, his *Elements of Mineralogy*, which has been described as the first systematic work on the subject in English. His *Geological Essays* (1799) brought him into conflict with James Hutton over the chemical composition of rocks. Kirwan was also involved in industrial chemistry. He received news from Karl Scheele of the bleaching properties of chlorine and quickly had it tested and marketed in both Lancashire and Ireland.

Kistiakowsky, George Bogdan

(1900–1982)

RUSSIAN–AMERICAN CHEMIST

Kistiakowsky (kis-ti-a-**kow**-skee) came from a family of academics in Kiev, now in Ukraine. He began his education in his native city but, after fighting against the Bolsheviks, completed it in Berlin. He moved to America in 1926, working first at Princeton before moving to Harvard where he was appointed professor of chemistry in 1937, a post he retained until his retirement in 1971.

His most important work during the war was as head of the Explosives Division at Los Alamos (1944–45). On being told of the project his initial reaction had been: "Dr Oppenheimer is mad to think this thing will make a bomb." The basic device, proposed by Seth Neddermeyer, consisted of a thin hollow sphere of uranium that would become critical only when "squeezed" together. In theory this was achieved by surrounding the subcritical uranium with conventional explosives whose detonation would compress the radioactive material into a critical mass. To work the process must take place in less than a millionth of a second and with great precision and accuracy. Right to the very end there was considerable doubt as to whether Kistiakowsky could solve the technical problems involved.

After the war Kistiakowsky, very much a figure of the scientific establishment, spent much time advising numerous governmental bodies. From 1959 until 1961 he served as special assistant for science and technology to President Eisenhower, later writing an account of this period in *A Scientist at the White House* (1976). Toward the end of his life he spoke out about the dangers of nuclear weapons.

Kitasato, Baron Shibasaburo

(1852–1931)

JAPANESE BACTERIOLOGIST

Born in Oguni, Japan, Kitasato (kee-tah-**sah**-toh) graduated from the medical school of the University of Tokyo in 1883 and then went to Berlin to study under Robert Koch. A close and long-lasting friendship developed between the two men.

While in Berlin Kitasato worked with Emil von Behring and in 1890 they announced the discovery of antitoxins of diphtheria and tetanus. They showed that if nonimmune animals were injected with increasing sublethal doses of tetanus toxin, the animals became resistant to the disease. Their paper laid the basis for all future treatment with antitoxins and founded a new field in science, that of serology. Kitasato returned to Japan and became director of the Institute of Infectious Diseases in 1892. Two years later there was an outbreak of bubonic plague in Hong Kong and he succeeded in isolating the plague bacillus, *Pasteurella pestis*. In 1898 he isolated the microorganism that causes dysentery.

He founded the Kitasato Institute for Medical Research in 1914 and became dean of the medical school, Keio University, Tokyo. In 1924 he was created a baron. In 1908 Koch visited Japan and Kitasato secretly obtained clippings of the visitor's hair and fingernails. When Koch died in May 1910, Kitasato built a small shrine for the relics in front of his laboratory; when Kitasato died, his remains were placed in the same shrine, next to those of his respected master.

Kittel, Charles

(1916–   )

AMERICAN PHYSICIST

Kittel is regarded by many as the leading authority on the physics of the solid state. Born in New York City, he graduated from Cambridge University, England, with a BA in 1938 and gained his PhD from the University of Wisconsin in 1941. He was an experimental physicist at the Naval Ordnance Laboratories, Washington (1940–42), and an operations analyst with the U.S. Fleet (1943–45). After a short spell as a physics research associate at the Massachusetts Institute of Technology, he worked as a research physicist with the Bell Telephone Laboratories (1947–50). From there he took up an associate professorship at the University of California at Berkeley, becoming full professor of physics in 1951. He retired in 1978.

During the 1950s Kittel published several important papers on the properties and structure of solids. These were concerned with: antiferroelectric crystals; electron-spin resonance in the study of conduction electrons in metals; the nature of "holes" in the process of electrical conduction; plasma-resonance effects in semiconductor crystals; ferromagnetic resonance and domain theory; and spin-resonance absorption in antiferromagnetic crystals. He is widely known for his textbook *Introduction to Solid State Physics* (1953), successive editions of which have served generations of physics students.

Kjeldahl, Johan Gustav Christoffer Thorsager

(1849–1900)

DANISH CHEMIST

Kjeldahl (**kel**-dahl), the son of a physician, was born at Jagerpris in Denmark and educated at the Roskilde Gymnasium and the Technical University of Denmark, Copenhagen. After working briefly at the Royal Veterinary and Agricultural University he joined the laboratory set up by the brewer Carl Jacobsen in 1876 to introduce scientific methods into his Carlsberg brewery founded the previous year. Kjeldahl directed the chemistry department of the laboratory from 1876 until his fatal heart attack in 1900.

Kjeldahl is still widely known to chemists for the method named for him, first described in 1883, for the estimation of the nitrogen content of compounds. It was much quicker, more accurate, and capable of being operated on a larger scale than the earlier combustion-tube method dating back to Jean Dumas. It utilized the fact that the nitrogen in a nitrogenous organic compound heated with concentrated sulfuric acid will be converted into ammonium sulfate. The ammonia can then be released by introducing an alkaline solution, and then distilled into a standard acid, its amount being determined by titration.

His name is also remembered with the *Kjeldahl flask*, the round-bottomed long-necked flask used by him in the operation of his method.

Klaproth, Martin Heinrich

(1743–1817)

GERMAN CHEMIST

Born in Wernigerode, Germany, Klaproth (**klahp**-roht) was apprenticed as an apothecary. After working in Hannover and Danzig he moved to Berlin where he set up his own business. In 1792 he became lecturer in chemistry at the Berlin Artillery School and in 1810 he became the first professor of chemistry at the University of Berlin.

His main fame as a chemist rests on his discovery of several new elements. In 1789 he discovered zirconium, named from zircon, the mineral from which it was isolated. In the same year he extracted uranium from pitchblende and named it for the newly discovered planet, Uranus. He also rediscovered titanium in 1795, about four years after its original discovery, and discovered chromium in 1798. Klaproth used the Latin *tellus* (earth) in his naming of tellurium (1798), which had been discovered by Muller von Richtenstein in 1782. In 1803 he discovered cerium oxide, named for the newly discovered asteroid, Ceres. He made important improvements to chemical analysis by bringing samples to a constant weight through drying and ignition.

Klaproth's son, Heinrich Julius, became a noted orientalist.

Klein, (Christian) Felix

(1849–1925)

GERMAN MATHEMATICIAN

Klein (klIn), one of the great formative influences on the development of modern geometry, was born in Düsseldorf, Germany, and studied at Bonn, Göttingen, and Berlin. He worked with Sophus Lie – a collaboration that was particularly fruitful for both of them and led to the theory of groups of geometrical transformations. This work was later to play a crucial role in Klein's own ideas on geometry.

Klein took up the chair in mathematics at the University of Erlangen in 1872 and his inaugural lecture was the occasion of his formulation of his famous *Erlangen Programm*, a suggestion of a way in which the study of geometry could be both unified and generalized. Throughout the 19th century, with the work of such mathematicians as Karl Friedrich Gauss, Janós Bolyai, Nikolai Lobachevsky, and Bernhard Riemann, the idea of what a "geometry" could be had been taken increasingly beyond the conception Euclid had of it and Klein's ideas helped show how these diverse geometries could all be seen as particular cases of one general concept. Klein's central idea was to think of a geometry as the theory of the invariants of a particular group of transformations. His *Erlangen Programm* was justly influential in guiding the further development of the subject. In particular Klein's ideas led to an even closer connection between geometry and algebra.

Klein also worked on projective geometry, which he generalized beyond three dimensions, and on the wider application of group theory, for example, to the rotational symmetries of regular solids. His name is remembered in topology for the *Klein bottle*, a one-sided closed surface, not constructible in three-dimensional Euclidean space. In 1886 Klein took up a chair at Göttingen and was influential in building Göttingen up into a great center for mathematics.

Klingenstierna, Samuel

(1698–1765)

SWEDISH MATHEMATICIAN AND PHYSICIST

Klingenstierna (**klin**-gen-shair-na) was born at Linköping in Sweden and, before embarking on his mathematical and scientific studies, studied law at Uppsala. He was appointed secretary to the Swedish treasury (1720) but also had interests in philosophy and science and was allowed to continue his studies at Uppsala. In 1727 he was awarded a scholarship, which enabled him to travel in Europe. He traveled to Marburg where he studied with the Leibnizian philosopher Christian Wolff and also to Basel to study mathematics with Johann I Bernoulli. Klingenstierna became professor of mathematics at Uppsala and later professor of physics there (1750). His last appointment was the highly prestigious one of tutor to the crown prince (1756–64).

Klingenstierna's most notable scientific work was in the field of optics. He was able to show that some of Newton's views on the refraction of light were incorrect and made practical use of this discovery in producing designs for lenses free from chromatic and spherical aberration.

Klitzing, Klaus von

(1943–)

GERMAN PHYSICIST

Von Klitzing (fon **klit**-sing) was born at Poznan but when the town was restored to Poland after 1945 his family moved to West Germany. He was educated at the universities of Brunswick and Würzburg, where he received his PhD in 1972 and where he remained as a teaching fellow until 1980. After serving as professor of physics at the Technical University, Munich, from 1980 to 1984, he was appointed director of solid-state research at the Max Planck Institute, Stuttgart.

In 1980 von Klitzing began work on the Hall effect, first described by Edwin Hall in 1879. Hall noted that when a current flows in a conductor placed in a magnetic field perpendicular to the sample's surface, a potential difference (the *Hall voltage*) is produced acting at right angles to both the current and field directions. It is possible to measure a *Hall resistance*, defined in the normal way by dividing the Hall voltage by the current it produces.

Von Klitzing set out to make extremely precise measurements of the Hall resistance working with a two-dimensional electron gas. This can be formed by using a special kind of transistor in which electrons can be drawn into a layer between an insulator and a semiconductor. When the layer is thin enough, of the order of 1 nanometer (10^{-9} meter), and the temperature is as low as 1.5 K, the electrons are forced into a two-dimensional plane parallel to the surface of the semiconductor.

Under normal conditions the Hall resistance increases directly with the strength of the magnetic field. In contrast von Klitzing found that under his experimental conditions the resistance became quantized, varying in a series of steps as the magnetic field was changed. Von Klitzing went on to establish that the Hall resistance at each step was a function of Planck's constant h, the fundamental constant of quantum theory, and could be used to measure h very accurately. For his discovery of the *quantized Hall effect* von Klitzing was awarded the 1985 Nobel Prize for physics.

Sources and Further Reading

HEISENBERG

Cassidy, David. *Uncertainty: the Life and Science of Werner Heisenberg.* New York: W. H. Freeman, 1992.

Powers, Thomas. *Heisenberg's War.* New York: Alfred A. Knopf, 1993.

HELMHOLTZ

Cahan, David, ed. *Herman von Helmholtz and the Foundation of 19th Century Science.* Berkeley, CA: University of California Press, 1993.

HELMONT

Pagel, Walter. *J. B. van Helmont: Reformer of Science and Medicine.* New York: Cambridge University Press, 1982.

HERSCHEL, Sir William

Armitage, Angus. *William Herschel.* London: Nelson, 1962.

Hoskin, Michael. *William Herschel and the Construction of the Heavens.* London: Oldbourne, 1963.

HERTZ, Heinrich

Aitken, Hugh J. G. *Syntony and Spark: the Origins of Radio.* Princeton, NJ: Princeton University Press, 1985.

Buchwald, J. Z. *The Creation of Scientific Effects: Heinrich Hertz and Electric Waves.* Chicago, IL: University of Chicago Press, 1994.

HEVELIUS

Taton, R., and C. Wilson, eds. *The General History of Astronomy. 2A: Tycho Brahe to Newton.* New York: Cambridge University Press, 1989.

HILBERT

Gjertsen, Derek. *The Classics of Science.* New York: Lilian Barber Press, 1984.

Lloyd, G. E. R., ed. *Hippocratic Writings.* New York: Viking Penguin, 1984.

HOFSTADTER, Douglas

Hofstadter, Douglas. *Gödel, Escher, Bach: An Eternal Golden Braid.* New York: Basic Books, 1979.

———. *Metamagical Themas.* New York: Basic Books, 1985.

HOLLERITH

Austrian, G. D. *Herman Hollerith: Forgotten Giant of Information Processing.* New York: Columbia University Press, 1982.

HOOKE

Hooke, Robert. *Micrographia*. New York: Dover Publications, 1961.

HOOKER, Sir Joseph Dalton

Turril, W. B. *Joseph Dalton Hooker: Botanist, Explorer and Administrator*. London: Nelson, 1963.

HORROCKS

Helden, Albert Van. *Measuring the Universe: Cosmic Dimensions from Aristarchus to Halley*. Chicago, IL: University of Chicago Press, 1985.

Woolf, Harry. *The Transits of Venus*. Princeton, NJ: Princeton University Press, 1959.

HOYLE

Hoyle, Fred. *Home is Where the Wind Blows: Chapters from a Cosmologist's Life*. Mill Hill, CA: University Science Books, 1994.

HUBBLE

Christianson, Gale E. *Edwin Hubble: Mariner of the Nebulae*. New York: Farrar, Straus and Giroux, 1995.

Hubble, Edwin. *The Realm of the Nebulae*. New York: Dover Publications, 1958.

HUBEL

Hubel, David H. *Eye, Brain and Vision*. New York: W. H. Freeman, 1988.

HUMBOLDT

Botting, Douglas. *Humboldt and the Cosmos*. New York: Harper Row, 1973.

HUTTON

Gillespie, C. C. *Genesis and Geology*. New York: Harper Torchbooks, 1959.

Porter, Roy. *The Making of Geology: Earth Science in Britain 1660–1815*. New York: Cambridge University Press, 1977.

HUXLEY, Thomas

Desmond, Adrian. *Huxley: The Devil's Disciple*. London: Michael Joseph, 1994.

HUYGENS

Huygens, Christiaan. *Treatise on Light*. New York: Dover Publications, 1962.

JACOB

Jacob, François. *The Statue Within: An Autobiography*. New York: Basic Books, 1988.

JENNER

Fisher, R. B. *Edward Jenner 1749–1823*. London: André Deutsch, 1991.

JOHANSON

Johanson, Donald, and M. A. Edey. *Lucy, the Beginnings of Humankind*. New York: Simon and Schuster, 1981.

JOULE

Cardwell. D. S. L. *James Joule*. New York: St Martin's Press, 1989.

KAMEN

Kamen, Martin D. *Radiant Science, Dark Politics*. Berkeley, CA: University of California Press, 1985.

KAMMERER

Koestler, Arthur. *The Case of the Midwife Toad*. New York: Random House, 1971.

KAPITZA

Badash, Lawrence. *Kapitza, Rutherford, and the Kremlin*. New Haven, CT: Yale University Press, 1985.

KEKULÉ

Brock, William H. *The Norton History of Chemistry*. New York: W. W. Norton, 1993.

Russell, C. A. *The History of Valency*. New York: Humanities Press Inc., 1971.

KELVIN

Burchfield, J. D. *Lord Kelvin and the Age of the Earth*. New York: Science History Publications, 1975.

MacDonald, D. K. C. *Faraday, Maxwell and Kelvin*. New York: Doubleday Anchor Books, 1964.

KEPLER

Caspar, Max. *Kepler*. New York: Abelard-Schuman, 1959.

Koestler, Arthur. *The Sleepwalkers*. New York: Macmillan, 1959.

KILBY

Reid. T. R. *Microchip: the Story of a Revolution and the Men Who Made It*. London: Collins, 1985.

Glossary

absolute zero The zero value of thermodynamic temperature, equal to 0 kelvin or −273.15°C.

acceleration of free fall The acceleration of a body falling freely, at a specified point on the Earth's surface, as a result of the gravitational attraction of the Earth. The standard value is 9.80665 m s^{-2} (32.174 ft s^{-2}).

acetylcholine A chemical compound that is secreted at the endings of some nerve cells and transmits a nerve impulse from one nerve cell to the next or to a muscle, gland, etc.

acquired characteristics Characteristics developed during the life of an organism, but not inherited, as a result of use and disuse of organs.

adrenaline (epinephrine) A hormone, secreted by the adrenal gland, that increases metabolic activity in conditions of stress.

aldehyde Any of a class of organic compounds containing the group –CHO.

aliphatic Denoting an organic compound that is not aromatic, including the alkanes, alkenes, alkynes, cycloalkanes, and their derivatives.

alkane Any of the saturated hydrocarbons with the general formula C_nH_{2n+2}.

alkene Any one of a class of hydrocarbons characterized by the presence of double bonds between carbon atoms and having the general formula C_nH_{2n}. The simplest example is ethylene (ethene).

alkyne Any one of a class of hydrocarbons characterized by the presence of triple bonds between carbon atoms. The simplest example is ethyne (acetylene).

allele One of two or more alternative forms of a particular gene.

amino acid Any one of a class of organic compounds that contain both an amino group ($–NH_2$) and a carboxyl group ($–COOH$) in their molecules. Amino acids are the units present in peptides and proteins.

amount of substance A measure of quantity proportional to the number of particles of substance present.

anabolism The sum of the processes involved in the synthesis of the constituents of living cells.

androgen Any of a group of steroid hormones with masculinizing properties, produced by the testes in all vertebrate animals.

antibody A protein produced by certain white blood cells (lymphocytes) in response to the presence of an antigen. An antibody forms a complex with an antigen, which is thereby inactivated.

antigen A foreign or potentially harmful substance that, when introduced into the body, stimulates the production of a specific antibody.

aromatic Denoting a chemical compound that has the property of aromaticity, as characterized by benzene.

asteroid Any of a large number of small celestial bodies orbiting the Sun, mainly between Mars and Jupiter.

atomic orbital A region around the nucleus of an atom in which an electron moves. According to wave mechanics, the electron's location is described by a probability distribution in space, given by the wave function.

ATP Adenosine triphosphate: a compound, found in all living organisms, that functions as a carrier of chemical energy, which is released when required for metabolic reactions.

bacteriophage A virus that lives and reproduces as a parasite within a bacterium.

bacterium (*pl.* **bacteria**) Any one of a large group of microorganisms that all lack a membrane around the nucleus and have a cell wall of unique composition.

band theory The application of quantum mechanics to the energies of electrons in crystalline solids.

baryon Any of a class of elementary particles that have half-integral spin and take part in strong interactions. They consist of three quarks each.

beta decay A type of radioactive decay in which an unstable nucleus ejects either an electron and an antineutrino or a positron and a neutrino.

black body A hypothetical body that absorbs all the radiation falling on it.

bremsstrahlung Electromagnetic radiation produced by the deceleration of charged particles.

carbohydrate Any of a class of compounds with the formula $C_nH_{2m}O_m$. The carbohydrates include the sugars, starch, and cellulose.

carcinogen Any agent, such as a chemical or type of radiation, that causes cancer.

catabolism The sum of the processes involved in the breakdown of molecules in living cells in order to provide chemical energy for metabolic processes.

catalysis The process by which the rate of a chemical reaction is increased by the presence of another substance (the catalyst) that does not appear in the stoichiometric equation for the reaction.

cathode-ray oscilloscope An instrument for displaying changing electrical signals on a cathode-ray tube.

cellulose A white solid carbohydrate, $(C_6H_{10}O_5)_n$, found in all plants as the main constituent of the cell wall.

chelate An inorganic metal complex in which there is a closed ring of atoms, caused by attachment of a ligand to a metal atom at two points.

chlorophyll Any one of a group of green pigments, found in all plants, that absorb light for photosynthesis.

cholesterol A steroid alcohol occurring widely in animal cell membranes and tissues. Excess amounts in the blood are associated with atherosclerosis (obstruction of the arteries).

chromatography Any of several related techniques for separating and analyzing mixtures by selective adsorption or absorption in a flow system.

chromosome One of a number of threadlike structures, consisting mainly of DNA and protein, found in the nucleus of cells and constituting the genetic material of the cell.

codon The basic coding unit of DNA and RNA, consisting of a sequence of three nucleotides that specifies a particular amino acid in the synthesis of proteins in a cell.

collagen A fibrous protein that is a major constituent of the connective tissue in skin, tendons, and bone.

colligative property A property that depends on the number of particles of substance present in a substance, rather than on the nature of the particles.

continental drift The theory that the Earth's continents once formed a single mass, parts of which have drifted apart to their present positions.

cortisone A steroid hormone, produced by the cortex (outer part) of the adrenal gland, that regulates the metabolism of carbohydrate, fat, and protein and reduces inflammation.

critical mass The minimum mass of fissile material for which a chain reaction is self-sustaining.

cryogenics The branch of physics concerned with the production of very low temperatures and the study of phenomena occurring at these temperatures.

cyclotron A type of particle accelerator in which the particles move in spiral paths under the influence of a uniform vertical magnetic field and are accelerated by an electric field of fixed frequency.

cytoplasm The jellylike material that surrounds the nucleus of a living cell.

dendrochronology A method of dating wooden specimens based on the growth rings of trees. It depends on the assumption that trees grown in the same climatic conditions have a characteristic pattern of rings.

dialysis The separation of mixtures by selective diffusion through a semipermeable membrane.

diffraction The formation of light and dark bands (diffraction patterns) around the boundary of a shadow cast by an object or aperture.

diploid Describing a nucleus, cell, or organism with two sets of chromosomes, one set deriving from the male parent and the other from the female parent.

DNA Deoxyribonucleic acid: a nucleic acid that is a major constituent of the chromosomes and is the hereditary material of most organisms.

dissociation The breakdown of a molecule into radicals, ions, atoms, or simpler molecules.

distillation A process used to purify or separate liquids by evaporating them and recondensing the vapor.

ecology The study of living organisms in relation to their environment.

eigenfunction One of a set of allowed wave functions of a particle in a given system as determined by wave mechanics.

electrolysis Chemical change produced by passing an electric current through a conducting solution or fused ionic substance.

electromagnetic radiation Waves of energy (electromagnetic waves) consisting of electric and magnetic fields vibrating at right angles to the direction of propagation of the waves.

electromotive force The energy supplied by a source of current in driving unit charge around an electrical circuit. It is measured in volts.

electromotive series A series of the metals arranged in decreasing order of their tendency to form positive ions by a reaction of the type $M = M^+ + e$.

electron An elementary particle with a negative charge equal to that of the proton and a rest mass of 9.1095×10^{-31} kilograms (about 1/1836 that of the proton).

electron microscope A device in which a magnified image of a sample is produced by illuminating it with a beam of high-energy electrons rather than light.

electroweak theory A unified theory of the electromagnetic interaction and the weak interaction.

enthalpy A thermodynamic property of a system equal to the sum of its internal energy and the product of its pressure and its volume.

entomology The branch of zoology concerned with the study of insects.

entropy A measure of the disorder of a system. In any system undergoing a reversible change the change of entropy is defined as the energy absorbed divided by the thermodynamic temperature. The entropy of the system is thus a measure of the availability of its energy for performing useful work.

escape velocity The minimum velocity that would have to be given to an object for it to escape from a specified gravitational field. The escape velocity from the Earth is 25,054 mph (7 miles per second).

ester A compound formed by a reaction between an alcohol and a fatty acid.

estrogen Any one of a group of steroid hormones, produced mainly by the ovaries in all vertebrates, that stimulate the growth and maintenance of the female reproductive organs.

ethology The study of the behavior of animals in their natural surroundings.

excitation A change in the energy of an atom, ion, molecule, etc., from one energy level (usually the ground state) to a higher energy level.

fatty acid Any of a class of organic acids with the general formula $R.CO.OH$, where R is a hydrocarbon group.

fermentation A reaction in which compounds, such as sugar, are broken down by the action of microorganisms that form the enzymes required to catalyze the reaction.

flash photolysis A technique for investigating the spectra and reactions of free radicals.

free energy A thermodynamic function used to measure the ability of a system to perform work. A change in free energy is equal to the work done.

free radical An atom or group of atoms that has an independent existence without all its valences being satisfied.

fuel cell A type of electric cell in which electrical energy is produced directly by electrochemical reactions involving substances that are continuously added to the cell.

fungus Any one of a group of spore-producing organisms formerly classified as plants but now placed in a separate kingdom (Fungi). They include the mushrooms, molds, and yeasts.

galaxy Any of the innumerable aggregations of stars that, together with gas, dust, and other material, make up the universe.

gene The functional unit of heredity. A single gene contains the information required for the manufacture, by a living cell, of one particular polypeptide, protein, or type of RNA and is the vehicle by which such information is transmitted to subsequent generations. Genes correspond to discrete regions of the DNA (or RNA) making up the genome.

genetic code The system by which genetic material carries the information that directs the activities of a living cell. The code is contained in the sequence of nucleotides of DNA and/or RNA (*see* codon).

genome The sum total of an organism's genetic material, including all the genes carried by its chromosomes.

global warming *See* greenhouse effect.

glycolysis The series of reactions in which glucose is broken down with the release of energy in the form of ATP.

greenhouse effect An effect in the Earth's atmosphere resulting from the presence of such gases as CO_2, which absorb the infrared radiation produced by the reradiation of solar ultraviolet radiation at the Earth's surface. This causes a rise in the Earth's average temperature, known as "global warming."

half-life A measure of the stability of a radioactive substance, equal to the time taken for its activity to fall to one half of its original value.

halogens The nonmetallic elements fluorine, chlorine, bromine, iodine, and astatine.

haploid Describing a nucleus or cell that contains only a single set of chromosomes; haploid organisms consist exclusively of haploid cells. During sexual reproduction, two haploid sex cells fuse to form a single diploid cell.

heat death The state of a closed system when its total entropy has increased to its maximum value. Under these conditions there is no available energy.

histamine A substance released by various tissues of the body in response to invasion by microorganisms or other stimuli. It triggers inflammation and is responsible for some of the symptoms (e.g., sneezing) occurring in such allergies as hay fever.

histology The study of the tissues of living organisms.

hormone Any of various substances that are produced in small amounts by certain glands within the body (the endocrine glands) and released into the bloodstream to regulate the growth or activities of organs and tissues elsewhere in the body.

hydrocarbon Any organic compound composed only of carbon and hydrogen.

hydrogen bond A weak attraction between an electronegative atom, such as oxygen, nitrogen, or fluorine, and a hydrogen atom that is covalently linked to another electronegative atom.

hysteresis An apparent lag of an effect with respect to the magnitude of the agency producing the effect.

ideal gas An idealized gas composed of atoms that have a negligible volume and undergo perfectly elastic collisions. Such a gas would obey the gas laws under all conditions.

immunology The study of the body's mechanisms for defense against disease and the various ways in which these can be manipulated or enhanced.

insulin A hormone that is responsible for regulating the level of glucose in the blood, i.e., "blood sugar." It is produced by certain cells in the pancreas; deficiency causes the disease diabetes mellitus.

integrated circuit An electronic circuit made in a single small unit.

interferon Any one of a group of proteins, produced by various cells and tissues in the body, that increase resistance to invading viruses. Some types are synthesized for use in medicine as antiviral drugs.

internal energy The total energy possessed by a system on account of the kinetic and potential energies of its component molecules.

ion An atom or group of atoms with a net positive or negative charge. Positive ions (cations) have a deficiency of electrons and negative ions (anions) have an excess.

ionizing radiation Electromagnetic radiation or particles that cause ionization.

ionosphere A region of ionized air and free electrons around the Earth in the Earth's upper atmosphere, extending from a height of about 31 miles to 621 miles.

isomerism The existence of two or more chemical compounds with the same molecular formula but different arrangements of atoms in their molecules.

isotope Any of a number of forms of an element, all of which differ only in the number of neutrons in their atomic nuclei.

ketone Any of a class of organic compounds with the general formula RCOR′, where R and R′ are usually hydrocarbon groups.

kinetic energy The energy that a system has by

virtue of its motion, determined by the work necessary to bring it to rest.

kinetic theory Any theory for describing the physical properties of a system with reference to the motion of its constituent atoms or molecules.

laser A device for producing intense light or infrared or ultraviolet radiation by stimulated emission.

latent heat The total heat absorbed or produced during a change of phase (fusion, vaporization, etc.) at a constant temperature.

lepton Any of a class of elementary particles that have half-integral spin and take part in weak interactions; they include the electron, the muon, the neutrino, and their antiparticles.

lipid An ester of a fatty acid. Simple lipids include fats and oils; compound lipids include phospholipids and glycolipids; derived lipids include the steroids.

liquid crystal A state of certain molecules that flow like liquids but have an ordered arrangement of molecules.

macromolecule A very large molecule, as found in polymers or in such compounds as proteins.

magnetohydrodynamics The study of the motion of electrically conducting fluids and their behavior in magnetic fields.

meiosis A type of nuclear division, occurring only in certain cells of the reproductive organs, in which a diploid cell produces four haploid sex cells, or gametes.

meson Any member of a class of elementary particles characterized by a mass intermediate between those of the electron and the proton, an integral spin, and participation in strong interactions. They consist of two quarks each.

metabolism The totality of the chemical reactions taking place in a living cell or organism.

mitosis The type of nuclear division occurring in the body cells of most organisms, in which a diploid cell produces two diploid daughter cells.

moderator A substance used in fission reactors to slow down fast neutrons.

monoclonal antibody Any antibody produced by members of a group of genetically identical cells (which thus constitute a "clone"). Such antibodies have identical structures and each combines with the same antigen in precisely the same manner.

morphology The study of the form of organisms, especially their external shape and structure.

muon An elementary particle having a positive or negative charge and a mass equal to 206.77 times the mass of the electron.

mutation Any change in the structure of a gene, which can arise spontaneously or as a result of such agents as x-rays or certain chemicals. It may have a beneficial effect on the organism but most mutations are neutral, harmful, or even lethal. Mutations affecting the germ cells can be passed on to the organism's offspring.

natural selection The process by which the individuals of a population that are best adapted to life in a particular environment tend to enjoy greater reproductive success than members which are less well adapted. Hence, over successive generations, the descendants of the former constitute an increasing proportion of the population.

neutrino An elementary particle with zero rest mass, a velocity equal to that of light, and a spin of one half.

nuclear fission The process in which an atomic nucleus splits into fragment nuclei and one or more neutrons with the emission of energy.

nuclear fusion A nuclear reaction in which two light nuclei join together to form a heavier nucleus with the emission of energy.

nuclear winter The period of darkness and low temperature, predicted to follow a nuclear war, as a result of the obscuring of sunlight by dust and other debris.

nucleic acid Any of a class of large biologically important molecules consisting of one or more chains of nucleotides. There are two types: deoxyribonucleic acid (DNA) and ribonucleic acid (RNA).

nucleotide Any of a class of compounds consisting of a nitrogen-containing base (a purine or pyrimidine) combined with a sugar group (ribose or deoxyribose) bearing a phosphate group. Long chains of nucleotides form the nucleic acids, DNA and RNA.

nucleon A particle that is a constituent of an atomic nucleus; either a proton or a neutron.

nucleus 1. The positively charged part of the atom about which the electrons orbit. The nucleus is composed of neutrons and protons held together by strong interactions. 2. A prominent body found in the cells of animals, plants, and other organisms (but not bacteria) that contains the chromosomes and is bounded by a double membrane.

oncogene A gene, introduced into a living cell by certain viruses, that disrupts normal metabolism and transforms the cell into a cancer cell.

optical activity The property of certain substances of rotating the plane of polarization of plane-polarized light.

osmosis Preferential flow of certain substances in solution through a semipermeable membrane. If the membrane separates a solution from a pure solvent, the solvent will flow through the membrane into the solution.

oxidation A process in which oxygen is combined with a substance or hydrogen is removed from a compound.

ozone layer A layer containing ozone in the Earth's atmosphere. It lies between heights of 9 and 19 miles and absorbs the Sun's higher-energy ultraviolet radiation.

parity A property of elementary particles depending on the symmetry of their wave function with respect to changes in sign of the coordinates.

parthenogenesis A form of reproduction in which a sex cell, usually an egg cell, develops into an embryo without fertilization. It occurs in certain plants and invertebrates and results in offspring that are genetically identical to the parent.

pathology The study of the nature and causes of disease.

peptide A compound formed by two or more amino acids linked together. The amino group ($-NH_2$) of one acid reacts with the carboxyl group ($-COOH$) of another to give the group $-NH-CO-$, known as the "peptide linkage."

periodic table A tabular arrangement of the elements in order of increasing atomic number such that similarities are displayed between groups of elements.

pH A measure of the acidity or alkalinity of a solution, equal to the logarithm to base 10 of the reciprocal of the concentration of hydrogen ions.

photocell Any device for converting light or other electromagnetic radiation directly into an electric current.

photoelectric effect The ejection of electrons from a solid as a result of irradiation by light or other electromagnetic radiation. The number of electrons emitted depends on the intensity of the light and not on its frequency.

photolysis The dissociation of a chemical compound into other compounds, atoms, and free radicals by irradiation with electromagnetic radiation.

photon A quantum of electromagnetic radiation.

photosynthesis The process by which plants, algae, and certain bacteria "fix" inorganic carbon, from carbon dioxide, as organic carbon in the form of carbohydrate using light as a source of energy and, in green plants and algae, water as a source of hydrogen. The light energy is trapped by special pigments, e.g., chlorophyll.

piezoelectric effect An effect observed in certain crystals in which they develop a potential difference across a pair of opposite faces when subjected to a stress.

pion A type of meson having either zero, positive, or negative charge and a mass 264.2 times that of the electron.

plankton The mass of microscopic plants and animals that drift passively at or near the surface of oceans and lakes.

plasma 1. An ionized gas consisting of free electrons and an approximately equal number of ions. **2.** Blood plasma: the liquid component of blood, excluding the blood cells.

plate tectonics The theory that the Earth's surface consists of lithospheric plates, which have moved throughout geological time to their present positions.

polypeptide A chain of amino acids held together by peptide linkages. Polypeptides are found in proteins.

potential energy The energy that a system has by virtue of its position or state, determined by the work necessary to change the system from a reference position to its present state.

probability The likelihood that an event will occur. If an event is certain to occur its probability is 1; if it is certain not to occur the proba-bility is 0. In any other circumstances the probability lies between 0 and 1.

protein Any of a large number of naturally occurring organic compounds found in all living matter. Proteins consist of chains of amino acids joined by peptide linkages.

proton A stable elementary particle with a positive electric charge equal to that of the electron. It is the nucleus of a hydrogen atom and weighs 1,836 times the mass of the electron.

protozoa A large group of minute single-celled organisms found widely in freshwater, marine, and damp terrestrial habitats. Unlike bacteria they possess a definite nucleus and are distinguished from plants in lacking cellulose.

pulsar A star that acts as a source of regularly fluctuating electromagnetic radiation, the period of the pulses usually being very rapid.

quantum electrodynamics The quantum theory of electromagnetic interactions between particles and between particles and electromagnetic radiation.

quantum theory A mathematical theory involving the idea that the energy of a system can change only in discrete amounts (quanta), rather than continuously.

quark Any of six elementary particles and their corresponding antiparticles with fractional charges that are the building blocks of baryons and mesons. Together with leptons they are the basis of all matter.

quasar A class of starlike astronomical objects with large redshifts, many of which emanate strong radio waves.

radioactive labeling The use of radioactive atoms in a compound to trace the path of the compound through a biological or mechanical system.

radioactivity The spontaneous disintegration of the nuclei of certain isotopes with emission of beta rays (electrons), alpha rays (helium nuclei), or gamma rays.

radio astronomy The branch of astronomy involving the use of radio telescopes.

radiocarbon dating A method of dating archeological specimens of wood, cotton, etc., based on the small amount of radioactive carbon (carbon–14) incorporated into the specimen when it was living and the extent to which this isotope has decayed since its death.

radioisotope A radioactive isotope of an element.

recombination The reassortment of maternally derived and paternally derived genes that occurs during meiosis preceding the formation of sex cells. Recombination is an important source of genetic variation.

redox reaction A reaction in which one reactant is oxidized and the other is reduced.

redshift The displacement of the spectral lines emitted by a moving body towards the red end of the visual spectrum. It is caused by the Doppler effect and, when observed in the spectrum of distant stars and galaxies, it indicates that the body is receding from the earth.

reduction A process in which oxygen is removed from or hydrogen is combined with a compound.

reflex An automatic response of an organism or body part to a stimulus, i.e., one that occurs without conscious control.

refractory A solid that has a high melting point and can withstand high temperatures.

relativistic mass The mass of a body as predicted by the theory of relativity. The relativistic mass of a particle moving at velocity v is $m_0(1 - v^2/c^2)^{-1/2}$, where m_0 is the rest mass.

rest mass The mass of a body when it is at rest relative to its observer, as distinguished from its relativistic mass.

retrovirus A type of virus whose genome, consisting of RNA, is transcribed into a DNA version and then inserted into the DNA of its host. The flow of genetic information, from RNA to DNA, is thus the reverse of that found in organisms generally.

RNA Ribonucleic acid: any one of several types of nucleic acid, including messenger RNA, that process the information carried by the genes and use it to direct the assembly of proteins in cells. In certain viruses RNA is the genetic material.

semiconductor A solid with an electrical conductivity that is intermediate between those of insulators and metals and that increases with increasing temperature. Examples are germanium, silicon, and lead telluride.

semipermeable membrane A barrier that permits the passage of some substances but is impermeable to others.

serum The fraction of blood plasma excluding the components of the blood-clotting system.

sex chromosome A chromosome that participates in determining the sex of individuals. Humans have two sex chromosomes, X and Y; females have two X chromosomes (XX) and males have one of each (XY).

sex hormone Any hormone that controls the development of sexual characteristics and regulates reproductive activity. The principal human sex hormones are progesterone and estrogens in females, testosterone and androsterone in males.

simple harmonic motion Motion of a point moving along a path so that its acceleration is directed towards a fixed point on the path and is directly proportional to the displacement from this fixed point.

SI units A system of units used, by international agreement, for all scientific purposes. It is based on the meter-kilogram-second (MKS) system and consists of seven base units and two supplementary units.

soap A salt of a fatty acid.

solar cell Any electrical device for converting solar energy directly into electrical energy.

solar constant The energy per unit area per unit time received from the Sun at a point that is the Earth's mean distance from the Sun away. It has the value 1,400 joules per square meter per second.

solar wind Streams of electrons and protons emitted by the Sun. The solar wind is responsible for the formation of the Van Allen belts and the aurora.

solid-state physics The experimental and theoretical study of the properties of the solid state, in particular the study of energy levels and the electrical and magnetic properties of metals and semiconductors.

speciation The process in which new species evolve from existing populations of organisms.

specific heat capacity The amount of heat required to raise the temperature of unit mass of a substance by unit temperature; it is usually measured in joules per kilogram per kelvin.

spectrometer Any of various instruments used for producing a spectrum (distribution of wavelengths of increasing magnitude) and measuring the wavelengths, energies, etc.

speed of light The speed at which all electromagnetic radiation travels; it is the highest speed attainable in the universe and has the value 2.998×10^8 meters per second in a vacuum.

standing wave A wave in which the wave profile remains stationary in the medium through which it is passing.

state of matter One of the three physical states – solid, liquid, or gas – in which matter may exist.

stereochemistry The arrangement in space of the groups in a molecule and the effect this has on the compound's properties and chemical behavior.

steroid Any of a group of complex lipids that occur widely in plants and animals and include various hormones, such as cortisone and the sex hormones.

stimulated emission The process in which a photon colliding with an excited atom causes emission of a second photon with the same energy as the first. It is the basis of lasers.

stoichiometric Involving chemical combination in exact ratios.

strangeness A property of certain hadrons that causes them to decay more slowly than expected from the energy released.

strong interaction A type of interaction between elementary particles occurring at short range (about 10^{-15} meter) and having a magnitude about 100 times greater than that of the electromagnetic interaction.

sublimation The passage of certain substances from the solid state into the gaseous state and then back into the solid state, without any intermediate liquid state being formed.

substrate A substance that is acted upon in some way, especially the compound acted on by a catalyst or the solid on which a compound is adsorbed.

sugar Any of a group of water-soluble simple carbohydrates, usually having a sweet taste.

sunspot A region of the Sun's surface that is much cooler and therefore darker than the surrounding area, having a temperature of about 4,000°C as opposed to 6,000°C for the rest of the photosphere.

superconductivity A phenomenon occurring

in certain metals and alloys at temperatures close to absolute zero, in which the electrical resistance of the solid vanishes below a certain temperature.

superfluid A fluid that flows without friction and has extremely high thermal conductivity.

supernova A star that suffers an explosion, becoming up to 10^8 times brighter in the process and forming a large cloud of expanding debris (the supernova remnant).

surfactant A substance used to increase the spreading or wetting properties of a liquid. Surfactants are often detergents, which act by lowering the surface tension.

symbiosis A long-term association between members of different species, especially where mutual benefit is derived by the participants.

taxonomy The science of classifying organisms into groups.

tensile strength The applied stress necessary to break a material under tension.

thermal conductivity A measure of the ability of a substance to conduct heat, equal to the rate of flow of heat per unit area resulting from unit temperature gradient.

thermal neutron A neutron with a low kinetic energy, of the same order of magnitude as the kinetic energies of atoms and molecules.

thermionic emission Emission of electrons from a hot solid. The effect occurs when significant numbers of electrons have enough kinetic energy to overcome the solid's work function.

thermodynamics The branch of science concerned with the relationship between heat, work, and other forms of energy.

thermodynamic temperature Temperature measured in kelvins that is a function of the internal energy possessed by a body, having a value of zero at absolute zero.

thixotropy A phenomenon shown by some fluids in which the viscosity decreases as the rate of shear increases, i.e., the fluid becomes less viscous the faster it moves.

transducer A device that is supplied with the energy of one system and converts it into the energy of a different system, so that the output signal is proportional to the input signal but is carried in a different form.

transistor A device made of semiconducting material in which a flow of current between two electrodes can be controlled by a potential applied to a third electrode.

tribology The study of friction between solid surfaces, including the origin of frictional forces and the lubrication of moving parts.

triple point The point at which the solid, liquid, and gas phases of a pure substance can all coexist in equilibrium.

tritiated Denoting a chemical compound containing tritium (^{3}H) atoms in place of hydrogen atoms.

ultracentrifuge A centrifuge designed to work at very high speeds, so that the force produced is large enough to cause sedimentation of colloids.

unified-field theory A theory that seeks to explain gravitational and electromagnetic interactions and the strong and weak nuclear interactions in terms of a single set of equations.

vaccine An antigenic preparation that is administered to a human or other animal to produce immunity against a specific disease-causing agent.

valence The combining power of an element, atom, ion, or radical, equal to the number of hydrogen atoms that the atom, ion, etc., could combine with or displace in forming a compound.

valence band The energy band of a solid that is occupied by the valence electrons of the atoms forming the solid.

valence electron An electron in the outer shell of an atom that participates in the chemical bonding when the atom forms compounds.

vector 1. A quantity that is specified both by its magnitude and its direction. 2. An agent, such as an insect, that harbors disease-causing microorganisms and transmits them to humans, other animals, or plants.

virtual particle A particle thought of as existing for a very brief period in an interaction between two other particles.

virus A noncellular agent that can infect a living animal, plant, or bacterial cell and use the apparatus of the host cell to manufacture new virus particles. In some cases this causes disease in the host organism. Outside the host cell, viruses are totally inert.

viscosity The property of liquids and gases of resisting flow. It is caused by forces between the molecules of the fluid.

water of crystallization Water combined in the form of molecules in definite proportions in the crystals of many substances.

wave equation A partial differential equation relating the displacement of a wave to the time and the three spatial dimensions.

wave function A mathematical expression giving the probability of finding the particle associated with a wave at a specified point according to wave mechanics.

wave mechanics A form of quantum mechanics in which particles (electrons, protons, etc.) are regarded as waves, so that any system of particles can be described by a wave equation.

weak interaction A type of interaction between elementary particles, occurring at short range and having a magnitude about 10^{10} times weaker than the electromagnetic force.

work function The minimum energy necessary to remove an electron from a metal at absolute zero.

x-ray crystallography The determination of the structure of crystals and molecules by use of x-ray diffraction.

zero point energy The energy of vibration of atoms at the absolute zero of temperature.

zwitterion An ion that has both a positive and negative charge.

INDEX

183, 203, 205, 213, 219; **2**: 41, 42, 44, 50, 130, 153, 164, 171, 180, 206; **3**: 28, 38, 41, 43, 46, 55, 68, 95, 107, 112, 121, 131, 170, 180, 192, 200, 214; **4**: 23, 29, 43, 44, 75, 96, 104, 106, 108, 115, 116, 121, 125, 131, 148, 173, 194, 220; **5**: 20, 27, 40, 55, 77, 106, 179, 193, 198, 215; **6**: 8, 37, 49, 74, 75, 90, 91, 155, 185, 201; **7**: 8, 30, 64, 69, 73, 105, 114, 121, 122, 176, 197, 210; **8**: 29, 99, 104, 105, 111, 130, 147, 175, 183, 211; **9**: 10, 14, 25, 26, 33, 34, 37, 44, 62, 63, 124, 128, 159, 173, 176, 195, 200, 211, 212; **10**: 11, 18, 19, 29, 53, 84, 90, 109, 128, 148, 154, 163, 175, 179, 182, 183, 196, 201, 202

American physiologists: **2**: 56, 99, 150; **3**: 157; **4**: 81, 170, 215; **5**: 8, 102, 109, 200; **6**: 30, 117, 151, 152, 182; **7**: 207, 213; **8**: 48; **9**: 11, 95, 150, 171; **10**: 112

American psychologist: **5**: 171
American rocket engineer: **10**: 47
American sociologist: **7**: 50
American zoologists: **3**: 12, 26; **4**: 163; **5**: 130, 208; **7**: 23
Amici, Giovanni Battista **1**: 42
Amino acids: **3**: 210; **5**: 89; **6**: 26; **8**: 171; **9**: 7; **10**: 32
Amontons, Guillaume **1**: 43
Ampère, André Marie **1**: 43
Anatomists: **1**: 23, 72, 101, 126; **2**: 58, 170, 181, 219; **3**: 17, 154, 169, 178, 182; **4**: 10, 50, 67, 74, 91, 151; **5**: 19, 25, 61, 117, 185; **6**: 95; **7**: 93, 96, 97, 205; **8**: 14, 30, 132, 134; **9**: 125; **10**: 31, 36, 64, 121, 141, 160
Anaxagoras of Clazomenae 1: 45
Anaximander of Miletus 1: 46
Anaximenes of Miletus 1: 46
Anderson, Carl David **1**: 47
Anderson, Philip Warren **1**: 48
Anderson, Thomas **1**: 49
Andrade, Edward **1**: 50
Andrews, Roy Chapman **1**: 51
Andrews, Thomas **1**: 52
Anfinsen, Christian Boehmer **1**: 53
Ångström, Anders Jonas **1**: 54
Anthropologists: **1**: 207; **2**: 52; **4**: 72; **5**: 155; **6**: 77, 78, 79, 95; **7**: 179; **8**: 46
Antibiotics: **3**: 85, 98, 100; **4**: 3
Antibodies: **3**: 119; **5**: 152; **8**: 77; **9**: 207
Antimatter: **3**: 75; **8**: 218
Antoniadi, Eugène Michael **1**: 55
Apker, Leroy **1**: 56
Apollonius of Perga 1: 56
Apothecary: **9**: 48
Appel, Kenneth **1**: 57
Appert, Nicolas-François **1**: 58
Appleton, Sir Edward **1**: 59
Arab astronomers: **1**: 22, 29
Arab geographer: **1**: 29
Arabian alchemist: **4**: 89
Arab mathematician: **1**: 29

Arago, Dominique François Jean **1**: 60
Arber, Werner **1**: 61
Archeologists: **2**: 18; **6**: 77; **9**: 188; **10**: 169
Archimedes 1: 62
Architects: **8**: 30, 185; **9**: 172
Argelander, Friedrich Wilhelm August **1**: 64
Argentinian biochemist: **6**: 101
Argentinian inventor: **1**: 191
Argentinian physiologist: **5**: 94
Aristarchus of Samos 1: 65
Aristotle 1: 65
Arithmetic: **3**: 40; **4**: 37, 122; **8**: 12
Arkwright, Sir Richard **1**: 68
Armenian astronomer: **1**: 40
Armstrong, Henry Edward **1**: 69
Arnald of Villanova 1: 69
Arrhenius, Svante August **1**: 70
Artificial intelligence: **6**: 106; **7**: 24, 82; **8**: 24
Aschoff, Karl **1**: 72
Aselli, Gaspare **1**: 72
Astbury, William Thomas **1**: 73
Aston, Francis William **1**: 74
Astrologers: **2**: 103, 211
Astronomers: **1**: 8, 10, 19, 20, 22, 29, 40, 42, 54, 55, 64, 65, 88, 92, 105, 124, 137, 146, 155, 179, 186, 202, 208, 218; **2**: 3, 4, 9, 16, 25, 32, 35, 37, 59, 64, 79, 80, 93, 98, 115, 126, 135, 136, 138, 152, 157, 162, 174, 182, 217; **3**: 22, 31, 45, 61, 82, 86, 90, 91, 92, 94, 111, 117, 147, 155, 165, 178, 218, 219; **4**: 5, 22, 43, 45, 64, 68, 95, 96, 112, 128, 144, 149, 160, 161, 189, 192, 198, 211, 215; **5**: 18, 23, 29, 30, 31, 36, 43, 45, 57, 92, 95, 99, 104, 108, 110, 111, 128, 132, 145, 146, 148, 177, 182, 183, 195, 202, 206, 211; **6**: 21, 22, 23, 34, 39, 45, 50, 51, 59, 62, 67, 80, 102, 111, 132, 148, 170, 173, 181, 187; **7**: 1, 6, 12, 13, 15, 44, 48, 55, 57, 63, 74, 76, 80, 83, 84, 104, 113, 150, 161, 186, 189, 193, 194; **8**: 16, 24, 41, 42, 43, 44, 54, 61, 67, 69, 78, 90, 92, 96, 98, 102, 103, 122, 125, 131, 137, 138, 139, 140, 145, 154, 167, 174, 186, 198, 206, 214, 215; **9**: 5, 16, 22, 35, 40, 45, 50, 52, 60, 61, 77, 86, 87, 97, 103, 109, 113, 114, 141, 142, 143, 169, 177, 183, 205, 210, 217; **10**: 7, 13, 21, 22, 26, 44, 99, 111, 130, 131, 149, 158, 159, 168, 201
Atanasoff, John Vincent **1**: 76
Atom bomb: **1**: 218; **2**: 172; **3**: 194; **4**: 49; **7**: 198; **9**: 40, 160, 173; **10**: 16
Atomic structure: **1**: 216; **4**: 12; **5**: 38; **7**: 134; **8**: 203; **9**: 27, 99
Atomic weight: **1**: 178; **2**: 97; **8**: 95, 142; **9**: 120
Audubon, John James **1**: 77
Auenbrugger von Auenbrugg,

Joseph Leopold **1**: 78
Auer, Karl, Baron von Welsbach **1**: 79
Auger, Pierre Victor **1**: 80
Australian anatomist: **3**: 17
Australian astronomers: **7**: 74; **10**: 130
Australian chemists: **2**: 190; **3**: 205
Australian earth scientist: **2**: 76
Australian immunologist: **7**: 71
Australian mathematician: **2**: 76
Australian pathologists: **2**: 83, 95; **4**: 8
Australian physicists: **7**: 74, 191
Australian physiologist: **3**: 115
Austrian astronomers: **1**: 186; **2**: 4; **8**: 98, 137
Austrian biologist: **10**: 198
Austrian botanist: **7**: 40
Austrian chemists: **1**: 79; **6**: 167; **7**: 209; **8**: 83; **9**: 29, 77; **10**: 197
Austrian earth scientists: **7**: 116; **9**: 146
Austrian entomologist: **4**: 47
Austrian ethologists: **4**: 47; **6**: 165
Austrian mathematicians: **2**: 4; **8**: 98, 137
Austrian pathologist: **8**: 165
Austrian philosopher: **3**: 199
Austrian physicians: **1**: 78, 187; **7**: 53; **9**: 75
Austrian physicists: **2**: 1; **3**: 88; **6**: 192; **9**: 27, 123
Austrian psychoanalyst: **4**: 39
Austrian psychologist: **1**: 14
Austrian zoologists: **4**: 47; **5**: 172
Austro-Hungarian physician: **1**: 117
Averroës 1: 81
Avery, Oswald Theodore **1**: 81
Avicenna 1: 82
Avogadro, Amedeo **1**: 84
Axelrod, Julius **1**: 85
Ayala, Francisco José **1**: 86
Ayrton, William Edward **1**: 87
Azerbaijani physicist: **6**: 53

Baade, Wilhelm Heinrich Walter **1**: 88
Babbage, Charles **1**: 90
Babcock, Harold Delos **1**: 92
Babcock, Horace Welcome **1**: 92
Babcock, Stephen Moulton **1**: 94
Babinet, Jacques **1**: 94
Babo, Lambert Heinrich Clemens von **1**: 95
Babylonian astronomers: **5**: 202; **9**: 45
Bache, Alexander Dallas **1**: 96
Backus, John **1**: 96
Bacon, Francis **1**: 97
Bacon, Roger **1**: 99
Bacteria: **1**: 82; **2**: 169; **3**: 47, 150; **4**: 154, 164; **5**: 142; **6**: 89, 89, 182; **8**: 180; **10**: 185, 195
Bacteriologists: **1**: 81; **2**: 66, 71, 168; **3**: 66, 127; **4**: 3, 60, 154, 205; **5**: 214; **6**: 3, 100, 153; **7**: 148, 164, 171; **8**: 36, 38; **9**: 83, 134; **10**: 8, 76, 95, 185
Bacteriophage: **3**: 47, 67; **5**: 33; **7**:

Boss, Lewis 2: 16
Botanists: 1: 32, 114, 136, 160, 199, 201; 2: 15, 63, 94, 96, 127, 168, 189, 190; 3: 34, 64, 100, 128, 149, 150; 4: 41, 46, 53, 124, 157, 191; 5: 75, 85, 86, 93, 121, 133, 139, 154, 166; 6: 22, 120, 135; 7: 40, 87, 133, 141; 8: 37, 89, 200, 212, 220; 9: 19, 20, 38, 50, 138, 162, 180, 208; 10: 1, 33, 79, 140
Bothe, Walther Wilhelm Georg Franz 2: 17
Boucher de Crevecoeur de Perthes, Jacques 2: 18
Bouguer, Pierre 2: 19
Boulton, Matthew 2: 20
Bourbaki, Nicolas 2: 20
Boussingault, Jean Baptiste 2: 21
Boveri, Theodor Heinrich 2: 22
Bovet, Daniel 2: 23
Bowen, Edmund John 2: 24
Bowen, Ira Sprague 2: 25
Bowman, Sir William 2: 26
Boyd, William Clouser 2: 27
Boyer, Herbert Wayne 2: 27
Boyle, Robert 2: 28
Boys, Sir Charles Vernon 2: 30
Brachet, Jean 2: 31
Braconnot, Henri 2: 32
Bradley, James 2: 32
Bragg, Sir William Henry 2: 33
Bragg, Sir William Lawrence 2: 34
Brahe, Tycho 2: 35
Brahmagupta 2: 37
Braid, James 2: 38
Brain: 4: 10; 5: 42, 65, 205; 9: 96; 10: 32
Bramah, Joseph 2: 39
Brambell, Francis 2: 39
Brand, Hennig 2: 40
Brandt, Georg 2: 40
Brans, Carl Henry 2: 41
Brattain, Walter Houser 2: 42
Braun, Karl Ferdinand 2: 43
Bredt, Konrad Julius 2: 44
Breit, Gregory 2: 44
Brenner, Sydney 2: 45
Bretonneau, Pierre Fidèle 2: 47
Brewster, Sir David 2: 48
Bricklin, Daniel 2: 49
Bridgman, Percy Williams 2: 50
Briggs, Henry 2: 51
Bright, Richard 2: 51
British aeronautical engineer: 10: 119
British agricultural scientists: 6: 72; 8: 196; 10: 2
British anatomists: 5: 117, 185; 6: 95; 7: 205; 10: 121
British anthropologists: 4: 72; 6: 77, 78, 95; 7: 179; 8: 46
British archeologist: 6: 77
British architect: 9: 172
British astronomers: 1: 8, 19, 105, 155, 202; 2: 32, 64, 79, 80, 152; 3: 22, 31, 45, 111, 117; 4: 22, 144, 198; 5: 2, 18, 29, 30, 31, 45, 95, 108, 146, 148; 6: 67, 148, 170; 7: 6, 12, 76; 8: 61, 67, 90, 206; 9: 87, 97, 109,

183; 10: 7, 168
British bacteriologists: 2: 66; 4: 3; 6: 100; 10: 8
British biochemists: 1: 196; 2: 129; 4: 207; 5: 54, 89, 193; 6: 25; 7: 85, 142, 143; 8: 32, 34, 50, 77; 9: 7, 204
British biologists: 1: 73; 2: 45, 203; 4: 164, 201, 209; 5: 124, 126, 127, 138, 183; 6: 176; 7: 21, 78, 211; 8: 13, 39, 157, 197; 9: 186, 190; 10: 135
British botanists: 1: 114, 136, 160, 199; 2: 63, 189; 4: 124; 5: 85, 86, 121; 6: 120; 8: 200, 220; 9: 38, 50, 162; 10: 79, 140
British chemical engineers: 1: 21, 149, 185; 2: 134, 208; 3: 34; 4: 75, 112; 7: 91; 9: 107; 10: 96
British chemists: 1: 4, 24, 49, 69, 74, 120, 131, 144, 196; 2: 24, 28, 196, 197, 207, 209; 3: 5, 9, 13, 29, 65, 87, 145, 173, 183, 187; 4: 1, 30, 147, 206, 209, 219; 5: 5, 21, 53, 56, 60, 69, 88, 134, 137, 160, 184, 202, 209; 6: 29, 64, 106, 136, 158; 7: 3, 4, 38, 46, 75, 143, 152, 162, 174, 183, 218; 8: 1, 27, 28, 39, 58, 66, 71, 75, 86, 95, 109, 151, 159, 160, 170, 200; 9: 64, 94, 100, 147, 157, 168, 176, 185, 187, 196, 197, 203, 215; 10: 6, 14, 65, 137, 139, 161, 186
British computer scientists: 2: 90; 9: 138; 10: 133
British crystallographers: 1: 168; 6: 159
British earth scientists: 1: 139; 2: 75, 139, 177, 205; 3: 22, 44, 216; 4: 54, 93, 195; 5: 80, 122, 148; 6: 47, 64, 120, 169, 184, 211; 7: 8, 70, 77, 125, 127, 163, 190; 8: 81, 85, 93, 120, 191, 210; 9: 41, 84, 85, 97, 102; 10: 39, 113, 118, 166
British ecologist: 3: 143
British Egyptologist: 10: 187
British electrical engineers: 4: 4; 5: 7
British embryologists: 5: 55; 10: 59, 162
British endocrinologist: 4: 213
British engineers: 1: 180; 2: 20, 39, 67; 5: 93; 7: 12, 23, 138, 151, 220; 8: 113; 9: 10, 69, 126, 172, 183; 10: 120
British entomologists: 5: 183; 10: 127
British ethologists: 3: 32; 9: 198
British explorers: 1: 133; 2: 178; 4: 54, 72; 5: 85
British geneticists: 1: 135, 186; 3: 16, 213; 4: 14, 186; 5: 147, 199; 7: 7; 8: 70; 10: 59
British herbalist: 4: 101
British horticulturist: 1: 186
British immunologists: 4: 145; 7: 31
British inventors: 1: 68, 106, 151, 180; 2: 39, 111, 124, 191; 4: 211; 7: 12, 51, 218; 9: 10, 126,

153; 10: 2, 82
British mathematicians: 1: 90, 128, 179; 2: 7, 123, 139, 175, 196; 3: 74, 117, 213; 4: 159, 208; 5: 67, 146; 6: 47, 145, 169, 198; 7: 76, 101; 8: 22, 93, 195; 9: 41, 75, 135, 155, 166; 10: 3, 113, 116, 117, 131
British metallurgists: 2: 191, 193; 3: 15, 60; 4: 179; 5: 60, 115
British meteorologists: 3: 13, 216; 6: 48; 8: 143; 9: 56, 72
British mineralogist: 4: 160
British naturalists: 1: 133; 2: 72; 3: 18; 4: 13; 7: 142; 10: 66, 114
British ornithologists: 6: 40; 7: 153
British paleontologists: 7: 205, 219; 10: 77, 164
British pathologists: 3: 153; 5: 70, 138
British pharmacologists: 6: 18; 10: 25
British philosophers: 1: 97; 2: 121; 5: 114; 7: 208; 8: 66, 73, 195; 9: 108; 10: 110, 116
British physicians: 1: 12, 30, 105, 144, 152, 196, 202; 2: 26, 38, 51, 54, 72, 73, 82, 158; 3: 21, 141, 197; 4: 77, 196; 5: 21, 87, 117, 118, 141, 150; 6: 118, 131, 143, 195, 201, 210; 7: 219; 8: 162, 172; 9: 74, 90; 10: 79, 121, 153, 170, 187
British physicists: 1: 50, 59, 73, 74, 87, 122, 125, 134, 153, 159, 197; 2: 8, 28, 30, 33, 34, 48, 100, 110, 128, 164, 179, 193, 196, 207; 3: 9, 56, 65, 74, 87, 171, 183; 4: 4, 33, 49, 57, 118, 166, 198; 5: 2, 7, 48, 146, 162, 163, 189, 198; 6: 37, 127, 134, 144, 149, 156, 177, 209; 7: 17, 51, 109, 111, 163; 8: 17, 21, 22, 49, 79, 80, 112, 113, 116, 119, 144, 158, 177, 189; 9: 31, 71, 130, 135, 144, 167, 192, 193; 10: 9, 76, 79, 80, 108, 117, 136, 145, 160, 161, 187
British physiologists: 1: 15, 137; 3: 6; 4: 17, 78, 187; 5: 54, 68, 123, 181; 6: 58, 177, 197; 7: 36, 211; 8: 95, 193; 9: 55, 59, 118
British psychologist: 2: 86
British zoologists: 1: 110; 2: 39; 3: 35; 4: 24, 139, 143; 6: 61, 212; 7: 127; 8: 79; 9: 198; 10: 180, 199
Broca, Pierre Paul 2: 52
Brockhouse, Bertram 2: 53
Brodie, Sir Benjamin 2: 54
Brodie, Bernard Beryl 2: 55
Brongniart, Alexandre 2: 55
Bronk, Detlev Wulf 2: 56
Brønsted, Johannes 2: 57
Broom, Robert 2: 58
Brouncker, William Viscount 2: 59
Brouwer, Dirk 2: 59
Brouwer, Luitzen 2: 60
Brown, Herbert Charles 2: 61

Metchnikoff, Elie **7**: 56
Meteorologists: **1**: 1, 164, 193, 194; **2**: 88, 210; **3**: 13, 14, 50, 162, 196, 216; **4**: 180; **6**: 14, 48, 160, 163; **7**: 209; **8**: 122, 143, 173; **9**: 56, 72; **10**: 86
Metius, Jacobus **7**: 57
Meton **7**: 57
Mexican chemist: **7**: 90
Meyer, Julius Lothar **7**: 58
Meyer, Karl **7**: 59
Meyer, Viktor **7**: 60
Meyerhof, Otto Fritz **7**: 61
Michaelis, Leonor **7**: 61
Michel, Hartmut **7**: 62
Michell, John **7**: 63
Michelson, Albert Abraham **7**: 64
Microscope: **6**: 145; **7**: 51; **10**: 193
Midgley, Thomas Jr. **7**: 66
Miescher, Johann Friedrich **7**: 67
Milankovich, Milutin **7**: 68
Military Scientists: **6**: 206; **9**: 163
Miller, Dayton Clarence **7**: 69
Miller, Hugh **7**: 70
Miller, Jacques Francis Albert Pierre **7**: 71
Miller, Stanley Lloyd **7**: 72
Millikan, Robert Andrews **7**: 73
Mills, Bernard Yarnton **7**: 74
Mills, William Hobson **7**: 75
Milne, Edward Arthur **7**: 76
Milne, John **7**: 77
Milstein, César **7**: 78
Mineralogists: **1**: 147; **2**: 207; **3**: 12, 48, 50; **4**: 60, 160; **5**: 1, 62, 212; **7**: 89; **8**: 127; **10**: 100
Mining Engineer: **1**: 127
Minkowski, Hermann **7**: 79
Minkowski, Rudolph Leo **7**: 80
Minot, George Richards **7**: 81
Minsky, Marvin Lee **7**: 81
Misner, Charles William **7**: 83
Mitchell, Maria **7**: 84
Mitchell, Peter Dennis **7**: 85
Mitscherlich, Eilhardt **7**: 86
Möbius, August Ferdinand **7**: 87
Mohl, Hugo von **7**: 87
Mohorovičić, Andrija **7**: 88
Mohs, Friedrich **7**: 89
Moissan, Ferdinand Frédéric Henri **7**: 89
Molina, Mario José **7**: 90
Mond, Ludwig **7**: 91
Mondino de Luzzi **7**: 93
Monge, Gaspard **7**: 94
Monod, Jacques Lucien **7**: 95
Monro, Alexander (Primus) **7**: 96
Monro, Alexander (Secundus) **7**: 97
Montagnier, Luc **7**: 98
Montgolfier, Etienne Jacques de **7**: 99
Montgolfier, Michel Joseph de **7**: 99
Moore, Stanford **7**: 100
Mordell, Louis Joel **7**: 101
Morgagni, Giovanni Batista **7**: 102
Morgan, Thomas Hunt **7**: 103

Morgan, William Wilson **7**: 104
Morley, Edward Williams **7**: 105
Morse, Samuel **7**: 106
Morton, William **7**: 107
Mosander, Carl Gustav **7**: 108
Moseley, Henry Gwyn Jeffreys **7**: 109
Mössbauer, Rudolph Ludwig **7**: 110
Mott, Sir Nevill Francis **7**: 111
Mottelson, Benjamin Roy **7**: 112
Moulton, Forest Ray **7**: 113
Mueller, Erwin Wilhelm **7**: 114
Muller, Alex **7**: 115
Müller, Franz Joseph, Baron von Reichenstein **7**: 116
Muller, Hermann Joseph **7**: 117
Müller, Johannes Peter **7**: 118
Müller, Otto Friedrich **7**: 120
Müller, Paul Hermann **7**: 120
Muller, Richard August **7**: 121
Mulliken, Robert Sanderson **7**: 122
Mullis, Kary Banks **7**: 123
Munk, Walter Heinrich **7**: 124
Murchison, Sir Roderick Impey **7**: 125
Murphy, William Parry **7**: 126
Murray, Sir John **7**: 127
Murray, Joseph Edward **7**: 127
Muscle contraction: **5**: 54, 90, 124; **9**: 159
Muspratt, James **7**: 129
Musschenbroek, Pieter van **7**: 130
Muybridge, Eadweard James **7**: 131

Naegeli, Karl Wilhelm von **7**: 133
Nagaoka, Hantaro **7**: 134
Nambu, Yoichipo **7**: 135
Nansen, Fridtjof **7**: 136
Napier, John **7**: 137
Nasmyth, James **7**: 138
Nathans, Daniel **7**: 139
Natta, Giulio **7**: 140
Naturalists: **1**: 26, 51, 77, 133, 146, 156; **2**: 6, 32, 72, 74, 133; **3**: 18; **4**: 13, 105; **7**: 142; **8**: 118, 188; **9**: 152; **10**: 66, 114
Naudin, Charles **7**: 141
Nebulae: **1**: 124; **5**: 108; **7**: 55; **10**: 159
Nebular hypothesis: **5**: 147, 174; **6**: 63; **10**: 95
Needham, Dorothy Mary Moyle **7**: 142
Needham, John Turberville **7**: 142
Needham, Joseph **7**: 143
Néel, Louis Eugène Félix **7**: 144
Ne'eman, Yuval **7**: 145
Nef, John Ulric **7**: 146
Neher, Erwin **7**: 147
Neisser, Albert Ludwig Siegmund **7**: 148
Nernst, Walther Hermann **7**: 148
Nerve action: **1**: 15; **3**: 97, 157; **4**: 81; **5**: 68, 182; **6**: 178
Nerve cells: **3**: 115; **7**: 119; **8**: 114, 132

Nervous system: **1**: 152; **4**: 10, 79, 136; **6**: 200; **9**: 60
Newcomb, Simon **7**: 150
Newcomen, Thomas **7**: 151
Newell, Allan **7**: 151
Newlands, John Alexander Reina **7**: 152
Newton, Alfred **7**: 153
Newton, Sir Isaac **7**: 154
New Zealand biochemist: **10**: 143
New Zealand physicist: **8**: 201
Nicholas of Cusa **7**: 160
Nicholson, Seth Barnes **7**: 161
Nicholson, William **7**: 162
Nicol, William **7**: 163
Nicolle, Charles Jules Henri **7**: 164
Niepce, Joseph-Nicéphore **7**: 165
Nieuwland, Julius Arthur **7**: 166
Nilson, Lars Fredrick **7**: 166
Nirenberg, Marshall Warren **7**: 167
Nitrogen fixation: **1**: 190; **4**: 177
Nobel, Alfred Bernhard **7**: 168
Nobili, Leopoldo **7**: 169
Noddack, Ida Eva Tacke **7**: 170
Noddack, Walter **7**: 170
Noguchi, (Seisako) Hideyo **7**: 171
Nollet, Abbé Jean Antoine **7**: 172
Nordenskiöld, Nils Adolf Eric **7**: 173
Norlund, Niels Erik **7**: 173
Norman, Robert **7**: 174
Norrish, Ronald **7**: 174
Northrop, John Howard **7**: 175
Norton, Thomas **7**: 176
Norwegian bacteriologist: **4**: 205
Norwegian biologist: **7**: 136
Norwegian chemists: **1**: 190; **4**: 132, 171, 218; **10**: 57
Norwegian engineer: **3**: 174
Norwegian explorer: **7**: 136
Norwegian industrialist: **3**: 174
Norwegian mathematicians: **1**: 6; **6**: 124; **9**: 76
Norwegian meteorologists: **1**: 193, 194
Norwegian physicist: **1**: 190
Noyce, Robert Norton **7**: 176
Noyes, William Albert **7**: 177
Nuclear fission: **4**: 49, 184; **7**: 35, 170; **9**: 173; **10**: 12
Nuclear magnetic resonance: **1**: 203; **6**: 209; **8**: 99
Nucleic acids: **2**: 31; **6**: 17; **7**: 67
Nucleotide bases: **3**: 210; **6**: 110; **9**: 205
Nucleus: **1**: 215; **4**: 125; **5**: 151; **7**: 112; **8**: 105
Nüsslein-Volhard, Christiane **7**: 178

Oakley, Kenneth Page **7**: 179
Oberth, Hermann Julius **7**: 180
Occhialini, Giuseppe Paolo Stanislao **7**: 181
Ocean currents: **3**: 140; **5**: 9, 113; **7**: 17
Oceanography: **2**: 200
Ochoa, Severo **7**: 182